Subterranean Britain

Subterranean Britain
Aspects of Underground Archaeology

Edited by

Harriet Crawford

Contributions by

J. W. BARNES   G. D. B. JONES
KENNETH HUDSON   G. de G. SIEVEKING
BARBARA JONES   RICHARD WARNER

John Baker · London

First published 1979
John Baker (Publishers) Ltd
35 Bedford Row, London WC1R 4JH
© 1979 John Baker (Publishers) Ltd
ISBN 0 212 97024 0

British Library Cataloguing In Publication Data

Subterranean Britain
   1. Great Britain – Antiquities 2. Underground
areas – Great Britain
I. Crawford, Harriet
936.1   DA90

ISBN 0-212-97024-0

Text set in 11/12 pt VIP Plantin, printed and bound in Great Britain at The Pitman Press, Bath.

Contents

Individual bibliographies are printed at the end of each chapter

Contributors

Biographical Notes

J. W. BARNES

Dr Barnes studied mining engineering and later became Deputy Director of the Geological Survey of Uganda; from here he went as advisor on mining geology to Turkey. Since 1965 he has lectured in economic and mining geology at University College, Swansea and has helped to direct an international programme of training in geological mine investigation held annually in Turkey, Iran or Pakistan. It was this programme which first excited his interest in ancient mining.

KENNETH HUDSON

Mr Hudson is a well-known author and one of the pioneers of industrial archaeology in this country. He wrote the first book on the subject in 1963 and has published eight more since then. He is now a full-time author and museums' consultant.

BARBARA JONES

Miss Jones was an artist and architectural historian whose best known book is probably *Follies and Grottoes*; she has also designed a number of major exhibitions and at the time of her death was working on a book called *The Popular Arts of Today*.

G. D. B. JONES

Professor Barri Jones is professor of archaeology at Manchester University and an acknowledged expert on the Roman period. He has himself carried out research on mining, notably at the Roman mines at Dolaucothi which he excavated with P. R. Lewis.

vi

G. de G. SIEVEKING

Mr Sieveking is a Deputy Keeper at the Department of Prehistoric and Romano-British antiquities at the British Museum. He co-directed the recent excavations at Grime's Graves and is the author of several papers on flint mining.

RICHARD WARNER

Mr Warner is an Assistant Keeper in the Department of Antiquities at the Ulster Museum, Belfast and has made a detailed study of the Irish souterrains.

Illustrations

Acknowledgements

As a novice editor my warmest thanks go to Anne Watts and Phil Harris, from whom I learnt about the business of book production, and also to Louisa Browne who set the ball rolling.

Introduction

The areas below the ground seem always to have had a fascination for man. They represent a challenge and arouse an instinct to explore, to conquer and to exploit. As soon as man discovered fire, the first artificial light, without which he was powerless below the ground, he seems to have begun to add another dimension to his world – that of depth. Some of the most spectacular and beautiful examples of Palaeolithic art come from the painted caves of France and Spain, and illustrate the conquest of darkness and the exploitation by man of the majestic and awe-inspiring qualities of caves and grottoes, perhaps the first attributes to become apparent to him. Caves also had more mundane and domestic uses; an extreme example of a cave used as a dwelling comes from the enormous cave of Shanidar in the Zagros mountains of Iraq which apparently housed a considerable community for at least part of the year. Great Britain and Ireland have not provided us with any colourful cave art or with any inhabited caves on the scale of Shanidar, but none the less man has been exploring and using the subterranean in this country since Palaeolithic times.

Broadly speaking, the subterranean has been used for three main purposes: the industrial, the domestic and the ritual; in this book we are primarily concerned with the industrial exploitation of the earth's resources. There is not a great deal of evidence in the British Isles for domestic usage, although caves in limestone regions such as the Mendips were certainly inhabited to the end of the Roman period and in some cases later still. The underground complexes of rooms and tunnels found in a number of areas and known as souterrains or fougous, seem to have been at least partially domestic in function. The ice-houses of the eighteenth and nineteenth centuries also fall into the domestic category, though the ice itself was probably used for medical and other non-domestic purposes. There are no underground villages like those in the Chinese loess belt. Here factories, schools, hotels and government offices are all built underground, as are literally millions of houses. It may be that the climate in Britain is not extreme enough to make the labour of such excavations worthwhile even where the soil is suitable.

Ritual usage is inadequately represented because it was decided not to include funerary monuments. The reasons for this decision are two-fold; many of the burial mounds are not strictly speaking underground, they belong to the category aptly described by Barbara Jones as the 'overground underground'; there are also a number of up to date books dealing specifically with them. Again, since the crypts and tombs of the medieval period fit more happily into an architectural rather than an archaeological context, they too have been excluded.

The main theme in this book then is the industrial exploitation of the earth's resources and it begins with a chapter which describes the mining of flint at Grime's Graves. Although these mines have been known for a long time and flint knapping is still a living tradition around Brandon, much new evidence has been gathered in recent years and some of it is presented here for the first time. Some of the conclusions reached must still be tentative as work is continuing on the processing of information obtained in the recent excavations. It becomes abundantly clear that at Grime's Graves we have an industrial operation, and the area today has much the same impact as a scrap-metal yard, or a derelict colliery. This industrial operation is subjected to an archaeological time and motion study and evidence is produced to indicate that the flint was mined by specialists in their trade, possibly on a seasonal basis.

Having mastered the technology of flint, man seems to have begun experimenting with metals, probably treating pieces of native metal just as if they were other types of stone; heating them to make them fracture more easily, and beating and chipping them into shape. It may have been this heating which led to the discovery of the unique properties of metals. In Chapter 2 Dr Barnes gives us a brief historical introduction to the development of mining in this country and details the geographical distribution of the ore fields in Great Britain and Ireland. A most interesting section of this chapter is his description of the geological processes involved in the laying down of the metalliferous deposits, information which is not easy for the archaeologist to find in a comprehensible form. The techniques of extraction are described, the tools are illustrated and several individual sites are discussed to illustrate the different extraction processes. An entirely convincing explanation of the legend of the Golden Fleece is included as a passing comment.

As techniques slowly improved old mines were reworked and this alone makes the recovery of archaeological evidence extremely difficult. Unless one is lucky enough to find dateable finds in a stratified context the dating of early mine workings is extremely unreliable. In spite of this, Dr Barnes has contrived to build up a convincing picture of the early working of metals in this country.

The story is carried into the Roman period by Professor Barri Jones, who has much new evidence to present from his own excavations. Like Dr Barnes, he stresses the problems of dating mining evidence and confines his discussion to those examples where it has been possible to date the workings accurately, usually by means of associated finds. He traces the development of several mines from adits and opencast workings to deep gallery extraction, which brought with it problems of drainage. At the Dolaucothi gold mine fragmentary remains of a water wheel were discovered which must have been used to keep the deepest shafts open – shafts up to 220 metres deep. Very interesting plans of the Llanymynech copper mine have recently become available, and these are discussed; here absolute dating was made possible by the discovery of coins, some buried with human bones, probably those of miners. The accompanying photographs provide a vivid commentary on the scale of the operations.

We are well accustomed to the thought of caves as habitation sites in the Stone Age, but they were still in use as late as the Romano–British period and extensive field systems associated with some of them show that they were not just emergency bolt-holes or hide-outs, but were part of the normal farming economy. Some caves, however, had less blameless and domestic functions. The find of a Roman counterfeiter's workshop at White Woman's Hole in Eastern Mendip throws light on the seamier side of Roman Britain. Forgery, in fact, seems to have been quite a flourishing industry, as another 'den' was found in the then abandoned lead mine at Draethen.

Underground structures of another kind are dealt with by Richard Warner in his chapter on the Irish souterrains. He presents a detailed picture of the distribution, construction and usage of these structures and sets them in their social and economic background. Over a thousand of them are known, unevenly distributed over the country, and seeming to date from the sixth to twelfth centuries A.D. One of his most interesting conclusions is that skilled craftsmen (one can perhaps legitimately call them engineers) were used to construct many of the more elaborate examples. Some of these engineers may have been migrants from other parts of the British Isles, in particular Scotland and Cornwall, where souterrains are known in earlier contexts. The evidence favours the interpretation of souterrains as emergency refuges and 'safe deposits' against marauders, although some of the roomier ones with easy access may have been used for storage; literary as well as archaeological evidence is quoted to support this contention. Apart from the examples from Scotland and Cornwall, other similar shelters are found in Brittany and even in Iceland, where an Irish element seems to have been present during its occupation in the ninth and tenth centuries. Much of the evidence in this chapter is published for the first time and provides interesting parallels with the evidence from mining contexts for construction techniques and similar problems with establishing firm dates for the material.

With Chapter 5 we are back in the industrial world again and the range is extended to include coal and iron mining, stone quarrying and the technological innovations of the Industrial Revolution. The earliest extant steam engine, for instance, developed to drain deep mines, dates back to 1720 and can be seen today at Dartmouth. Perhaps for the first time mining began, directly or indirectly, to influence the lives of a substantial proportion of the population and to transform large sections of the landscape. The whole scale is dramatically altered by the introduction of the new technology; it is estimated that three million tonnes of ore were removed from the Greenside mine in the Lake District in the 300 years of its working life; the profits escalated and so, of course, did the risks. The death toll was high among miners as was the cost in disease and disability. Whole families were often employed in the mine, and visitors to Dolcoath mine in Cornwall noted the deformation of the shoulders of many of the girls employed to break up and shovel the lumps of ore. Some slate quarries retained elements of early nineteenth-century technology until their closure at the beginning of World War II and first-hand descriptions of working conditions still survive. The chapter ends on a more cheerful note with a description of the stone mines at Box/Corsham which would seem to qualify for an Ideal Home award by contrast.

The final chapter is complementary to its predecessor in that it provides a look at the less serious and practical uses of the subterranean. It begins with a description of a unique chalk cave at Royston, Herts., decorated with a bewildering and fascinating series of carvings, mostly of medieval date. Then, with the age of the Romantics, came the heyday of the grotto. Barbara Jones describes the delights of such underground curiosities as the Goldney lions' den, the Hawkstone labyrinth and the Margate grotto. She also looks at some of the extraordinary tunnels below the cities of Liverpool and Nottingham, and at the underground ballroom and other amenities constructed by the fifth Duke of Portland at Welbeck. There are a number of other amazing cepts, and the German usage in this instance seems to cover both mining underground and surface quarrying, leading to the recognition of Mesolithic and Upper Palaeolithic flint mines in Poland and even an alleged Mousterian flint mine, 30 000 years ago in Switzerland. In contradistinction, the French prehistorians reserve the word mine for truly underground structures and call their prehistoric quarries 'extraction pits', which is much more helpful since it places the quarrying procedure in the context of pits in general.

In fact, pits of many different kinds are found in European Upper Palaeolithic settlements, particularly in those settlements which are relatively permanent or long term instead of just temporary camps. The loess settlements of Czechoslovakia and European Russia have large numbers of associated pits and these seem to be used for many different purposes, probably as quarries for clay and loess used for house construction and other purposes, and also (possibly after this process was complete) as rubbish or storage pits, and even for ceremonial purposes – as shrines. Even a short term winter settlement such as Gönnersdorf in the Rhineland has a considerable number of internal storage pits in the dwelling houses, and similar pits are reported from cave dwellings of this period. Though the Palaeolithic digging tools are largely missing or have not yet been identified by archaeologists, they must have existed both for pit digging and for grubbing up roots and vegetables and digging deadfall traps for animals, which seem to have been well known practices in all the non-agricultural societies of pre-Neolithic Europe. As pit digging was already an established technique it is scarcely surprising that we should have clear Palaeolithic and Mesolithic evidence for surface quarrying concerned with the extraction of flint and other suitable raw materials for making stone tools. The collection of particularly attractive or high-quality rocks from considerable distances and the reliance on particular sources of supply, is attested from the earliest Palaeolithic periods and the standardisation of stone tool design is itself evidence for the importance of these tools to the Stone Age communities. Quarrying of one sort or another on sea cliffs, steep hills and outcrops must always have supplemented mere collection of raw material from loose scree deposits and river or sea beach gravels.

The known distribution of prehistoric flint quarries or mines is controlled by two things: by the availability of raw material and by likelihood of preservation. There is, of course, no purpose in excavating for raw material unless suitable rock is to be found beneath the surface, and the distribution of flint and therefore of flint quarries and mines is largely controlled by the distribution in Western Europe of cretaceous chalk, the rock containing the typical chalk-flint. In Britain, flint mining is thus confined to Southern England: though chalk deposits are known in Northern Ireland and Yorkshire so far they have produced no real mines.* In Europe, flint quarries and mines are known from Denmark and possibly South Sweden, from Holland, Belgium and France – that is, from the total area of the distribution of cretaceous chalk rock. In addition, very similar quarries and mines occur in limestones, mostly of cretaceous age, in Hungary, Poland, Germany, Switzerland, Southern France, Italy and even Sicily, from which is extracted a chert somewhat similar to flint in appearance and equally suitable for stone tool manufacture. As well as chert and flint (really a special variety of chert in petrological terms), which are prized partly for their sharp cutting edges, a variety of igneous and other 'hard-rocks' were also quarried in Western and Northern Europe, particularly for the manufacture of Neolithic axes, but no case of underground mining of igneous rocks has been recorded, except possibly in Australia. One may as well complete the picture by saying that once near the Mediterranean we move into the zone of obsidian exploitation, where this sharp and easily broken volcanic glass was quarried as a source of stone tool material from open air sites in the West Mediterranean islands and peninsulas, from North Africa, from East Mediterranean sources including Melos and also from numerous sources in Asia Minor and Iran. Here again there is no trace of underground mining, though considerable amounts of chert and obsidian were exchanged and traded throughout the region.

While flint extraction sites are known in quantity from Western and Northern Europe these are nearly all of Neolithic date. It is only in Switzerland, Poland and Hungary that we have at present well-attested examples of pre-Neolithic practice of flint or chert extraction. From the available descriptions it seems that the principal Polish region exploited in pre-farming times was an outcropping ridge of highly coloured and easily identifiable chert several square miles in extent. Like a very similar large-scale outcrop quarry site at Grand Pressigny in France, it was known and used for raw materials from the Lower Palaeolithic onwards. As the

* Some claims have been put forward for surface quarries on exposed headlands in Yorkshire. One site of this character in Ireland, Ballygalley Head, Co. Antrim has been examined and briefly reported as a flint mine (Collins 1958).

chert is easily recognisable it can be shown that rock from the Polish quarries was carried hundreds of miles from its source. Probably because it was so easy to extract locally many of the early Polish and Hungarian chert quarries are grouped close together and are thus archaeologically 'visible'. The British pre-Neolithic examples, if they existed, are dispersed and therefore invisible.

We learn little of mining and quarrying technology from the pre-Neolithic quarries. As quarrying below the surface is related to extracting rock from outcrops, it is not surprising that the workmen quickly learned to follow a particular seam of rock underground. Outcrops are often sub-horizontal, at a slight angle to the ground surface, and the Swiss Mousterian chert quarry is a linear sloping pit or trench very similar to the igneous rock quarry at the Neolithic axe factory site of Myndydd Rhieu, in North Wales, and indeed to the prehistoric copper mines in Ireland and Yugoslavia. At some of the Hungarian Palaeolithic flint quarries the tools for levering the rock were apparently made from deer antler. Red deer antler picks are characteristic of Neolithic flint mining, particularly in Britain, and the Palaeolithic Hungarian examples are sometimes cited as evidence of the antiquity of the Neolithic mining tradition. But the Neolithic miners' picks are a standardised, if very simple, tool, an L-shaped lever and pick, with a handle made from a short portion of the main antler beam, and retaining only the first prong nearest the head of the animal known as the brow tine (See Fig. 1:1) as the point of the pick. Even if the Palaeolithic tools closely resembled these Neolithic picks one would not be surprised, as it is a simple and obvious use for the antler. In fact, the early examples of these tools are much more diverse in design than those of the Neolithic. Deer antler was used a great deal in making tools in the latest Palaeolithic and earliest post-glacial industries, and various types of club and sharpened tools made from the heavy beam, with perhaps an antler blade or point at right angles to it, are commonplace in this period. When used for quarrying they are best regarded as generalised digging tools and not as part of a specialised mining technology.

Radiocarbon dating allows us to draw a neat line between Neolithic flint mining and quarrying practices and the earlier technology. Though rock extraction and collection must have continued throughout the intervening period, the underground mining which is characteristic of the later Neolithic seems to be more of a large-scale industry than the earlier quasi-domestic practice. It is also accompanied by a great increase in surface quarrying on sites which do not merit underground mining. Perhaps it would be fair, after all, to point to this as the first of the series of European Industrial Revolutions.

In Northern, Central and Western Europe including Britain underground flint mining first appears between 4000–3000 B.C., if we follow the uncalibrated Radiocarbon chronology. As the first Neolithic farmers enter the continental area before 5000 B.C. (using the same time-scale), this means that there is a clear 1500-year period of Neolithic occupation on the continent before the appearance of the underground flint mining industry. In respect to the British Isles the position is no different. The earliest British flint mines, those in Sussex, are dated to between 3250–3010 B.C., as are those of Belgium, Holland and Poland, the only centres of mining for which reliable dates presently exist.

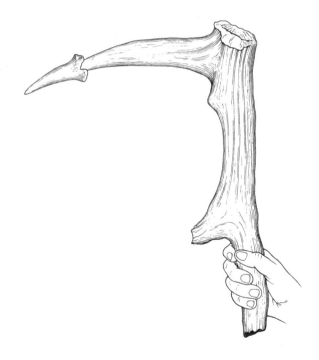

Fig. 1:1 A perforated ox bone mounted on an antler pick. The drawing shows the difference in scale between the antler pick and the ox bone adze. *By kind permission of the Trustees of the British Museum.*

The traditional explanation of the development of the flint mining industry is that it took place in response to the need for heavy flint axes, as tools for clearing farming land. The earliest European farmers, those of the so-called Danubian cultures, only colonised the most easily cultivated and cleared light soils – such as the loess soils in Germany and Holland. The Danubian farmers made little use of axes, or indeed of flint as a raw material for their tools. The normal Danubian tool was a small flat adze made of hard igneous rock, and these are generally scarce compared with the number of heavy axes found on later farming sites. After 4000 B.C. the position has changed. The less attractive soils are beginning to be cleared for farming, and the settlements of the farmers are well supplied with heavy flint axe heads, particularly in the deciduous forest zones of the Baltic and Western Europe. The expansion of flint quarrying and the innovation of deep mining for flint and chert tools took place at this time and the relationship between the two events is demonstrated by the existence of factories for axe manufacture close to the mouths of mine shafts, on many of the major flint mines.

Though there may be traces of pastoral farming practice in Britain at an earlier period, the colonisation of the British Isles by farmers engaged in tillage agriculture should be regarded as part of the general movement onto poorer soils after 4000 B.C. (There are no traces of the Danubian farmers though they do seem to have reached Jersey.) One may notice the strength of social organisation demonstrated by these farmers when they first arrive in Southern Britain. Considerable co-operative ventures such as the construction of ceremonial long barrows and other monuments are well known. On some early farming sites pottery vessels, or the ingredients used in pottery making, were transported to the spot from upwards of 100–150 km away. Though engaged in clearing primary forest for plough or pasture these were not merely small groups of isolated settlers leading a hand to mouth existence as subsistence farmers. Though their settlement traces are not easy to examine or to define we can be certain that they had a social organisation permitting and validating co-operation in many forms. The expansion of farming, leading to the general colonisation of poor soils throughout Europe, is presumably a function of a population increase and the greatly increased flint quarrying which the application of underground mining techniques represents may also be a result of increased demand from a larger population, as well as a change to farming practices requiring the use of flint axes.

Whatever the cause the few facts we have are clear enough. Large-scale flint quarrying and mining was inaugurated on the Sussex coast near Worthing around 3300 B.C. It continued unabated until the end of the Neolithic period when polished stone axes went out of fashion, around 1800 B.C. Whereas the earliest miners specialised in the manufacture and export of half-finished axes, the industries associated with the latest flint mines, those at Grime's Graves in Norfolk, produced in addition to axes a preponderence of blanks for flake tools such as knives and spearheads. This again is in line with events on the continent, as the earliest dated mines in Poland or at Spiennes in Belgium specialise in axe manufacture, whilst the latest quarry sites in Denmark and in France specialise in the export of dagger and knife blanks or fully manufactured weapons. The decline in the importance of the heavy polished or flaked flint axe in Britain at the end of the Neolithic is accompanied by the abandonment of much of the arable land and the regeneration of woodland. The poorer soils had apparently become impoverished by over-exploitation, and as pasture replaced ploughed land axes were required less for tree-felling and land clearance. However, it is notable that the Grime's Graves flint mine dated from around this period is if anything considerably larger in output than the earliest British mines. These are the most developed examples of mining practice, in terms of size and output from individual mines and of organisation, i.e. numbers of workmen engaged in one mine at the same time. It looks as if flint mining, like several modern technological practices (e.g. windmills in the late eighteenth century and clipper ships in the 1860s), had its greatest and most efficient application when it was already under serious threat from an eventually successful competitive technology – in this case the manufacture of tools of copper and bronze.

Grime's Graves, therefore, though a late example of flint mining, can be taken as an epitome of British mining practice. This is particularly so since on the site are represented many different types of mining and quarrying from the smallest quarry pits to the deepest shafts known in Britain, associated in many cases with a complex of underground galleries operated in a most systematic manner. As usual, local conditions control the application of the available extraction techniques on different parts of the site. Thus the main deep shafts are found massed close together on the relatively flat top of a chalk hill, where the main flint seam to be exploited is between 6–14 metres below the ground, while on the hill slopes to the north and east deep mining is less frequent and is replaced by several less productive extraction techniques. A similarly varied exploitation pattern can be found on the sites of several other British flint mines, though in some cases the most developed form of shaft and gallery system is not suitable to local conditions on *any* part of the site.

Grime's Graves was first explored in detail between 1914–1938, when its investigator was preoccupied with problems of the origin of mining. Flint occurs in the chalk at Grime's Graves as elsewhere as successive flat sub-horizontal rows of nodules, or layers of flat tabular rock. The problem was to decide how prehistoric man first found the Grime's Graves flint. The main investigator, A. L. Armstrong, adopted the apparently reasonable explanation that the most valuable seam of flint at Grime's Graves, the so-called floorstone buried deep beneath the chalk at the top of the hill, was first discovered outcropping on the hillside, where the chalk had been eroded into the valley below the flint level. The advantage of this explanation, adopted from earlier work at the Belgian flint mine at Spiennes, was that it suggested that the minor forms of quarrying present on the hillside must be earlier than the deep shaft and gallery mines at the top of the hill, and so provided both a plausible reason for starting work at Grime's Graves and an explanation of the evolution of mining on the site. As the area dominated by the small quarries, the so-called primitive pits, became worked out, the miners were forced to move up the hill, digging ever deeper pits, undercutting their sides with a series of niches or rudimentary galleries, until finally the shafts became so deep that it became efficient to dig out horizontal galleries for flint extraction at the base of each shaft.

Two fatal flaws to this explanation have since appeared, the first connected with the supposed chronology of this site. If Armstrong's hypothesis were correct the opencast mining and the so-called primitive pits should be the earliest on the site. Radiocarbon dating has shown that they are not. There is some evidence as far as dates of individual mines are concerned to show that the apparent order of exploitation could be reversed, e.g. that the deep mines at the top of the hill are in fact earlier than some of the exploitation on the surface of the hillside (Sieveking *et al* 1973. Fig. 1:2). In general however, the dates for shaft and gallery mining and those for surface quarrying have proved to cover precisely the same time bracket, between 2100–1800 B.C., suggesting that there was a single major period of activity at Grime's Graves when the attractive fine quality local black flint was most fashionable. We have dates

Fig. 1:2 Grime's Graves. The deep shafts from the air. *Cambridge University Collection.*

for fifteen separate quarries, and six deep shaft and gallery mines, the latter from all parts of the site (a total of more than 100 Radiocarbon dates), all of which fall into this main period.

Apart from the Radiocarbon chronology a further objection to supposing that the pits on the hillside are the progenitors to the shafts on the hilltop exploiting the fine seam of tabular 'floorstone' *in situ* in the solid chalk, is that this tabular flint layer appears to run

10

out and become more sporadic before it reaches the side of the hill. The best quality seam is severely localised on the hilltop, at least at the mine site, though it reappears elsewhere in the district (e.g. south and east of Brandon). We have been unable to find evidence of the floorstone level in some of the smaller pits and quarries on the north and west of the hill when these have been cut into the solid chalk. Where it does exist on the south boundary (e.g. Pit 11), the seam is already much thinner. At one of the major shafts on the boundary to the east of the mining area (recently explored by the Department of the Environment) galleries were contemplated but not cut because the flint had apparently run out eastwards.

If the supposedly more primitive pits at Grime's Graves are not earlier than the main period of exploitation, this is less surprising now that we know flint mining had already been in vogue elsewhere in Britain almost continuously for a thousand years. There is no need today to suppose the Grime's Graves miners ignorant of local geology when they first started work. The fine floorstone flint elsewhere in the district had been exploited by prehistoric man in previous periods. Doubtless the value of the site lay principally in the evidence of a continuous thick seam of flint. This was discovered by trial mining in the hilltop and almost entirely worked out.

Seen from the map the deep mine shafts are clustered together at the top of the hill. The total area of exploitation terminates abruptly to the east but stretches out to the west where the hillside slopes gradually into a shallow dry valley and northwards where the fall is more abrupt. Earlier exploration of the site enabled Armstrong in 1926 to plot the limits of exploitation beyond which there are no more signs of disturbance. The hillside within the boundary is a maze of exploratory shafts, and small and larger sized pits, very different from the situation on the hilltop. There are several reasons for this. As the hillside falls away the preferred flint seam would necessarily approach the surface before it petered out, and opencast quarries would replace shaft and gallery systems. However, the slope of the solid chalk is steeper than is indicated by the surface contours, since the dry valleys are partly filled by sands and by shattered chalk and chalk-mud (coombe rock) formed by periglacial processes. The latter, which have been moved both downslope in a frozen mass and also vertically upwards by cryoturbation, contain only isolated flint nodules distributed in a random fashion, but these are often large enough to be worth collection. Most, if not all, of the shallow flint quarries exploit the nodules in the shattered

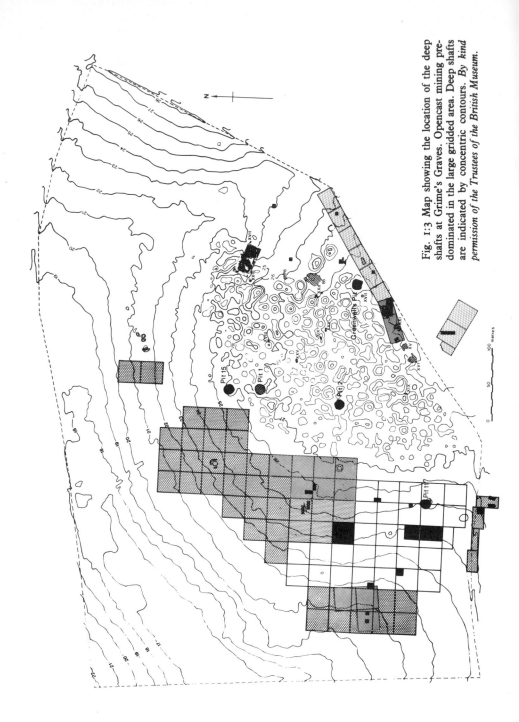

Fig. 1:3 Map showing the location of the deep shafts at Grime's Graves. Opencast mining predominated in the large gridded area. Deep shafts are indicated by concentric contours. *By kind permission of the Trustees of the British Museum.*

chalk/chalk-mud zone, and do not penetrate the solid chalk as the flint seam has already given out or has been cut away by surface erosion.

Several isolated pits were explored by the most recent investigations at Grime's Graves (carried out by the British Museum). From these we can get some idea of their typical dimensions and how they were worked. A typical small pit is 3 × 5 metres in plan and 2–3 metres deep. It has steeply overhanging sides and when one examines the pit walls rounded holes can be seen, where flint nodules have been levered from the chalk-mud. These surface pits are cut down to the surface of the solid chalk, but not into it. Abandoned antler picks like those used in the mines are found on the pit floor, under the overhangs and elsewhere in the filling. The scale and productivity of these operations can be estimated from the isolated pits, which could have been excavated in one or two days, producing from 10–30 fair-sized flint nodules. On the old ground surface, close to the edge of the pit, are workshops where these nodules were broken up and flaked into roughed out blanks for axes and other tools. These again provide a useful estimate of the scale of work to be expected from such operations. One or two hammerstones are found associated with a ring of flakes and broken nodules and between 4–12 rough-outs broken or abandoned in the half finished state. Experiments carried out as part of the British Museum excavation at Grime's Graves indicate that it takes between 10–14 minutes to make one Neolithic rough-out axe – the most complex and hence the slowest tool to make. So if we assume 10 per cent failure rate in the manufacture of rough-outs the workshop floors again represent between half a day and at the most two days' labour. The whole operation with its emphasis on small profits and quick returns, if one contrasts it with the labour investment of the deep mining operation, suggests that these miners were aiming to supply themselves and their immediate relatives and associates with a useful tool kit for their own use. The domestic scale of operation is clearly apparent.

Though small isolated pits have been found, it is more usual to find a maze of such pits, all of the same scale, each succeeding pit cutting the walls of the pit before until the patch of hillside has been completely turned over. The edges of the individual pits seldom remain intact, but their scale can be reconstructed since each pit has been back-filled by the workmen exploiting the adjacent area, and pit diameters show up as layers of back-filling confined by now vanished walls of the earlier pit.

In addition to areas of small scale opencast operations of this sort, a variety of other structures can be recognised on the hillside. These include small pits full of habitation refuse, cylindrical exploratory shafts and a variety of larger pits which exploit or attempt to exploit the solid chalk as well as the overlying chalk-muds. The morphology of these structures provides evidence for the nature of the exploration techniques employed in the flint mining operations. In the first place there are narrow cylindrical shafts scarcely more than a metre in width. One of these examined proved to be between 6–7 metres deep cut through the chalk-mud and 3–4 metres into the solid chalk; approximately to the level of the floorstone if allowance is made for the slope of the hill. One must assume that the depth of the floorstone was taken from an open shaft still in operation and that some form of levelling device was employed by the miners to calculate its depth in the shaft. At the appropriate point the cylindrical shaft has been undercut in the search for the flint seam, leaving a significant bulge.

Further evidence of Neolithic mining techniques at Grime's Graves is provided by the larger-scale structures in the hillside, formerly assigned to the class of 'primitive' pits. Two new examples of these structures have been excavated, and a third was recognised when the first of the primitive pits (Pit 3) was re-examined and more fully excavated in 1976. All three pits are very similar and belong to a class of two-level structures, previously recognised at Neolithic flint mines at Cissbury in Sussex and probably at Easton Down near Salisbury. But while those elsewhere in Britain are cut in the solid chalk, the Grime's Graves two-level mines are cut through and exploit both cryoturbated drift (chalk-mud) and solid chalk, drawing attention to the relationship between opencast quarrying and deep mining as practised in this period. These two-level quarries are roughly circular shafts 5–8 metres in diameter at the surface and of similar depth. The upper stage has a considerable parapet as a working floor surmounted by a series of semi-circular niches or short galleries driven into the cryoturbated chalk drift round the circumference of the shaft. Below this level the shaft reaches a lower stage where short galleries between 2–3 metres in length and diameter are driven into the chalk at the base of the shaft. It is evident that the purpose of the low-level operation is to find a good flint supply. In the case of the marginal pits at Grime's Graves, the flint supply does not appear to have been good. Certainly little trace of flint remains in these tiny galleries, while the walls of the deep galleries usually contain nodules or seams of flint

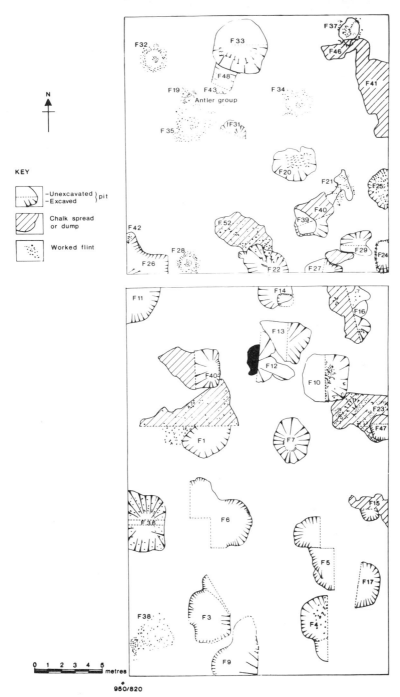

KEY

- - - Unexcavated } pit
—— Excaved

▨ Chalk spread or dump

⋮ Worked flint

950/820

Fig. 1:4 Plan of isolated and adjacent opencast pits at Grime's Graves and workshop floors on surface. (In course of excavation.) *By kind permission of the Trustees of the British Museum.*

15

which the miners have been unable to extract. So it seems that such two-level mines as we have examined were unsuccessful in locating flint in the solid chalk. In the case of the Sussex mines however the search for flint was successful, as very similar two-stage mines are associated with the driving of considerable galleries at the lower

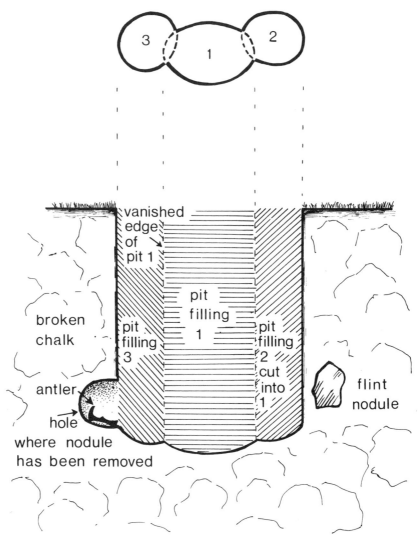

Fig. 1:5 Reconstruction of sequence of opencast working at Grime's Graves. Plans of adjacent pits in order of cutting indicated above. (Not to scale.) *By kind permission of the Trustees of the British Museum.*

level. What we have at Grime's Graves therefore, is a record of the earliest stage of shaft sinking, preserved in these unsuccessful examples. This focusses attention on the pit morphology and in particular on the evidence of the parapet at the higher level, which would have been of value as a stage for extracting chalk and flint from the base of the shaft. Traces of a similar parapet in a degraded condition may perhaps be claimed for Greenwell's Pit, one of the deeper shaft and gallery mines at Grime's Graves.

One can also appreciate the economy of the mining method which allowed the miners to exploit erratic nodules in the disturbed chalk before proceeding to cut down to the level of the preferred tabular flint. Early investigators of the deep mines noted that the flint tools produced on the surface at Grime's Graves were not always made from the tabular floorstone. Layers of nodules cut through by the shaft were also collected and used for tool making, though the galleries were universally driven at floorstone level. We may suggest that the pattern of exploitation implied by the two-level mines formed part of the essential routine of shaft digging in the deep shaft and gallery mines, though traces of the upper level are difficult to find today, and went unnoticed by the previous investigators.

The evidential value of the two-level mines so far explored at Grime's Graves relates to their being unsuccessful ventures on the lower level, preserving features that were eliminated once a good seam of flint was found in the chalk. On the lower level small circular or elongate chambers or niches are cut into the chalk walls in the shaft, in the search for flint. As the flint seam was absent or not sufficiently promising these chambers are abandoned instead of being transformed into long galleries. Traces of preliminary work are thus preserved.

The advantage of the underground situations at the flint mines is that as they have been back-filled fairly rapidly, they preserve traces of their original excavation in the form of marks on the walls and floor, and also abandoned tools where they have been dropped after use, instead of swept aside. In the case of the two-level mines we find a special tool was in use, unknown until recently from elsewhere at Grime's Graves, and the walls of the unfinished chalk galleries preserve traces of its use. The tool is made from the tibia of an ox, broken about halfway along its length and sharpened into a blade or pick form and perforated longitudinally through the remaining articular end. The tools were originally known as hand picks, and since they were only found in the supposedly less developed and therefore earlier 'primitive pits', while the red deer antler picks were in the earliest investigations found only in shaft and gallery mines, the ox-bone picks were thought of as an earlier tool, abandoned when the red deer antler pick had been developed. Recently, more careful examination revealed several deer antler picks in the two-level mines, and of course such antler picks were already in general use in Sussex at the earliest known British flint mines, perhaps a thousand years previous to their application at Grime's Graves. With this in mind, if we look again at the ox tibia picks, we see that they are a much smaller tool than the big red deer antler pick, and could scarcely be used except with a handle. The carefully made perforation is conical in cross-section, that is to say greater at the articulation and tapering towards the working edge. In many cases the business end is a wedge or adze rather than a point, and on the chalk walls of the preserved niches at the foot of the shaft we find many marks of the blades of small adzes of precisely the dimensions of these tools, showing that these implements must have been swung with their edges parallel to the walls and roof of the niche which one could not achieve by hand without barking one's knuckles. So it is likely that these are a form of perforated adze mounted in a handle. Their size and conical perforation suggests the ox-bone tools were mounted on the brow tine of the antler pick, as an auxiliary tool for transforming the pick into an axe or adze. If used in this manner, every time the pick was swung the ox-bone would jam more firmly into the point of the tine. The perforated ox-bones which we found were broken longitudinally along the shaft, suggesting that strain was applied in this manner. These auxiliaries could be discarded and replaced as soon as they were blunt or damaged, and so they are found in some numbers, but the antler picks on which they were mounted are generally absent. These could still be used by replacing the blade, and were carried away to the next exploratory pit.

The interesting thing is that these little ox-bone blades seem to have been little used in the actual mining. When we come to look at the successful shaft and gallery mines, we find that the point of the antler is generally preferred to the blade, and despite a careful search we have only identified one ox bone pick from the galleried mines, along with hundreds of antler picks. There are several possible explanations for this contrast. It may be that the exploratory work required the use of a different tool. The distribution of axe marks on the walls of underground galleries might suggest that these were more generally used close to the shaft before the major

Fig. 1:6 *Above* A two-stage mine at Grime's Graves. Upper stage parapet with cavities where nodules have already been extracted from the broken chalk. The lower stage is just visible below the metric rod. *Below* A flint mine shaft at Grime's Graves during excavation. *By kind permission of the Trustees of the British Museum.*

galleries were driven. But it seems most likely that the perforated ox-bone adzes are mounted on the brow tines of antler picks (see Fig. 1:1) whose points have been worn or broken off in gallery mining – that they are the equivalent of a re-sharpened tool. The point of the tine is the working part of the antler tool and, as we shall see, these tools were used and discarded in large quantities underground. The supply of red deer antler was limited (we know very few have been found in the back-filled shafts and virtually none in the exploratory shafts). It is likely that first-class tools were reserved for mining and worn out tools were reserved for the less arduous and rewarding tasks of exploration.

Though the open quarries and exploratory structures provide some insight into prehistoric flint mining techniques and problems, the underground galleried mines at Grime's Graves are the only ones from which we can reconstruct a reasonably complete picture of the pattern of work and of the process of flint extraction, and provide an estimate of the likely returns in terms of quantity of flint extracted in relation for labour time invested in mining. In some ways these galleried mines seem almost uniquely enlightening: the mining methods employed, the condition of the chalk galleries and the circumstances under which they were abandoned would seem to have combined to preserve many different types of evidence not usually available.

A great many galleried flint mines have been explored in Britain since Canon Greenwell in 1869 demonstrated at Grime's Graves that these structures were used for mining flint, but it was only with the most recent excavation at this site that it was realised that the conditions underground could allow a detailed reconstruction of the mining procedure. Previous investigations by archaeologists had concentrated almost without exception on the age and cultural relationships of the prehistoric miners, as evidenced by stylistic analysis of their pottery and finished stone implements. Any description of the mining itself had been limited to generalities. The British Museum investigation at Grime's Graves was carried out in co-operation with the prehistoric mining section of the Netherlands Geological Association at Maastricht, a group including both ex-professional miners and mining engineers, whose interest naturally centred on the methods employed in mining, and whose experience was of great value in providing a really practical reconstruction of mining behaviour. Archaeologists have seldom been professional engineers and miners (or even professional architects or farmers) and their pictures of the past have often been

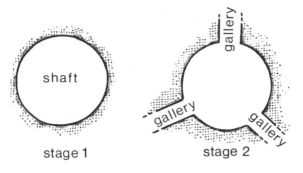

shaft

gallery

gallery

gallery

stage 1   stage 2

Fig. 1:7 Theoretical model of the stages of excavation at (a) the shaft, and (b) a gallery. *By kind permission of the Trustees of the British Museum.*

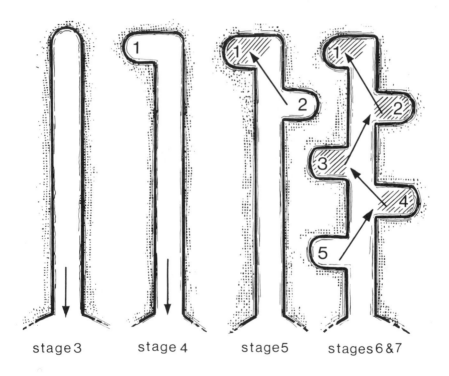

stage 3   stage 4   stage 5   stages 6 & 7

impractical as well as second-hand. Engineer P. J. Felder, who led the underground investigation at Grime's Graves, had been a professional coal miner himself for many years. He it was who realised that it was possible to provide reasonable estimates of the labour employed in each mine, and the time required to complete the mining operation, based on the limiting circumstances these structures provided. The experience and professional knowledge of Mr Felder and his colleagues allow us to formulate a provisional model of the flint mining procedure more practical and realistic than would otherwise be the case, taking into account local opportunities and difficulties that would not have been apparent to the ordinary above ground archaelogist. An outline of the model, and of the evidence on which it is based may now be given.

As field monuments flint mines are best seen from the air. The position of the vertical shafts is marked by a series of semi-circular holes in the ground, usually turf-lined. These are half-filled shafts surrounded by a ring of debris thrown up in the course of sinking the shaft itself or its nearest neighbours. Two points are worth noting. The smooth semi-circular profile of the partly filled shafts indicates that chalk and soil has slipped back into the shaft and also that the shafts are not quite so wide as they appear on the surface. The cylindrical, slightly tapering shafts cut in the chalk, are nevertheless between 5–12 metres in diameter near the surface and become only gradually smaller. In profile they sometimes appear almost as wide as they are deep, and their excavation must have required a considerable effort. Many hundreds of tons of chalk had to be removed before the flint was reached at the shaft bottom. The shafts are sunk through the superficial sands or clays into the chalk rock. Above the solid chalk the mouth of the shaft must have been wider to allow the surface sediments to reach an angle of rest, and some shafts also appear to be somewhat undercut at the base giving a bell-shaped profile due perhaps to the excavation of galleries and collapse caused by consequent changes in loading of the rock. Such a profile may be accentuated by the irregularities in the shaft wall such as shelves, alluded to already.

Each flint mine has a series of low horizontal galleries radiating from the foot of the shaft. The vertical profile shows that the shafts generally cut through two or more horizontal layers of flint nodules in the chalk, before reaching the preferred flint seam just above floor level. The method used at Grime's Graves is to cut down to the base of the flint seam, so that the flint can be levered up in blocks. The galleries driven from the shaft thus follow the same level in relation to the flint and are generally sub-horizontal. It was found that the floor level varied by less than a metre within the galleries of one mine. The blocks of flint left by the miners can still be seen in the walls of the galleries at floor level. The scale of these galleries appears small in contrast to the wide shafts, each gallery having minimum dimensions between 60 cm–1½ metres in height and equivalent breadth, though broadening out into niches or small rooms cut out of the chalk, both near the shaft and at various points along the length of each gallery. The dimensions of the shaft thus allow galleries to be driven in several directions and provide room for manoeuvre when extracting chalk and flint from the galleries. A broad shaft also ensures that a considerable amount of flint can be extracted from the foot during excavation, before the first galleries are begun. Some have gone so far as to suggest that the galleries play a subsidiary rôle in the mining at Grime's Graves, and the shaft provides the greatest amount of extracted flint, but (as will be seen later) our figures do not support this proposition.

Nevertheless the morphology of the galleried mines at Grime's Graves raises the question of alternative strategies of flint extraction. Granted that all the shafts at Grime's Graves are comparatively massive, increasing depth is generally accompanied by increasing shaft diameter. On the surface the large shafts are close together, only separated by the ring of debris surrounding each shaft. Underground, the intervening territory between the shafts is explored by a large number of short galleries and associated niches. A more economical mining procedure might be to dig an occasional large shaft (requiring a massive investment of time and labour) and from this to cut a network of extremely long galleries, a complete mine associated with the single shaft, in the manner of eighteenth- and nineteenth-century mines. There are practical reasons why this procedure was not adopted.

The dimensions of flint mine galleries are dictated by considerations of safety. At Grime's Graves or elsewhere in Britain the chalk is closely jointed. The rock is broken into roughly horizontal layers 30–60 cm apart, with vertical joints at the same intervals. If one cuts a horizontal corridor or gallery into the chalk it has to carry the weight of the rock above it, and the joints limit the width of the gallery, unless it is supported by a system of pit props and ceiling rafters like a modern mine. Careful examination of the flint mines shows that they were designed with a series of narrow galleries, with load-bearing walls, and that pit props and supports were not used. Under these conditions a single shaft with radiating horizontal galleries is an inefficient method of extracting flint except in the immediate vicinity of the shaft. Niches and side galleries cannot be cut without altering the roof loading and endangering the whole system. So that as the straight narrow corridors become more distant from the shaft they become further apart, the dead ground between them increases and the percentage of total available flint extracted diminishes exponentially. The system adopted with a series of large shafts close together and numerous short galleries between them extracts a far greater percentage of the flint seam in the immediate vicinity of the shafts, and this may be an overriding consideration if the seam is thought to be discontinuous in regional terms and likely to run out at any moment.

At Grime's Graves the flint seam is in fact too regular and the mine shafts cover too large an area for one to be certain of the manner in which the most valuable part of the site was progressively explored and exploited. But if we examine other flint mines whose shafts are visible from the surface or from air photography we find isolated shafts, lines of shafts and small or large groups of shafts, suggesting that exploitation consisted of sinking a number of adjacent shafts on all sides of a successful mine until the flint seam had run out and then moving to a more profitable site a few hundred metres away.

We can reconstruct some of the mining techniques with confidence, as both the conditions and the tools used closely resemble those found in coal mining before this was mechanised. The flint miner's pick made out of deer antler closely resembles a modern mining tool. Though it is smaller it too has one short prong mounted on a handle with a sharp point at the working end. The host rock surrounding the coal seam in the mine is also familiar, since it is enclosed in a system of joints like those in the chalk. From this we deduce that the antler picks were used like those of modern miners under such conditions, to take advantage of the joint system to extract convenient sized blocks of rock. Mining is not like digging potatoes, or digging a trench in soft soil or sand. The problem to be faced in cutting through solid rock, is to find a way of breaking the rock into convenient sizes at right-angles to the surface. The rock wall or floor holds together in one piece. It may be described as being in tension: the problem is to break the tension in the rock by progressive removal of small blocks. This can best be done by following faults, fractures and joints in the rock. The point of the tool is used to pick out a convenient fissure or joint. This is followed until the cross-joints are laid bare. A line of blocks is

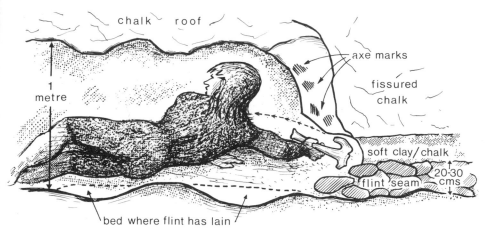

Fig. 1:8 Reconstruction showing the use of an antler pick in mining flint. *By kind permission of the Trustees of the British Museum.*

extracted, a parallel joint is explored and further blocks extracted. The principal tool at Grime's Graves (in fact the only tool found except in a very few cases), the red deer antler pick, shows conclusively that it was used for this purpose. Nearly always the points of the picks are worn and numerous holes the size of the point of the brow tine are found in the walls of the mine galleries. Many broken points of these picks have been found in the galleries, in one case (in the most recent investigation at Greenwell's Pit) a brow tine point was still in position stuck in one of these holes.

If we examine the gallery walls we find traces of the mining technique described above, most notably at the level of the flint seam itself. Along the flat top of the flint seam a deep groove has often been cut with an antler pick. If this groove is illuminated with a side-light one can see traces of the individual blows struck by the miner in cutting the groove; a series of horizontal jabs. One can judge the direction of the blows and thus where the miner was placed, and in which hand the pick was held at this point. The mining procedure underground seems to have been to tackle the flint seam last. The chalk is especially soft above the impervious flint, as water migrating downwards from the surface has been held up at this point, and a deep groove is easily cut. Once this is effected it is easy to extract a first layer of rocks and then to bring down the rest of the rock above, until sufficient room is provided to lever up the flint from the gallery floor.

In addition to the point of the pick the red deer antler often shows considerable battering and deep-cut marks at the head of the shaft, behind the point of departure of the brow tine. It was first thought that this might be due to using a mallet to drive the pick further into the chalk before levering out a block, but this does not seem to be likely. During the British Museum investigation several flint mining experiments were carried out using professional miners and picks made from modern red deer antler. In some cases hammers of the hardest box-wood and of antler were used to drive the pick into the wall, but this did not appear to be as efficient as swinging the pick in the usual manner. Also it was not possible to reproduce the marks found on the ancient picks in this way, as the red deer antler was too hard to damage with these materials. The only thing that could bruise the antler was the flint itself and fragments of flint were found in some of the ancient grooves in the antler. This suggests that the pick itself was sometimes reversed and used as a hammer to shift the flint when it was levered up from its bed.

The mine galleries themselves are always rather damp, and chalk dust produced in the mining is compressed into hard mud on the floors and is found on the handles of the picks, where fingerprints of the miners are sometimes preserved. In addition to the fingerprints (which though unusual are generally too fragmentary for identification purposes), one can find places where the grip-marks made by the miners are preserved. The mud has been squeezed up into a row of parallel ridges, which enable us to get some idea of the grip of the tool adopted by the miners. The mud-covered handle of one of these tools shows that the fingers of the miner curled round the pick handle away from rather than facing the direction of the brow tine. This confirms the use of this tool as a hammer, suggested by the battering commonly found on its crown. Unlike the chalk, the flint at Grime's Graves is not jointed though it has been shattered at intervals by some natural cause, possibly by off-loading after a heavy glacier had passed across the surface of the hill, or by permafrost (which might well include freezing to this depth in chalk), during a glacial phase of the Pleistocene period. However, such fractures are irregular, so that additional hammering must often have been required to break the flint into convenient pieces. The so-called flint seam is usually made up of a large number of blocks of irregular size and thickness joined together on the upper surface by a continuous thin horizontal layer of flint. Between the individual blocks this layer is only 5–10 cm thick. It is

Fig. 1:9 A view of a mine gallery wall showing the jointed chalk, the black flint seam at the foot of the wall, and an antler abandoned in the mine. (20 cm scale.) *By kind permission of the Trustees of the British Museum.*

easy to break the flint at these points, so that while the antler picks could only be used as hammers to shift jammed blocks if these have already been shattered by natural causes, they undoubtedly also served to break the thin flint crust between them.

If the red deer antler picks are the only tools found in large numbers at Grime's Graves, they are not the only tools used, though there is no trace of the so-called shoulder blade shovel made from cow or deer shoulder blades which seems to have been used in the earlier flint mines in Sussex. Nor can we find underground any other tools for shifting rock once it has been mined. Such tools could have been of wood, for wood would not be preserved in the flint mines: but there is evidence to suggest that shovels need not have been used, at least in the galleries. All the blocks of chalk

27

could have been put into baskets by hand or piled up into heaps without the use of additional tools. But in addition to pick marks the walls of the galleries do show other traces, including marks left by the blades of axes or adzes, most probably stone axes with a somewhat wider blade than the perforated ox-bone adzes already described. Considerable numbers of these axe marks have been found in the galleries, usually close together in groups and generally at points where the wall bulges out into the gallery, or above a block of flint which has not been extracted but shows traces of preparation for extraction. It seems that the mining procedure – or one of the mining procedures – was to lay bare a block of flint by extracting the irregular chalk blocks above it, and to remove any irregularities in the face, cutting these away with a stone axe mounted or held sideways or as an adze and so creating sufficient room to lever up and remove the flint block without advancing any further into the chalk (Fig. 1:8).

The methods used to shift chalk and flint cannot be completely documented. During facework a good deal could be accomplished by hand. The chalk came away in convenient sized blocks. These were picked up one by one and placed behind the faceworker. In one niche where the flint was being extracted it is possible to see the flattened area of crushed chalk where the faceworker was seated facing the wall with his tools still in position beside the flint seam. Behind his seat is a sloping ramp of chalk blocks piled against the back wall of the niche. The air spaces and the lack of chalk dust between the blocks and the way the heap slopes away from the working position show that each block had been placed by hand. After cutting at the chalk face both chalk debris and flint need to be moved at least some distance away to keep the gallery clear and allow freedom of movement. This must have been accomplished by a combination of containers such as bags and baskets, possibly with additional tools such as rakes and spades. The latter would have to have extremely short handles if they were to be used in the confined space of an underground gallery. In all, the mining technique seems to offer considerable opportunities to the use of the human hand as an instrument of transport, though we must keep in mind the claims for bone shovels and antler rakes at the (much earlier) but similar flint mines in Sussex. As these are not present in the Norfolk mines perhaps they had been replaced by wooden versions of the same tools as woodland was comparatively plentiful in the vicinity of Grime's Graves.

The methods so far outlined were employed to dig both shafts and galleries at Grime's Graves. As Mr Felder has pointed out, the dimensions of the shafts and of the galleries each in different ways limit the maximum number of people that can be employed to excavate them, and thus enable one to work out the most probable size of the mining teams. More than a certain number of men cannot be packed into a confined space, particularly if they require room to swing a pick and to dispose of spoil in the form of broken chalk or sand before it is carried away and, though there is room for considerable variation in the amount of space required for this purpose, there are certain limits between which the operations of digging and transport can be carried on efficiently. For the purposes of calculation we have supposed that one man requires a square metre of working space. With this in mind, we may discuss the probable working of one of the flint mines at Grime's Graves, Greenwell's Pit, re-examined by the British Museum between 1974–6, which has one of the deepest shafts at this site.

At the top of the shaft the horizontal dimension provides 24 square metres of working space. Allowing for a margin of error this would allow for a team of approximately twenty persons engaged in mining. One may suppose that one man in two could have been excavating on the surface of the ground while a second man would be shifting the soil in baskets. As the level of the shaft sinks more people are required to shift the rock debris, and the total number of excavators or pick-men falls progressively. In fact, the shaft's dimensions narrow, so as to provide less than 16 square metres at the base. But, as the pit deepens, the real constraint becomes the ever-increasing task of lifting rock to the surface. If between 6–8 men are still employed excavating at the foot of the shaft, the rest would easily find employment moving the rock. Spoil could be hauled to the surface by ropes, or alternatively carried, probably up a series of stages established in the side of each shaft. Evidence for the use of both forms of transport have been found at Grime's Graves. The shaft excavated in 1972–3 preserved slots for horizontal wooden beams across the shaft which could have acted as the base for a platform fairly low down in the shaft (approximately 3–4 metres from the shaft floor) and in the shaft of Greenwell's Pit a natural ledge existed at the same level. These should probably both be considered as evidence for the use of stages, perhaps a number of which were in use one above the other, joined by short ladders. At Greenwell's Pit there is also evidence at the mouth of a gallery of a rope-groove cut into the roof. A rope has been lowered from the surface to drag some weight apparently from the interior of the gallery. The miners must have required ladders to reach the foot of the shaft, but we have no means of knowing which method was preferred for carrying rock.

The second stage in mining, that of driving galleries, necessarily employs less labour since the working space is smaller. There is evidence (discussed below) that at Greenwell's Pit only four galleries (out of a total of seven piercing the walls of the shaft) were actually cut from this shaft. (The remainder are attributed to neighbouring shafts.) The horizontal opening of each shaft is sufficient only for one face-worker wielding a pick. This workman requires for efficiency one assistant to move spoil, which at first is placed in a heap in the centre of the shaft. Such heaps, pyramids 3–5 metres high in the shaft centre, are as far as we know always found in the shafts of these mines when they are re-excavated.

If our reconstruction is accepted the four galleries that we find at Greenwell's Pit would require a total of eight men to service them. It is when the gallery system at Greenwell's Pit is examined that further deductions can be made. To do this we must interpret the plan of the galleries, which is a little confusing. The jointing of the chalk and the existence of occasional large faults in the rock make the gallery walls most irregular and increase their height and width in an unsystematic manner. There are also both large and small rooms, whose function has to be inferred, and these still further complicate the task of reading the pattern of operations from the gallery plan. Fortunately the contents of the interior of the galleries supply us with further information, which allows us to see how the work was carried out.

The first excavators to explore Grime's Graves and other British galleried mines, naturally expected to find a series of empty corridors underground like those of a modern worked out mine, where all the ore and rock debris had been taken to the surface. When the galleries of the flint mines were found to be filled up with chalk this was at first attributed to falls from the roof, so that re-examining the prehistoric mines was thought to be very dangerous. In fact, the greater part of the galleries are intact, as the miners kept within strict limits of roof loading. The chalk debris in these galleries was left there intentionally. Once this is realised the debris itself becomes a most useful archaeological tool, as it seals up the original wall and floor surface and ensures it is undamaged. It also preserves the tools and activity traces, and can be used to work out the comparative age of different mines and of separate galleries, by means of stratigraphy.

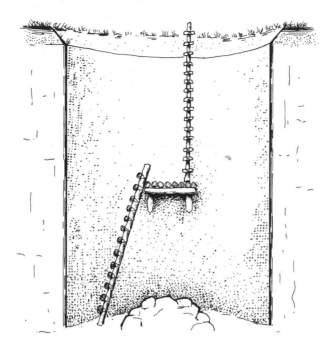

Fig. 1:10 Section of mine shaft showing means of access. Reconstructed from evidence of excavation (depth 14 metres). *By kind permission of the Trustees of the British Museum.*

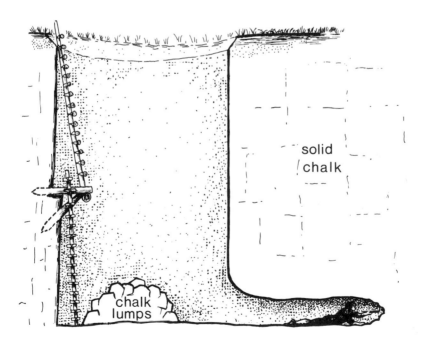

When an abandoned gallery is first re-visited it is usually found to be partly blocked with rock mining debris, back-filled by the miners themselves after the flint has been extracted and it is the slope of this debris that provides the essential stratigraphical information. After all the slope details from the different galleries have been correlated, we can work out the direction from which the gallery was back-filled and also the sequence of operations along different parts of the gallery. This allows us to see that there are essentially two successive stages in gallery mining, a first stage when a long narrow straight gallery is cut, flint is extracted from the floor of the gallery, and the chalk also removed, though not taken to the surface; and a second stage when niches or rooms are cut in the walls of the gallery, starting at the far end and working backwards towards the shaft. In stage one the chalk debris is removed, probably to be dumped on the shaft floor or in other already abandoned galleries, but stage two debris is left close by the workings. As a niche is widened the dimensions of the roof increase until it becomes too dangerous to continue. At this point a further niche is cut in the opposite wall of the gallery and the discarded rock from this is packed into the first niche when it is finally abandoned. A long gallery contains a series of heaps from these niches piled against the walls on both sides. These heaps interdigitate like the fingers of two hands touching one another. Each heap overlies the one behind, demonstrating conclusively the order in which the niches were exploited, starting at the end of the gallery furthest from the shaft. This mining method appears to be in general use in all the mines examined at Grime's Graves. A good visible example of such a gallery with its row of heaps filling side niches has been left untouched so that it can be seen and studied.

The gallery system of Greenwell's Pit includes four straight galleries, each with its characteristic niches, but the length of each gallery differs. Working round the shaft these are approximately 4, 8, 16, and 24 metres in length. The disparity between the lengths of the various galleries may be explained, if we assume the existence of a limited labour force to carry out the underground mining, and also take into account the increasing transport difficulties involved in progressively lengthening each gallery. The stratigraphy of the debris in the mine shows that the four galleries were abandoned and re-filled in inverse order of length, with the shortest gallery being the first to be abandoned and re-filled. If each face-man requires at first one assistant to move and re-pack his chalk debris and deliver flint for removal to the surface, after the gallery has been leng-

Fig. 1:11 A flint mine gallery discovered at Greenwell Pit. Heaps are piled up filling niches on either side of a long straight gallery. The scale in the photograph is metric (cf. plan of stages of reconstruction shown in Fig. 1:7). *By kind permission of the Trustees of the British Museum.*

thened a certain distance it will be necessary to supply a second assistant, and later a third assistant. The gallery dimensions suggest that the crisis occurred every four metres and that it was not always possible to supply extra labour from those working at the top of the shaft. Thus the galleries were depleted of staff and in turn abandoned as the labour team had to be reinforced in the other galleries which were still in use.

If one adopts a suitable figure for the amount of chalk cut by the pick of each labourer during the course of the day, it is possible to come up with a total figure for the time involved in excavating and exploiting each flint mine. The British Museum carried out a number of detailed experiments in cutting chalk with flint picks, and these results are still being analysed. A typical result suggests for example that a miner can produce 300–400 kg of chalk an hour for the period of an eight hour day, including both cutting and clearing operations and relaxation time. This has yet to be converted into actual cubic metres. For purposes of argument we have supposed that each worker can produce approximately a cubic metre of debris per day. Applied to the Greenwell's Pit this suggests that a team of twenty labourers could excavate the shaft in between 80–100 days. The exact figure arrived at appears to be 86 days. A further 42 days is required to excavate the galleries and remove the flint. These figures are not reliable, and will no doubt be changed as various computations and corrections are applied; but they do give some real idea of the time required to totally excavate one of the mines at Grime's Graves. The time required is short and the mine was abandoned before all the galleries had been fully exploited. This suggests that the mines were usually dug and worked in one operation and a limited period, and we may infer that flint mining was probably only a seasonal activity. In the following years further galleries were driven from nearby shafts (as shown by the direction of back-fill of these galleries) to complete the exploitation of this area, but the mine was not re-opened.

Various pieces of evidence support this picture of the mining as a short term activity. When we penetrate underground to the end of our galleries furthest from the shaft we generally run into other shafts or other galleries, already exploited. The miners have cut through the rock wall and come upon another already abandoned and back-filled gallery. Sometimes they merely cut a small window, too small to crawl through, before deciding that it was not worth going any further. Sometimes they cut such a window and stopped because a shaft filled with brown earth confronted them. There can be little doubt that neighbouring mine shafts were exploited within a very few years of each other, while the whereabouts of previous exploitation was still well remembered. No one would risk driving galleries into chalk already weakened by earlier operations if he could help it, and once abandoned each part of the minefield is unlikely to have been re-opened. We can also show that the shafts of abandoned mines were back-filled almost immediately, i.e. before the galleries of adjacent mines had been cut. This is not universally true: at one site at Grime's Graves two shafts were operated at the same time with an exit gallery kept open between them. But the evidence for reasonably rapid back-filling of shafts seems quite firm. One must suppose that the abandoned mine shaft was the most convenient place to jettison the rock from the next shaft when this was cut. It filled up a dangerous hole and disposed of a large amount of spoil which would otherwise form a heap of inconvenient height and size, and cover the ground required to sink adjacent shafts. In general, spoil heaps sufficiently large to represent the filling of a shaft do not occur at Grime's Graves. The only example of such a heap, close to a very deep mine shaft, may be on the site of the first mine excavated on the hilltop before such a convenient method of disposal was available.

Perhaps the best evidence for the rapid back-filling and closure of the shafts at Grime's Graves was recorded during the 1974-6 excavation at Greenwell's Pit. While the pit was being re-examined every year a large quantity of wild animals would fall down the pit during the winter season when no-one was about. On one occasion the bones of thirty different animals were found, including voles, rabbits and frogs. No bones of any ancient wild mammals were found in Greenwell's Pit: there are, of course, several hundred red deer antler picks and the complete skeleton of a domestic dog, apparently deliberately buried in back-fill. Most careful search was made for any trace of animals which might have fallen down the shaft. The fact that they are not present suggests simply that the mine was closed a very short time after it was abandoned. It seems likely that the shafts at Grime's Graves were generally filled right up to the surface and that the hollows seen in the ground today represent later subsidence.

Figures can be provided not only for the time and labour required to operate the flint mines but for the success of the operation. The amount of flint recovered from the mines can be directly calculated from casts left in the chalk floors of the galleries and the position of the flint in the walls. Each nodule of flint has been levered up from a bed in the chalk on or below floor level, and the position of these nodules is clearly registered by holes in the floors of the galleries, when they have been carefully cleaned of trampled chalk. Furthermore the upper surface of the flint seam is nearly horizontal and can be accurately estimated from its position in the adjacent gallery walls. The figures for Greenwell's Pit suggest a total of approximately 45 tonnes, approximately 80 per cent of which was obtained from the four galleries. Very little flint was available before the shaft was totally excavated, when 5-6 tonnes could be extracted. Thereafter a total of nearly a tonne of flint a day was available until the mine was abandoned.

More than 250 miners' picks were found in the back-fill of the Greenwell's Pit galleries, suggesting that the miners used up their tools fairly rapidly. Allowing for use by all members of the underground mining team, there is a wastage of approximately one pick a day per man. The large total of deer antlers required to make these tools suggests the existence of a good local supply of deer, itself a forest animal. Zoological examination of the antler also suggests that they represent one population, rather than the result of sporadic and widespread collection of the antlers after they have been shed by these animals; so we can envisage that the deer lived in the immediate vicinity of the mines.

In our discussion we have necessarily omitted many interesting details and even subjects. Lighting is a difficult question. Though chalk lamps have been found at other flint mine sites there is no trace of the use of artificial light underground at Grime's Graves. Reflected light from the chalk shaft was sufficient to light the galleries for mining purposes once the eyes were adjusted. Archaeological debris is another matter. There is no habitation refuse such as pottery or flaked flint in the galleries. One stone axe (said to fit the axe marks on the wall) was found in Greenwell's Pit in 1870 but the axes are not normally discarded which is one reason why their use can be regarded as confined to light work. However, the miners do seem to have carried food and drink to the foot of the shaft. Whole pottery containers (usually broken) are found at gallery entrances and on the top of the central chalk heap where they must have sat and relaxed between spells of labour.

The pattern of shaft and gallery mining displayed at Grime's Graves may be in common use at the other galleried British flint mines. We have little direct evidence except that the profile of the shafts and galleries of the other British examples seem very similar to those of the Norfolk mines. All the British mines make use of antler picks in large numbers. The British chalk exploited is always closely jointed and the mining technique makes full use of this characteristic. The shafts, though of different depth, are generally wide in proportion to their depth and there seems a close relationship between mining and quarrying. Each is carried out in a similar manner and each produces similar scars on the countryside.

Some of the continental flint mines, those in Holland and Belgium, our nearest neighbours, contrast strongly with the British examples. The mineshafts of these mines are generally perfectly cylindrical and not much more than $1\frac{1}{2}$ metres in diameter to whatever depth they are sunk. Their galleries are also generally narrow and low, and have smoothly carved rounded walls. In the Dutch mines antler picks were seldom if ever used in underground mining. They were replaced by flint pick-heads, at least thirty thousand of which have been recovered in the small number of mines examined at Rijkholt. The flint picks are sometimes found in heaps in the galleries, together with stone hammers used to

Fig. 1:12 A typical gallery at Grime's Graves after clearing by archaeologists. *By kind permission of the Trustees of the British Museum.*

re-sharpen them underground. (Supply heaps of antler picks have been found at Grime's Graves.) The general method of mining and back-filling employed in these Dutch flint mines resembles that in use in Grime's Graves, but the scale appears to be different. Many of the mineshafts in both Dutch and Belgian mines exceed those of Grime's Graves in depth. Sometimes they are more than 25 metres deep, sunk first through 10–15 metres of overlying gravel or soft sediment, and then cut through several metres of chalk, without varying in width or diameter. These remarkable structures seem to have been lined with basketry to contain the soft sediments, while footholds are cut in the chalk shaft to let the miners climb up and down.

The reason for the different approach employed by the Dutch and British miners may be sought in the properties of the chalk in the two areas. The British chalk is hard, but may easily be levered up, or extracted with antler picks. The Limburg chalk is soft and carves more easily than a British chalk, but the joints in the rock are far apart, and the antler pick would be no use as a mining tool here.

But to discuss the two types of galleried flint mines solely in terms of mining geology is to miss the essential point. The Dutch and the British mines represent different mining strategies in respect to their employment of labour. The Dutch mine is essentially a two-man operation, resembling an open air quarry. There is no room for more than two people to dig the shaft or to extract the flint. Thus the length of gallery associated with each shaft is shorter than at Grime's Graves and the shafts are closer together. The number of shafts at Rijkholt may exceed a thousand, and other continental mines are of similar size. It is doubtful however, if their productivity of extracted flint per mineshaft exceeded that of a single gallery at Grime's Graves. But a high proportion of the available flint appears to have been extracted in the vicinity of the mines. So the Dutch small-scale mines were not noticeably less efficient than those in Britain.

If we return to Grime's Graves we see that the contemporary opencast mining is another instance of this alternative mining strategy. It is a small-scale 2–3 man operation as opposed to the large team operation in use at the galleried mines on the site. Each open air quarry could be dug, exploited and abandoned in a few hours, a day or two at the most. From the beginning of our research we were struck by the size contrast between the two forms of mining structures. We tended to see this as a social difference, with quarrymen as local farmers requiring to supply their own small-scale needs, and the galleried mines operated by professional miners supplying wider regional needs for flint. However, another explanation is possible. Even if the two forms of exploitation are contemporary the Radiocarbon chronology only places them within a 40–50 year time-bracket. The shafts and galleries of the large structures represent a considerable labour investment with a large return in flint supplies, perhaps enough to supply the miners or their market with flint for two to three years. As with other seasonal operations the mining may not have been carried out every year. If a two- or three-year interval was observed in the mining operations, it was open to the miners to renew their flint supplies, perhaps for local needs only, by short term quarrying operations, at a minimal cost in terms of labour supplies or man hours. But it is difficult to judge of the motives of the prehistoric miner. While the quarrying at Grime's Graves does not seem very rewarding to us, compared with the mining, it is a general observation with all forms of primitive mining that full advantage is taken of the supplies of raw material wherever they may be. The sites appear to have been fully exploited before they were abandoned. Our chronological information of the quarrying at Grime's Graves is insufficiently detailed, and it may be that much of the opencast quarrying is later than the exploitation of the finest supplies of floorstone in the mines on the crest of the hill.

Elsewhere in Great Britain flint mines also show a gradation of operations from the small quarry to the galleried mine and the strategy adopted in each case must be a function of the depth of flint from the surface, and the geological circumstances. Some extensive mine-fields are almost entirely limited to using quarries, and the total output of flint from these structures must rival that of a field of galleried mines. This output can be judged not only from the estimated amount of flint extracted from the mines but from the large amounts of factory debris found at the head of the mineshafts. These are circular spreads of flint flakes and chunks and rejected or broken tool blanks sometimes at Grime's Graves more than a metre thick and several metres in diameter, overlying and sometimes sliding down into the tops of abandoned mineshafts. It seems as if some considerable part of the flint produced by the miners was roughed into shape, either as tool blanks or squared nodules before they were carried away. This may have been an essential part of the processing procedure, carried out as the flint was hauled to the surface, so that it could be packed up for transport by pack or by river.

The quantity of flint produced by each mine and the amount of tools made in these pit-head workshops was out of all proportion to the domestic supplies required by a group of twenty to thirty men. If we accept a figure of 30 tonnes of flint as an average yield from each mine, this is considerably more than one might expect to be consumed locally at regular one- or two-year intervals. We can see this if we look at the output of 30 000 axes a year suggested by archaeologists for a workshop associated with a similar flint mining complex in Poland. If a fair proportion of other smaller products were being manufactured at Grime's Graves in addition to axes the total production might be considerably greater.

The increase in scale of operations represented by Neolithic mining and quarrying, as compared with the earlier sporadic exploitations of this raw material is confirmed when the site of Grime's Graves is looked at as a whole. There are between 350–500 galleried mines, of similar dimensions to those already described. The Radiocarbon date suggest a 200–300 year period for the greater part of the mining. Exploitation on this scale has some claim to be

considered as something in the nature of an industrial revolution
when it is compared with the small-scale operations which precede
it, in the periods before 3500 B.C. It may be that Grime's Graves
represents the highest point in terms of organisation and output,
and that earlier developments are not so considerable. But evidence
for similar changes elsewhere in late Neolithic society are hard to
find. Some very large monuments were constructed by the cultural
group thought to have exploited Grime's Graves, the makers of
pottery known as grooved ware. The big henge monuments such as
Durrington Walls, constructed by this group at exactly the same
date as Grime's Graves, have extremely large ditches which represent a much larger investment in terms of labour than the largest
single galleried flint mine. But these are ceremonial monuments,
whose construction was perhaps the collective responsibility of
many different scattered communities and could have taken many
years to complete. Organised labour, ceremonial monuments and
galleried flint mines are all known from the earlier Neolithic
peoples 700–1000 years before Grime's Graves was in serious
operation.

It is fair however to regard the increase in flint mining and
quarrying activity which starts in Western Europe about 3500–3000
B.C. and continues until 1700 B.C. as one manifestation of an
increasing concern with the acquisition and exchange of raw
materials, some of which are definitely luxuries in this period as are
gold, copper, and also perhaps fine quality flint. The evolution (if
we may call it so) of copper mining can usefully be compared with
that of flint mining. Early copper mines are known for Yugoslavia
and Bulgaria, Southern Spain, Israel, and Southern Ireland, all of
which which may be as early or in some cases considerably earlier
than the British flint mines. Copper mining in Yugoslavia and
Bulgaria dates from the fourth or even from the fifth millennium
B.C. The Yugoslav mines have shafts 20 metres deep. Thirty or
more deep shafts have been found, as well as considerable traces of
other mining quarries and structures. Apparently antler picks were
used in the mining operation. The earliest copper mines in Israel
(dated to 2000 B.C. by their explorer Dr Rothenburg) have gallery
plans and shafts very similar to those of the Norfolk flint mines.
One cannot help being impressed by the parallels between early
copper mining and the flint mines. However, though copper was
known and used in Europe for several thousand years before 2000
B.C., it appears to be of no economic importance whatsoever. The
settlements and burials of the prehistoric copper users contain a few

trinkets, rings, armlets, of copper; a handful of pins and possibly a copper axe or two. The impression is that the metal was purely a luxury at this period.

Shortly after 2000 B.C. bronze tools became of economic importance, and we find that the copper mines increase in extent and compare in output with the flint mines. A newly examined copper mine field in County Cork in Ireland (dated to around 1500 B.C.) had an estimated total output of 1000 tonnes. One well known group of copper mines in Austria had an estimated annual output of 20 tonnes over a period of 300 years. Bronze tools were now of importance to the economy, and bronze replaced flint as the dominant raw material. The flint mines at Grime's Graves ceased production at this time, and it looks as if they were replaced as an economic phenomenon by metal mining on a very similar scale. Thus we may say that after following a very similar course of development over more than a thousand years a decisive shift took place in mining and exploitation from one raw material to the other.

Our model of the flint mining industry at Grime's Graves is of a part-time activity producing a considerable surplus of flint over local needs and transforming a high proportion of this raw material into blanks for implements required as counters in some extended regional exchange network.

One must end on a note of caution. It is easy to get an exaggerated idea of the scale of operations in the flint mines and of the professionalism of the miners. All that we have learned of flint mining at Grime's Graves suggests the existence of a strong and consistent tradition of flint mining – a professional approach involving a carefully worked out procedure, which was no doubt necessary if the underground extraction of flint was to be both safe and successful. While the tools used for extraction were common in the communities from which they came their application was systematic and controlled. As we have seen, the mining could have been undertaken on a part-time or seasonal basis and this need occasion no surprise. There are good descriptions of part-time mining in medieval England carried out by farmers in the slack periods of late Spring and early Autumn, and lead mines in Yorkshire were operated in this manner by farmers in the nineteenth century. The professionalism of such farmers can well be explained if mining was an essential and continuous occupation. Many types of traditional rural husbandry are as systematic and demanding, and it is not so long since similar cottage industries were a recognised part of rural life.

BIBLIOGRAPHY

ARMSTRONG, A.L. (1923) 'Discovery of a New Phase of Early Flint Mining at Grime's Graves, Norfolk' *PPSEA* 4, 113–25.
(1926) 'The Grime's Graves Excavation in the Light of Recent Research' *PPSEA* 5, 91–136.
BECKER, C.J. (1951) 'Late-Neolithic Flint Mines at Aalborg' *Acta. Arch.* XXII, 135–52.
(1951) 'Flintgruberne ved Aalborg. En 3500-aarig Dansk Ekaportvisksomhed' *NM Arbm.* 107–12.
(1959) 'Flint Mining in Neolithic Denmark' *Antiquity* 33, 87–92.
BRIART, A. (with CORNET, F.L.) (1872) 'Sur l'age de la pierre polie et les exploitations prehistoriques de Silex dans la province de Hainaut' *Congr. int. d'anthr. et d'arch. prehistoriques*, C.r.6ᵉ sess. Bruxelles 1872, 279–99. cf. C.r.10ᵉ sess. Paris 1889, 569–612.
CLARK, J.G.D. and PIGGOTT, S. (1933) 'The Age of the British Flint Mines' *Ant.* VII (1933), 166–83.
CLARK, W.G. (ed) (1915) 'Report on the Excavations at Grime's Graves, Weeting, Norfolk, March–May 1914' *Prehistoric Society of East Anglia Research Report*.
CLASON, A.T. (1971) 'The Flint-Mine Workers of Spiennes and Rijckholt – St Geertruid and their Animals' *Helinium*, no. 1, 13–33.
COLLINS, A. E. P. (1958) 'Ballygalley Head, Co. Antrim' *Proc. Prehistoric Society* 24 (1958), 218.
CURWEN, E. and E. C. (1926) 'Harrow Hill Flint Mine Excavation, 1924–25' *S.A.C.* LXVII, 1–36.
et al (1924) 'Blackpatch Flint-Mine Excavation, 1922' *S.A.C.* LXV, 69–111.
CURWEN, E.C. (1937) *The Archaeology of Sussex* London 1937.
ENGELEN, F.H.C. (1970) 'De oudste mijnbouw in Nederland' *Geologie en Mijnbouw* 49(1), 23–40.
FÜLÖP, J. (1975) 'Relics of Prehistoric Flint Mining in Hungary' *Staringia No. 3* Second International Symposium on Flint, Maastricht 1975, Nederlandse Geologische Vereniging, 72–7.
GINTER, B. (1969) 'Z problematyki badawczej schylkowopaleolitycznch pracowni krzemieniarskich cyklu mazowszanskiego w rejonie Wyzyny Wielunskiej/Summary: Problèmes des études sur les ateliers litiques épipaléolithiques de "Cycle Mazovien" de la région du Plateau de Wielunl' In *Prace i Materialy Muzeum Archeologicznego i Etnograficzego w Lodzi 16*
GREENWELL, W. (1871) 'On the Opening of Grime's Graves in Norfolk' *Jnl. Ethnological Soc.* 2, 419–40.
JAHN, M. (1960) *Der Älteste Bergbau in Europa* Abhandlungen der Sächsischen Akademie der Wissenschaften zu Leipzig.
KRUKOWSKI, S. (1939) *The Flint Mine of Krzemionki Opatowski* Warsaw 1939.
LECH, J. (1975) 'Neolithic flint mine and workshops at Saspów, near Cracow' *Staringia No. 3* Second International Symposium on Flint, Maastricht 1975, Nederlandse Geologische Vereniging.
MERCER, R. (1972) 'Excavation of a New Pit at Grime's Graves' *Department of the Environment Report*.
PIGGOTT, S. (1954) *The Neolithic Cultures of the British Isles* London.
SANDARS, H. W. (1910) 'On the Use of the Deer-Horn Pick in the Mining Operations of the Ancients' *Archaeologia* 62 (1910) 101–24.
SCHILD, R. (1971) 'Lokalizacja przetwórczych punktów eksploatacji krzemienia czekoladowego na pólnocno-wschodnim obrzezeniu Gór Swietokrzyskich/Summary: Location of the so-called Chocolate flint extraction sites on the North-eastern footslopes of the Holy Cross Mountains' In *Folia Quaternaria* 39.
SCHMIDT, E. (1972) 'A Mousterian Silex mine and dwelling place in the Swiss Jura' In *The Origin of Homo Sapiens* (ed) Bordes, F. Proceedings of the Paris INQUA Symposium for 1969, Unesco, Paris 1972, 129–33.

SIEVEKING, G. de G. *et al* (1972) 'Prehistoric Flint Mines and their Identification as Sources of Raw Material' *Archaeometry* 14, 2 (1972) 151–76.

et al (1973) 'A new survey of Grime's Graves, Norfolk' *Proceedings of the Prehistoric Society* 39, 1973.

STONE, J.F.S. (1931) 'Easton Down, Winterslow, S. Wilts., Flint Mine Excavation, 1930' *W.A.M.* XLV (1931), 350–65.

(1933) 'Excavation at Easton Down, Winterslow, 1931–32' *W.A.M.* XLVI (1933), 225–42.

(1933) 'A Flint Mine at St Martin's Clump, Over Wallop' *Hants F.C. Procs.* XII, 177–80.

VERHEYLEWEGHEN, J. (1967) 'Le Néolithique Minier Belge. Son Origine et ses Relations Culturelles' *Palaeohistoria* XII (1967), 529–57.

VERTES, L. (1964) 'Eine Prähistorische Silexgrube am Mogyorósdomb bei Sumeg' *Acta Archaeologica, Academiae Scientiarum Hungaricae* XVI, Budapest 1964.

2

The First Metal Workings and their Geological Setting

J. W. BARNES

Few realise that until little over a century ago the British Isles was the world's leading producer of metals, smelting them mostly from domestic ores. Lead came from Wales, Somerset, Devon and Derbyshire, and from the 'North Pennine Orefield' of Yorkshire, Cumbria, Northumberland and Durham. Copper, in which Britain led the world, came from Ireland, Anglesey and Devon, but mostly from Cornwall which had the largest copper deposits then known. Tin came from Cornwall too. Ironstone was found in many parts of Britain, often conveniently close to coalfields. When zinc, in the mid-eighteenth century, began to establish itself as a metal, it gave a further bonus to the mining of the lead ores with which it was associated although long before then zinc had been used unwittingly in the form of its carbonate 'calamine', in the manufacture of brass. Silver was a by-product of many lead mines and even gold was mined in Wales, Scotland and Ireland in what were in pre-Californian gold-rush days, by no means insignificant amounts. Of the 'seven metals of antiquity', only mercury was missing, and even that did occur, although its discovery had to await the 1960s.

In the history of civilisation, the British Isles was a late-comer to metal usage, not entering the Bronze Age until *c.* 1800 B.C. and the Iron Age some 1300 years later. However, it was soon established as an exporter of tinstone, one of the ingredients of bronze, and it produced all the copper it needed for its own use. Bronze Age Irish metalwork was traded as far as central Europe whilst Irish gold was also known from an early date. Lead, and its by-product silver, were said by some to have been the principal reason why the

References are listed on page 83.

44

Romans came to what Julius Caesar described as a 'grey land hidden in eternal mists'. The Romans were enthusiastic miners and produced metals during the whole of their occupation but when they left, four hundred years later, mining declined as it did everywhere during the Dark Ages. Smiths all over Europe then had to depend on metal scrap for their trade except, oddly enough, for lead, for in Britain lead mining survived, although the metal produced was no longer desilvered.

Mining in Europe revived under Charlemagne with the reopening of the silver-rich lead mines of Chemnitz and Kremnitz in the Erzegebirge, towards the end of the eighth century, and in later centuries mining flourished within the limited metal requirements of those times. In Britain, there was often government encouragement, such as the establishment of the *Mines Royal*, but such encouragement was by no means disinterested: it ensured revenue and the materials of war. With the coming of the Industrial Revolution British mining expanded further, production increased, new fields were exploited, and smelting methods improved with the use of new fuels. Britain was not the only metal producer, but it was the most important and it had the technological lead. During the last 150 years, other countries have caught up, equalled and surpassed this initial lead, but in any case, British metal requirements are now far beyond anything that domestic sources could supply. The British Isles still produces large tonnages of iron ores but they are low grade and need 'sweetening' with imported ores. Tin is mined in limited quantities, but copper, once our largest metal export, is now mined only in Eire. Lead and zinc are today exploited in new, rich fields in Eire, but only minor quantities come from the old traditional lead-zinc fields of England where these metals are now merely by-products from the mining of the fluorspar so desperately needed as a flux for the steel industry.

The later stages of the history of British mining are well recorded but the earliest have to be inferred mainly from indirect evidence, such as artefacts. Direct evidence of ancient mining is as rare in Britain as in other countries, probably rarer, for mining is a destructive industry and each succeeding generation of miners erases the evidence of its predecessors as it extends their workings in the search for more ore. Seldom are really ancient workings found intact and, even when they are, they are difficult to date, for mining methods changed remarkably little until the advent of machine mining. Even the tools used are often similar: a Roman miner's pick looks very like one from modern Cornwall, if cruder and of poorer material, and a wooden shovel of 1500 B.C. differs little from one of A.D. 1500 (Bromehead, 1954).

In the past, miners have had little regard for recording any ancient workings encountered, and unfortunately, modern mining methods, with the pressure on reducing costs by moving more and more ground more cheaply with larger and larger machines in open pits, give little opportunity for ancient workings to be seen before they are destroyed, let alone examined and mapped. Certainly, in Britain, direct evidence of any mining activity before Roman times is almost, but not quite, non-existent.

But what methods of mining were used in the earliest days of metal mining in the British Isles? Both gold and tin were probably mined exclusively from alluvial placer deposits,* but this does not mean miners may not have gone underground to reach payable gravels buried beneath thick overburdens of barren sands and gravels, as was done in Thrace and Egypt. There is evidence that this is just what they did do in Cornwall. In general, however, the earliest mines were probably surface workings, exploiting weathered oxidised outcrops of copper ores and the eluvial materials shed into the soils of the immediate area. Tin was possibly mined at first from gravels in streams close to the veins, for the tinstone was possibly coarser there than further downstream, and lay beneath only a thin cover of barren gravels and sands. Gold was mined from gravels too. Such ancient surface workings are most unlikely to be recognisable now from the appearance of the surface itself, although when dug into by an experienced 'streamer', the ground may well indicate gravelly back-filling instead of naturally deposited sands and gravels. At times, even artefacts of horn, stone or wood have been found within such gravels, and the workings can sometimes then be dated.

Although there is abundant evidence that the British Isles produced gold, copper, tin, lead and iron before the Romans came, no early gold, lead or even iron workings have ever been positively identified. Tools have been found showing a few sites where tin was once mined although no details of the workings can be seen, and

---

*Placer, pronounced 'plasser', a corruption of the Spanish word *plaza*. Placers are accumulations of heavy, insoluble, erosion-resistent minerals, such as gold and tinstone, which have been weathered out of nearby rocks and concentrated by natural sorting in beach or river gravels. The valuable heavy minerals are usually found with the coarser gravels, and at their base, especially on the bedrock the gravels lie on. Placers in rivers are called 'alluvial placers' to distinguish them from 'beach placers' found along coastal shorelines.

only copper workings can still be examined, and only then in a very few places. However, from indirect evidence and by comparisons with ancient mines elsewhere, some idea of Bronze and Iron Age mining can be synthesised.

MINING FIELDS OF THE BRITISH ISLES

'Gold is where you find it' was once, with some justification, the byword of prospectors. Its high price encouraged them to seek and find gold in nearly every country of the world, though its extraction frequently proved uneconomic. It needs but a few parts per million to turn barren rock into gold ore and gold has been found in many different types of rocks whose ages range over 3000 million years of geological time. Copper, lead and iron are also generously distributed throughout the world although much more generously in some countries than in others, but mercury and tin, metals which also interested ancient miners, are more restricted in occurrence. Mercury was never mined at all in these islands until the present decade and is still known only in one place. Tin is another matter. It occurs in few parts of the world and Cornwall is fortunate to be one of them. Silver, the last of the 'seven metals of antiquity', is largely a by-product metal for there are, in fact, very few true 'silver mines' known, and those are mostly in the Americas. Lead ores are the main source of silver. Some lead ores are richer than others and silver was probably extracted from them as long ago as the Early Iron Age, when gold used for jewellery was sometimes debased with silver. Copper was then added to counteract its paler colour and it is the correlation of high copper with high silver which shows that these were contrived alloys and not the natural gold–silver alloy, *electrum*. Some believe that such golds were imported from Europe; others disagree (Hartmann, 1970; Briggs *et al.*, 1973), but whenever it was that the British first recovered silver from its ores, it was certainly before the Roman invasion for Strabo gives it, together with gold, iron, tin and lead, in his list of British exports (Frere, 1974).

Where did the ancient miner find his metals in the British Isles? Fig. 2:1 shows the ore fields known today, although few now produce any metals. Fig. 2:2 shows where ores are thought to have been worked before Roman times. Most of the pre-Roman workings found are in the smaller ore fields, presumably because there was little chance that really ancient mines could survive in the later more intensively exploited larger fields.

47

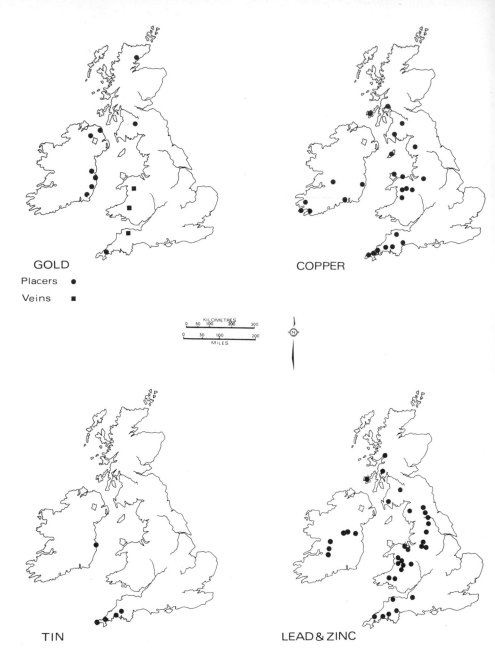

Fig. 2:1 The main mineral localities in the British Isles which have at some time been worked. The map for copper exaggerates the position to some extent, for many of the deposits are small, whilst the map for lead and zinc undervalues the present importance of Ireland because again the importance of individual areas is not shown.

48

GOLD

Fig. 2:1 shows that gold occurs in a number of small isolated areas, none of which could be called a 'goldfield' in world terms. Economically, the North Wales area is the most important but, so far as is known, it was never worked for gold until the last century. The gold occurs in veins which cut Cambrian slates on the south-east flanks of the Harlech dome and has been related to the dolerite dykes of the area. It would appear more probable that it is related to unexposed diorities, such as those found a few miles further east. Gold occurs sparsely in Devon and Cornwall too, nearly all of it in tin placers. Some was also recovered from 'gossan-lodes' (cf. p. 49), overlying copper veins in the Molton area of Devon in the 1850s (Maclaren, 1903) and gold-bearing gossans are not unusual where the copper ores are slightly auriferous, but they can never be extensive for they have no roots. All other golds found in the British Isles, including those of Ireland and Northern Scotland, originated in Lower Silurian rocks and were, in most cases, weathered out to form placer deposits in nearby stream and river gravels. Only at Ogofau in southern Wales can gold veins be seen too. There the gold occurs with *pyrite* (iron pyrites or iron sulphide) in quartz veins, but its origin is obscure. The veins show all the characteristics of those formed at moderate temperatures close to igneous rocks, yet no such rocks are known within many miles.

Gold occurs mainly as the 'native' metal itself, unlike most metals which are found in nature as compounds of oxygen and sulphur or as salts of one kind or another. Gold grains range from sub-microscopic, through just visible 'colours' and pin-head sizes, to lentil and barley size 'nuggets'. Larger nuggets do occur but the larger they are, the rarer. The main characteristics of native gold are that it is almost twice as heavy as lead, soft and insoluble, and that it may contain a considerable proportion of silver. Gold originates in veins, which may be anything from a finger-width stringer, to bodies many feet wide and thousands of feet long. During erosion, the gold is released from the veins and washed into streams and, because of its high density, tends to accumulate with the coarser gravels and especially with the boulders, cobbles and gravels which lie on the solid bedrock of the river bottom. Small amounts of gold are often associated with other ores, especially those of copper, and much gold today is produced as a by-product of base metal mining, particularly in the U.S.A. Where copper–gold ores are eroded, the copper may be removed in solution, whilst the gold, present perhaps only as a fractional part per million of the original ore, may be washed into nearby streams as tiny grains and concentrated with coarser gravels by natural sorting processes to form a viable ore. This, according to Jackson (1971), may well have been the origin of the placer gold in western Ireland, the gold originating from copper lodes in Wicklow, near Avoca, although Jackson believes that glaciation helped the transport and erosion too. All gold mined in Ireland during the Bronze and Iron Ages was placer gold and this can be determined by trace elements contained in the gold, and all of it is believed to have been mined in the Wicklow mountains, an area which had a short-lived gold-rush at the end of the eighteenth century (Raftery, 1971; Reeves, 1971) although Briggs *et al.* (1973) point out that gold also occurs in central Ulster.

Gold occurs in several other parts of Britain too. It occurs in small placers at Kildonan in Sutherland although its source has never been located except by inference. It was found and exploited in Ayrshire in the Middle Ages and it was also almost certainly recovered from Cornish streams whilst exploiting Bronze Age tin, for although we have no proof of it, it is most unlikely that the gold found with tinstone was ignored. Most abundantly, it occurs in Wales, near Dolgellau, which formed an active and lucrative mining field during the earlier part of the nineteenth century, and even today, sporadically comes into the news. However, there is no evidence that the Dolgellau gold field was ever exploited in prehistory, not even by those enterprising miners, the Romans, who certainly knew the surrounding country, for one of their roads passed just south of what became the mines at Bontddu. Perhaps the evidence has been merely lost. Gold also occurs at Dolaucothi,

Fig. 2:2 Localities where there is either direct or strong inferential evidence of pre-Roman metal working. Lead has been excluded, for it is much more difficult to pinpoint areas, such as in the Mendips and Flintshire. The Wicklow goldfield is included because it is so generally accepted as the source of Irish gold.

1 Wicklow goldfield	6 Bunmahon
2 Ogofau (Dolaucothi)	7 Avoca
3 Mount Gabriel and	8 Parys Mountain
Derrycarhoon	9 Alderley Edge
4 Allihies	10 Cwmystwyth (Snowbrook)
5 Killarney	11 Molton
12 Carnon	

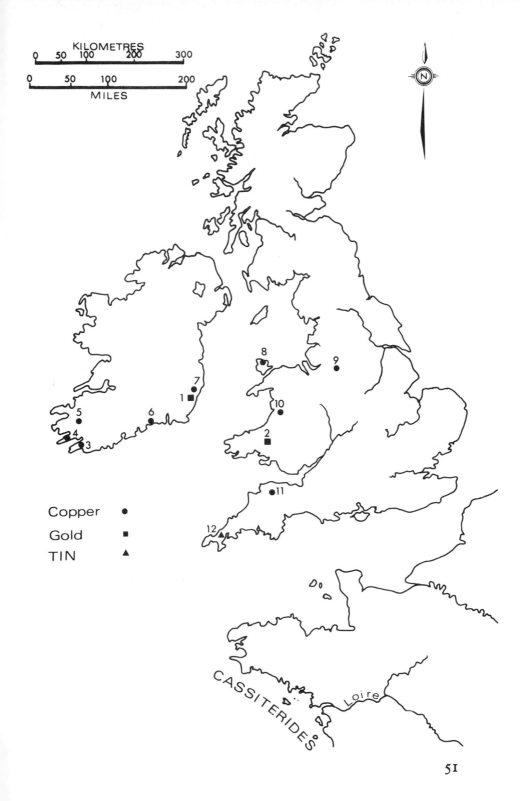

KILOMETRES
0   50   100   200   300

0   50   100   200
MILES

Copper   ●

Gold   ■

TIN   ▲

CASSITERIDES

Loire

51

near Pumpsaint in Dyfed, and this was exploited by the Romans. The history of that mine is described elsewhere. [See Chapter 3, p. 86 *et seq.*]

Much has been made of the large quantities of gold exported from Ireland in the Bronze and Iron Ages. None came from underground mines that we know of, and Hartmann (Raftery, 1971; Hartmann, 1970) has concluded from trace elements in a large collection of Irish golden artefacts, that few of them could in fact be attributed to gold of Irish origin. Not only does he question the widely held assumption that Ireland was a major source of European gold, but he maintains that the sources of gold used in Europe varied from time to time and that Irish gold played its part only in the Early Bronze Age, and not necessarily a significant part at that. Others are less than convinced by such arguments and point out that Hartmann, and his supporter Raftery, assume all Irish gold came from Wicklow and have ignored the alternative Irish and British sources in their investigations. They suggest that these may have been responsible for the trace element variations which Hartmann makes so much of (Briggs *et al.*, 1973). Briggs and his colleagues (ibid.) point to central Ulster in particular as a strong contender as one alternative gold source, for not only are small amounts of gold known in several streams but a large number of Early Bronze Age gold lunulae have been found there too. They suggest there is a connection. The almost religious faith that all Irish gold must have come from Wicklow is based on the fact that it is the only area in which workable gold has been found in historic times. Yet we do not know what a workable grade of ore was in the Bronze and Iron Ages. People of those days may have valued gold so highly that they may well have been happy to work very small deposits with grades far below what we would consider worthwhile today. The 'cut-off' grade of any metallic ore depends only on what you can mine profitably, and profitability depends on the balance between metal price and working costs. If the metal price is high, you can afford to mine low-grade ore: were economic considerations so very different in prehistoric times?

So far, little trace of any prehistoric gold workings have ever been found in the British Isles although we do know, if Strabo is to be believed, that gold was still being mined here shortly before the Roman occupation. Some very probably came from Dolaucothi, but whether from surface workings only, or from underground too, is not known. Dolaucothi is, in fact, the only place where any signs of pre-Roman gold mining has ever been found, and they are preserved only because the workings were shallow pits dug into quartz veins on high ground. No trace of any other gold workings, lode or placer, have ever been found, so that it is impossible to say exactly where most of the prehistoric gold came from in the British Isles: perhaps most did come from Europe as Hartmann and Raftery suggest. However, placer gold is so easy to look for, and so easy to mine when found, it was probably worked in many, many places, often perhaps in deposits which were very small indeed and which would be ignored by modern miners. No trace of these workings remain.

COPPER

The general distribution of copper in the British Isles is shown in Fig. 2:1, but most of the occurrences are small and isolated. South-west England was the most important area from the mid-eighteenth to the mid-nineteenth century, with a brief period between 1770 and 1790 when Anglesey copper dominated markets, and all but killed the Cornish industry. Copper was also worked at Avoca, south of Dublin, in Eire, during the nineteenth century and there has been a revival during the last two decades. County Cork was also a copper producer during the last century, but as in Cornwall, was killed off by the overseas copper industry before the end of the century. Copper is now produced in Tipperary and, with Avoca, Ireland is at present the only producer in the British Isles. Nearly all other copper deposits in Britain are small, and although they satisfied the limited needs of former centuries, they are not viable by present standards. The most prolific areas, apart from south-west England were, perhaps, mid- to North Wales and the Lake District, and many of these areas were mined sporadically from Roman times onwards. In recent years, great interest was shown in the Dolgellau area where there was a possibility of a large, low-grade disseminated copper deposit, analogous to the 'porphyry copper' deposits which supply more than half the copper of the world today. Unfortunately, early hopes of payable ore did not materialise. The nearest to any single large copper ore body in Britain was at Parys Mountain in Anglesey, worked from before Roman times. Its main period of development was in the eighteenth century when the Parys and Mona mines were briefly the most productive in Europe, and although the ore was low grade, the body was large enough to be worked by cheap mass-mining methods. The two huge opencasts can still be seen. The Parys

Mountain ores were largely disseminations of copper minerals in rock, but copper in other parts of Britain was mainly in quartz veins although there were exceptions. In two instances where pre-Roman workings are known, in County Cork, and at Alderley Edge in Cheshire, the ore was in impregnations in sandstones, but there the similarity ends, for their ages are very different, the Irish being Devonian, those in Cheshire, Triassic, nearly 200 million years younger. In Devon and Cornwall the copper ores are closely related to tin mineralisation and owe their existence to the granites which now form moorlands such as Dartmoor: these ores are discussed with tin on page 61. Otherwise, there is much variety in the details of copper mineralisation.

Which was the first metal to be found in the British Isles, copper or gold? Both were probably found at much the same time, and most likely in Ireland, where metal-working Beaker people settled early in the second millenium. Irish trade contacts were quickly established with mainland Britain, for Irish metalwork was soon in demand.

Copper can be found in a number of places in Ireland and Early Bronze Age workings have been discovered at several of them. But copper also occurs in many scattered localities in mainland Britain and was undoubtedly worked at many of these too, although there is evidence of pre-Roman mining at a very few of them. More surprisingly, in Cornwall, the prime world copper producer of the eighteenth and nineteenth centuries, there is hardly any sign of early copper working at all: in fact, there is no evidence to show that the Cornish copper industry even came into existence until just before the Industrial Revolution.

Despite the lack of concrete evidence, it seems impossible that ancient Cornish tin miners could have ignored the copper that lay on their own doorsteps, any more than they could have ignored the gold, especially as copper was the metal with which tin was alloyed to produce bronze. Admittedly, Gowland (1917–18) did believe a piece of copper he found in a hearth at Hengistbury Head in Hampshire came from Cornwall, because of its high silver content, but this was mere surmise. The copper mines may well have been shallow surface workings in oxidised outcrops which, even if any signs of them still remained in the eighteenth century, were obliterated by the scramble for copper to feed the Industrial Revolution. Another reason why we hear little of ancient Cornish copper is, perhaps, because the fame of Cornwall was as an exporter of the rare metal tin to bronze founders overseas, founders who had ample copper of their own and needed only the scarce and more expensive tin to mix with it. We also hear little of domestic bronze founding, only of the products made from the alloyed metal. But in many parts of Britain, tin and copper were brought together to make bronze, and one place where it was done must surely have been south-west England, a source of both metals.

We have no evidence of what early copper workings were like in Cornwall, if any even existed, but in Ireland Jackson (1968) has surveyed the only two accessible Early Bronze Age workings of the twenty-five found on Mount Gabriel in County Cork. These are short adits driven into a copper-bearing silty to sandy stratum lying at the contact between coarse grits and slates of Old Red Sandstone age. The formation dips into the hillside so that most of the adits which have followed down the ore zone are now flooded. The map of drift No. 1, made by Jackson (Fig. 2:3) shows a narrow adit portal three-quarters of a metre wide and of about the same height, which broadens out inside to over 4 metres wide by 4 metres long, gently inclined and of much the same height as before, although the true floor level is hidden by a layer of rubble. At the very end, headroom increases to about $1\frac{1}{2}$ metres. None of the adits appear to penetrate far into the ore horizon, possibly because the miners were defeated by accumulating water, or perhaps the rock became harder away from the surface outcrop, so that whenever the going got too hard, they started a new adit a little further along the crop. However, Jackson notes that the walls show spalling due to fire-setting, showing that the miners did at least work some rock harder than that which could be removed directly by primitive tools. Perhaps ventilation and smoke was their problem. Stone mauls, some plain, others rilled, were found in profusion, both inside workings, and on the spoil heaps outside, but are of little use for dating. Fortunately, charcoal from a trench has given a recently revised Radiocarbon age of 1500 B.C. $\pm$ 90 years (personal communication), establishing the workings as almost certainly Early Bronze Age although possibly continuing into later times.

In Wales there are a number of possible mining sites although most of the evidence is inferential. Almost certainly the ores of Parys Mountain in Anglesey were mined before the Romans came. The Romans appear to have taken over an active cottage industry on an agency basis, much as is still done in many parts of the world today. The native miners became 'tributers' who mined and smelted the ore for sale to the Roman metal factors. Richmond (1963) considers these were the most important copper deposits in

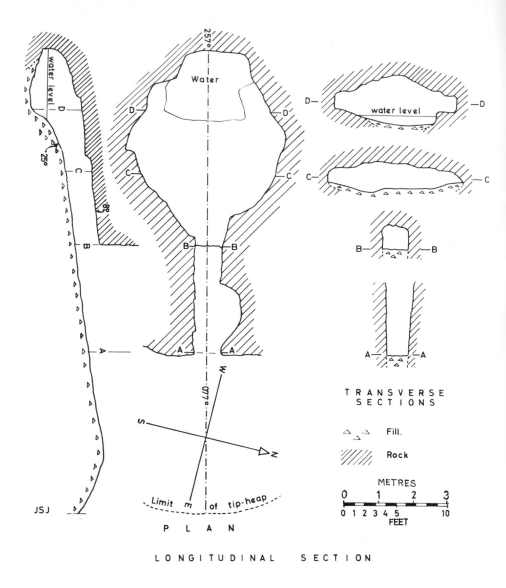

Water

Water level

water level

D

C

B

A

257°

077°

Limit m of tip-heap

JSJ

TRANSVERSE SECTIONS

△ △ Fill.

/// Rock

METRES
0   1   2   3
0 1 2 3 4 5   10
FEET

PLAN

LONGITUDINAL SECTION

Fig. 2:3 Early Bronze Age copper workings at Mount Gabriel, Co. Cork, Eire (after Jackson, 1968). *By courtesy of the Director of the National Museum of Ireland.*

Roman Britain, so important to the economy that a fort was built at Caernarvon to protect them. At Great Orme's Head near Llandudno the Romans established mines of their own and there is some controversy over whether mining had been done there before. Horn picks have been found, together with stone wedges, which might suggest Bronze or Early Iron Age activity (Davies, 1935; Davies, 1949). However, in Roman times the mines were worked by prisoners who were confined underground and perhaps were not entrusted with the best of tools. Bronze picks which have also been found there indicate that more sophisticated methods of mining were used too.

In the old county of Merioneth, now a part of Gwynedd, there are many likely copper prospects and Bronze Age palstaves are known to have been produced there. It does appear to be likely that the copper they were made from was also mined in the same hills although there is nothing to prove it (Bowen and Gresham, 1967). Bick (1977) also mentions copper mining of great antiquity at Snowbrook (Nant-yr-Eira) on the northern slopes of Plynlimmon, a mine more famed for its lead mined during the last century. Small picks and wedges and a broken stag-horn pick were found with extensive shallow workings in the more copper-rich part of the deposit and suggest an early age for the mine, but little more can be said. Roman mining accounted for other workings there which are nearly 300 metres long, $1\frac{3}{4}$ to $2\frac{1}{2}$ metres wide, and of unknown depth. Further westwards, in the Welsh Borderland at Llanymynech in Shropshire, ochre and malachite were mined from shallow pits dug into clay 'wayboards' interbedded with the Carboniferous limestone, but Roman coins and underground workings of very obviously Roman style prove only Roman occupation. [See also Chapter 3.] If the shallow pits were from earlier times, as some wish to believe, nothing has yet been found to prove it.

Copper was also produced by the Romans at Coniston in the Lake District, an area which has been mined sporadically until the present century. Shaw (1971) implies that there is a possibility of pre-Roman mining, but that appears to be merely wishful thinking. Lead ores too were worked here in Elizabethan times to provide the lead for extracting silver from the copper by liquating it before cupellation, a process certainly known to Iron Age Britons. These silver-rich ores may well have been attractive to pre-Roman miners, but proof has yet to be found.

The best known prehistoric copper workings in Britain are those at Alderley Edge in Cheshire. They appear to have been largely ignored by the Romans who perhaps thought the flat-lying ore beds too thin for economic working, although medieval miners did not think so, nor miners in the last century either. Evidence for ancient working includes earth circles and ramparts, together with flint knives, scrapers, flakes and cores, all within the mining area (Roeder, 1901). Undateable stone mauls also abound and an oaken shovel has been found. The ore here is composed of a number of thin flat-lying beds of sandstones, marls and conglomerates of Lower Keuper (Triassic) age, with impregnations of malachite, the copper silicate *chrysocolla*, and some galena and cerussite.

In ancient times the mine was worked largely as opencast in a manner which now gives a pock-marked appearance to the ground. According to Roeder and Graves (1909) a line of shallow open pits was first sunk to the first flat-lying ore bed, and then joined to each other. A second line was then sunk behind the first, then a third, and so on, until the whole ore bed was exposed. New pits were then sunk into the pit floor to reach the next lower ore bed, to develop a bench system much as is done on far larger scales in modern open pit mines today. These Bronze or Iron Age miners did not mine indiscriminately. Before sinking new pits to the next ore bed they first dug smaller holes 30 cm in diameter to ensure that there was ore below. As the ore beds were only 60 cm thick and lay only 10–30 cm apart, this was a most practical method of exploration, similar to that done by drilling for much the same reasons in open pit mining today.

Roeder and Graves (ibid.) speak also of the undercutting of rock faces to break down the ore, and of fire-setting where the rock was hard. Of particular interest is their observation that fire-setting fires were confined by hearths built of lead ore, suggesting that lead was not sought at the time that this was done and implying that parts of these workings were very ancient indeed.

Ancient copper mining in the British Isles would appear to have been largely from shallow surface workings. Only in Ireland have any underground workings been found and they are small, although the individual workings in each area are numerous. But even in Ireland open pits were worked too, at least one of them of considerable depth. Mining at Parys Mountain was again probably from shallow pits because there was unlikely to be any need to mine the huge ore body underground. Any ancient, or even Roman age, workings would have been obliterated by the two huge open pits developed in the eighteenth century. The only signs of ancient copper workings in south-west England are at Molton in Devon, where there is considerable evidence that ores were worked in 'very remote times' (Maclaren, 1903). However, no details of the workings appear to have been recorded, nor was their age determined. Alderley Edge is the only confirmed pre-Roman copper mine in England and it appears to have been, as far as is known, entirely an opencast at that time, although underground workings may well have been destroyed by mining in later years. [For another view cf. Chap. 3, p. 89.] All that can be said of ancient copper mining in these islands is that factual evidence is sparse, but at least more abundant than that for lead.

BRONZE

The alloying of copper with other metals to produce a harder, more durable, material developed in the eastern world in the fourth millenium. The first 'bronzes' were made from copper with arsenic and often antimony. They were almost certainly accidents of smelting, probably due to turning from the more easily smelted oxidised ores to the more abundant polymetallic sulphides. Some of these sulphides – the 'grey copper' ores – contained arsenic and antimony and their superiority was obvious. Not only was the resultant metal harder, but it melted at a lower temperature, and had less porosity than purer coppers (Coghlan and Case, 1957). However, it did have drawbacks, notably the toxic arsenical fumes produced during smelting. In the third millenium a newer alloy became available, a *bronze* made from copper and tin, and these bronzes could be 'tailored' to meet requirements; low-tin bronzes for strength, high-tin bronzes (+ 10% tin) for cutting edges. However, how it was first discovered that tin could be substituted for arsenic is an intriguing but unsolved problem, for these tin bronzes were developed in a part of the world where tin in more than minute trace amounts has yet to be discovered. Numerous tin-bearing areas are shown on archaeological maps of the Middle East and these sites have only one thing in common – no tin has ever been found at any of them, and most are, in any case, geologically improbable as tin sources. The source of the tin used in the Early Bronze Age of the Middle East is still a fascinating mystery, but what does appear obvious, is that sources were inadequate and that by mid-sixteenth century B.C. tin was being imported into the more advanced countries of the eastern Mediterranean from far to the west, most probably from Britain.

The Bronze Age spread westwards to the British Isles and

Northern Europe, probably reaching us in the early part of the second millenium. The earliest bronzes found in Britain, such as a rivet in a dagger dated at 2000–1900 B.C. (Muhly, 1973)*, were probably imported: Hawkes and Woolley (1963) put the first European bronzes at *c*. 1900 B.C.; Muhly (1973) puts them later, at between 1800 and 1700 B.C. In the British Isles, the bronze-using economy dates from the first Wessex phase (1650–1550 B.C.) of the Early Bronze Age, with copper, arsenical bronzes and low-tin bronzes being produced, and high tin-bronzes, containing up to 17% tin, coming into use during Wessex II (1550–1400 B.C.). The Wessex cultures established trade contacts for amber with the Baltic, and for faience with Mycenae and the Aegean. Tin was probably traded in exchange. There is, however, no direct proof of this tin trade at that time, but it is a logical assumption to account for the tin entering the Aegean region. The route was presumably overland via Brittany, Nantes, up the Garonne and thence to the Mediterranean; or to the Rhine, then via the Brenner to the Adriatic (Muhly, 1973). The Phoenician sea trade, made so much of in school books, came much later, in about 600 B.C. How direct the contact was between Britain and its tin trading customers is unclear. The Greeks attributed tin to the Cassiterides, the 'Tin Islands', which we British have chauvinistically assumed to be Britain. However, this view is no longer so firmly held, even by the British, and Sir Gavin de Beer (Richardson, 1974) has suggested that the Cassiterides were in fact the Belle Islands at the mouth of the Loire and they acted merely as an entrepôt trading port dealing in many commodities, among them tin from Britain (and possibly from Brittany too). Muhly (1973), in his detailed investigation of ancient tin-trading routes, also takes this view, although he includes Ushant and the Scilly Isles, too.

Where did British tin come from? This is easy to answer for Cornwall and west Devon are almost the only tin-bearing areas in the British Isles. But who first found the tin there and why is it so glibly assumed that British bronze was made of Cornish tin but of Irish or Welsh copper? Cornwall was rich in copper. It is surely more logical that copper, the easier metal to find, was found first in Cornwall, and tin was discovered whilst exploiting it. Even if the tin were found first, it is difficult to believe that Bronze Age miners would have missed the copper which occurred there too. However,

---

* Eaton and McKerrel suggest British metal usage as early as *c*.2200 B.C. (Eaton, E. R. and McKerrel, H., 1976. *World Archaeology*, 8(2), p. 182).

it is interesting, if puzzling, that in historic times Cornwall first mined only tin, and as a minor industry at that. Copper mining did not develop until about A.D. 1700 when production exploded to swamp the tin industry to such an extent that one copper mine alone could produce metal worth all the tin produced (Williams, *c.* 1970). Cornish copper mining flourished until the mid-nineteenth century when the discovery of more cheaply exploited copper ores overseas rapidly killed it off and tin once again dominated the Cornish economy. There is one other suggestion of how Cornish tin was first found, namely during gold prospecting, for small amounts of gold occurred in many Cornish streams, and almost certainly the one small deposit of Irish tin was found in this way.

TIN

The geology of British tin is easy to describe for it is virtually all concentrated in south-west England, apart from an insignificant alluvial occurrence on the coast of western Ireland. The tin occurs as cassiterite, or 'tinstone', in veins associated with the 'Hercynian' granites which intruded slates of Devonian age, locally called 'killas', some 250 million years ago. As molten granite crystallised deep beneath the surface of the earth, aqueous fluids separated out and streamed through fractures in the rocks enclosing the granite. These fluids deposited quartz veins containing tin within the granite and in the killas close to it. Veins bearing both tin and copper were deposited further from the granite, whilst copper alone is found farthest away. Erosion of the rocks above the granites has slowly brought the veins closer to the surface until they themselves have been exposed to erosion. This has released the tinstone from the veins containing it and carried it into streams and rivers where, owing to its high density and resistance to abrasion, it worked its way down into the gravels of the river beds to form placers. It was these stream deposits which were the main source of tin from the Bronze Age to medieval times. Copper occurred in the same lodes in the form of the brassy-looking copper-iron sulphide *chalcopyrite*, closely associated with the iron sulphide pyrite. When erosion brought these two minerals above the level of permanent ground-water – the *watertable*, which lies probably less, often very much less, than 6 metres down in most of Britain – oxygen, with the help of bacteria, broke down these sulphides to new chemical states. Iron sulphide was oxidised to a number of red-brown to black hydrated iron oxides, collectively called *limonite*. Limonite is insoluble and accumulated at the surface during erosion to form jagged red-brown erosion-resistant outcrops surrounded by reddish iron-rich soils, known as *gossan*. Other insolubles, such as gold, accumulated with the gossan too and this is how the gold-rich gossan-lodes of Molton were formed. Gossans have been known as pathfinders to ore by prospectors since the search for metals began.

The copper sulphides were oxidised in the oxygenated zone above the watertable. But the copper salts formed were soluble, and percolated downwards to precipitate as the green and blue basic copper carbonates *malachite* and *azurite*. The upper part of the oxidised zone was leached of copper and the lower part enriched. Some copper even reached the watertable to react with and enrich the existing sulphides there too, forming a 'zone of secondary sulphide enrichment'. The ancient miner was well aware of these richer ores beneath the surface, even though he was ignorant of how they were formed (Fig. 2:4).

How did Bronze Age miners recover tin? It is most improbable that they mined lodes and there is in fact no evidence to show that Cornish tin lodes were ever mined until the Middle Ages, when the hitherto plentiful placer supplies began to run out. Up to then, Cornish tin was won exclusively by 'streaming' from placers (Williams, *c*. 1970) and in fact tin-streaming was carried on until well into the present century.

Tinstone, or *cassiterite*, is the principle tin ore mineral: there are others, but for various reasons cassiterite was the only one likely to have been mined by prehistoric miners in Britain. Cassiterite is a hard, abrasive-resistant, insoluble form of stannic oxide, three times heavier than the quartz of the veins in which it is found. When the veins weather and erode at the earth's surface, the tinstone is freed from the enclosing vein minerals, and finds its way into streams where it concentrates with the coarser gravels in the same manner as placer gold. This was the material sought by Bronze Age miners.

The simplest method of mining would be to examine the gravels at the upper end of streams, close to gossan outcrops, for Bronze Age miners were undoubtedly aware of these indicators of mineralisation. Among the stream gravels, a few small very dark lumps of tinstone might be found and picked out, but the method would be, at best, poorly rewarding. Instead, they probably dug out the sands and finer gravels from between the boulders and cobbles of the river bed and then, as did Bronze Age miners in Tyrol (Bromehead, 1940), screened them through riddles of woven twigs to concentrate

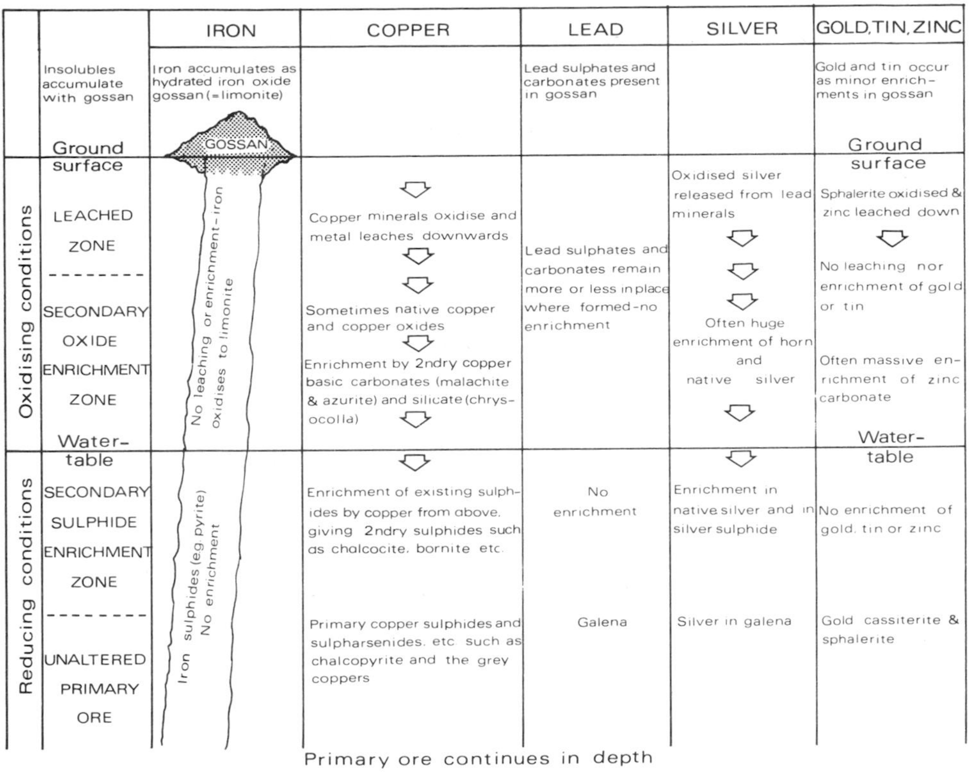

	IRON	COPPER	LEAD	SILVER	GOLD,TIN,ZINC
Insolubles accumulate with gossan	Iron accumulates as hydrated iron oxide gossan (=limonite)		Lead sulphates and carbonates present in gossan		Gold and tin occur as minor enrichments in gossan
Ground surface	GOSSAN			Oxidised silver released from lead minerals	Ground surface
LEACHED ZONE	No leaching or enrichment—iron. Oxidises to limonite	Copper minerals oxidise and metal leaches downwards	Lead sulphates and carbonates remain more or less in place where formed–no enrichment		Sphalerite oxidised & zinc leached down. No leaching nor enrichment of gold or tin
SECONDARY OXIDE ENRICHMENT ZONE		Sometimes native copper and copper oxides. Enrichment by 2ndry copper basic carbonates (malachite & azurite) and silicate (chrysocolla)		Often huge enrichment of horn and native silver	Often massive enrichment of zinc carbonate
Water-table					Water-table
SECONDARY SULPHIDE ENRICHMENT ZONE	Iron sulphides (eg pyrite). No enrichment	Enrichment of existing sulphides by copper from above giving 2ndry sulphides such as chalcocite. bornite etc.	No enrichment	Enrichment in native silver and in silver sulphide	No enrichment of gold. tin or zinc
UNALTERED PRIMARY ORE		Primary copper sulphides and sulpharsenides. etc such as chalcopyrite and the grey coppers	Galena	Silver in galena	Gold cassiterite & sphalerite

Left margin (oxidising/reducing conditions): Oxidising conditions; Reducing conditions

Primary ore continues in depth

Fig. 2:4 Oxidation processes in mineral deposits during erosion and the ensuing secondary enrichments at different levels for different metals.

the small tinstone granules with the finer sands which passed through the sieves. This concentrate was then washed, either by 'panning' in a wooden *batea* or flattish wooden bowl, such as is still used in parts of the world today or, on a larger scale, in a sluice made from a hollowed log, possibly lined, as in gold mining, with animals skins to catch the finer heavy tinstone particles.

One place where tin was once mined was at Carnon in Cornwall, where a wooden shovel, a human skull, and an antler pick were found in tin-bearing gravels (Bromehead, 1954). The horn pick has been dated as Early Bronze Age by comparison with a similar pick from Nointel, in France. The interesting point about this discovery is that these were found 'far below present sea level', under a bed of oyster shells *in situ* (ibid.). Again, relics have been discovered 12 metres deep beneath a stratum yielding the remains of an extinct whale in stream workings at Pentuan in southern Cornwall (loc. cit.). That they were found below sea-level merely means that the relative sea-level has fluctuated during the last few thousand years, as it has done in many places. These finds do not indicate mining before the beds containing the oysters or whale were deposited either, but that the gravels were mined underground. This is a logical method of mining deeply buried placer gravels, and is used in many countries today, including Alaska and Australia. It may well have seemed logical to Bronze Age miners too, even at relatively shallow depths, so that they could avoid the tedious task of removing barren overburden with wooden shovels and horn picks to reach a relatively thin pay-gravel below. It was certainly resorted to in Thrace in Roman times to reach gold-bearing gravels merely 3 metres below surface (*Northern Miner*, 1972). The Egyptians also worked placers in the same way, sometimes nearly 20 metres below surface (Llewellyn, 1933). Other signs of ancient mining found in Cornish stream workings include numerous bronze axes, and hollowed stone mortars used to crush ore. Evidence also includes the discovery of the age-blackened oak square-framed top of a sand-filled shaft of indeterminate age in 1852, and in 1812 of a wooden rag and chain pump about 2 metres below the surface in what was thought to be virgin ground on Drift Moor near Penzance (Richardson, 1974). The pump was probably of Roman age, and possibly later, but many of the finds provide direct evidence of pre-Roman mining. There is little else to determine how Bronze and Iron Age placer deposits were mined, but it is interesting that Posidonius noted in 130 B.C. that the Cornish were expert miners, and he also thought them both civilised and hospitable, characteristics he credited to contact with traders from abroad. In about 55 B.C. the export tin trade ceased, presumably owing to the discovery of the Iberian deposits, and did not revive until *c.* A.D. 250 when the more easily won Iberian sources were exhausted, or perhaps because of the increasing use of pewter by the Romans. Surprisingly, the Romans ignored the potentially lucrative Cornish tin trade for 200 years, perhaps through protectionist policies such as they imposed on lead.

There is one other mystery regarding tin. It has long been puzzling that although ingots of copper are frequently found in Bronze Age hoards, ingots of tin are not, yet tin metal appeared to be an essential material for bronze-making. However, Charles (1975) has recently shown that bronze, as suggested but not tested by Coghlan and Case (1957), can be made by sprinkling tinstone itself onto the surface of molten copper in a crucible, a process termed 'cementation'. Charles infers that in all probability the tin trade was not conducted in smelted metal ingots at all, but as tinstone concentrate carried probably in jars, or even bags. Broken bags and jars would spread their cassiterite as a sand on the floor, indistinguishable to most people from other sandy material upon the floor, and therefore easily missed. This does appear to be a most reasonable explanation for the puzzling absence of tin ingots of any shape or form, found either close to tin mining areas, or to bronze founders elsewhere. However, slags have been found both in the Belle Islands, and on St Michael's Mount off the coast of Cornwall (Richardson, 1974), and so some tin at least appears to have been traded, either in the form of metal, or perhaps as bronze.

LEAD AND SILVER

Of all the metals found in the British Isles, with the possible exception of iron, lead is the most widely distributed (Fig. 2: 1). It is found in the Pennine Chain from Northumberland to Derbyshire, in the Lake District, in North Wales, mid-Wales and the Welsh Borderland and in the Isle of Man, the Mendips, Devon and Cornwall. Lead also occurs in many parts of Ireland, and Eire has now become one of the major lead and zinc producers of Europe. There are also many other places in the British Isles where lead has been produced at one time or another in relatively small quantities. Lead was until recently a major British domestic metallic commodity. Over three million tonnes of metal were produced in the hundred years preceding 1950 and over a million tonnes in the century before that. Since 1950 lead production in mainland Britain has been almost entirely a by-product of fluorspar mining in Derbyshire and Weardale, but Irish production has soared owing to the discovery of several new mines, the latest at Navan north of Dublin, on the largest lead ore body in Europe.

Lead fields can be broadly classified as those in Carboniferous limestone and those in older rocks. There is no significant lead mineralisation in rocks younger than 300 million years old, the age of the Carboniferous limestone. The mineralisation is, of course, younger than the rocks which encloses it and in the Derbyshire Carboniferous is about 230 million years old. Silver content in the lead from the different fields also depends to some extent upon the rocks in which it is found, and the highest values tend to be found in the older rocks. Perhaps the richest silver fields were those in Devon and Cornwall, and in the Isle of Man, where some 20–30 ounces of silver were recovered from every tonne of lead metal, but in most fields less, often very much less, than 10 ounces could be extracted. Despite this, Britain has at times produced well over half a million ounces of silver a year from its own lead ores.

The lead normally occurs with zinc minerals in vein-like bodies a metre or so wide and often of many tens of metres in length and depth. In limestones the ore bodies may often be less vein-like and sometimes highly irregular with boundaries which are difficult to define. Some ores are obviously closely associated with hot aqueous fluids which emanated from igneous bodies and were deposited in fractures in similar fashion to the formation of tin lodes in Cornwall, but others have been deposited from much cooler solutions which percolated through collapsed limestone cavern systems. These fluids were squeezed out of great thicknesses of accumulating muddy materials and deposited in flanking sedimentary basins far younger than the limestones themselves. Such fluids have never been in contact with hot molten 'igneous' rocks and the mineralisation associated with them is much poorer in silver than that of igneous origin. Derbyshire is typical of this type of ore field.

Lead–zinc–silver deposits are affected by oxidation with often very considerable increases in silver content just above the watertable and just below it (see Fig. 2:4). The oxidised zinc mineral 'calamine' can also be very significantly concentrated above the watertable, although never below it. Lead, however, shows neither concentration nor leaching in the veins during oxidation, although it is normally converted to its carbonate *cerrusite*, which often tends to occur in large nodule-like masses, easier to recover than the primary ore. Perhaps it was these near surface accumulations which stimulated Pliny to comment on the ease with which lead could be mined in Britain.

In Cornwall and the Lake District silver is associated with copper ores and oxidation of copper–silver ores at Perranzabuloe in Cornwall has produced one of the rare examples of secondary native silver in Britain, where it is found with the secondary chloride 'horn silver' too. The quantity of silver recovered from copper in Britain is, however, relatively small compared with the amounts recovered from lead.

The evidence for pre-Roman mining of lead and silver is inferential. No workings have been found in the British Isles which can be identified as having been worked before the Romans but the speed with which the Romans started to mine lead soon after their arrival does suggest that they took over established native mining operations in at least some areas. In the Mendips, La Tène brooches and fibulae strongly suggest pre-Roman mining there (Poss, 1975), whilst we also know the Romans were certainly producing lead from the area by A.D. 49, only six years after their invasion, because ingots have been found there stamped with that date. They may, of course, have been mining there even earlier. On similar evidence, Flintshire mines were producing Roman lead by A.D. 74 and the Nidderdale mines in Yorkshire by A.D. 81 and these areas were not annexed until nearly two decades after the Roman arrival in southern Britain in A.D. 43 (Richmond, 1963). The Romans mined lead in numerous other places too, including Derbyshire, Northumberland, Durham and Cumbria, but again, whether they developed these fields as a result of their own prospecting activities, or merely appropriated existing mines, is unknown. The lack of pre-Roman evidence is by no means surprising when one considers Pliny's remarks concerning the ease with which lead could be recovered in Britain from shallow workings: native workings were perhaps even shallower than those of the Romans.

Tylecote (1962) gives the date of the earliest lead objects found in Britain as Late Bronze Age, consisting of pommels for bronze swords from Northumberland and lead patterns for making clay moulds for socketed axes from Lincolnshire. Although finds are rare, they are possibly not a true measure of the extent of lead usage in the Bronze and Iron Ages. Lead is easily salvaged and melted down and it was probably continuously re-cycled, much as it is today.

The earliest silver can only be dated to the Iron Age, but Tylecote (ibid.) infers that the susceptibility of silver to corrosion may well have removed traces of earlier artefacts or reduced them to a greyish powder of silver salts unnoticed by archaeological investigators.

Lead ore is the main source of silver. The silver occurs in 'solid solution' within the lead sulphide mineral *galena*. When galena is smelted to lead, the silver remains dissolved in the lead and can only be recovered by further processing. This is done by either *cupellation*, a method developed in about 2500 B.C. in the Chalybes of the Turkish Pontic Mountains – Homer's '. . . place where silver's born . . .' – or more expeditiously by *liquation* followed by cupellation. The Romans did de-silver leads, but whether they de-silvered all of them is uncertain. Cupellation is expensive and the costs relate almost entirely to the amount of lead treated rather than the quantity of silver recovered and many British leads, including those of Derbyshire, contain so little silver it would hardly be worth recovering. The imprint of EX ARG which is stamped on many of the Roman ingots found does not, apparently, mean that silver had been removed from them, as has often been supposed. Rieuwerts states that some ingots from Derbyshire bearing this imprint contain the same amount of silver as that in the ore they were smelted from (Ford and Rieuwerts, 1968). Despite several other suggestions, we still do not know what EX ARG really means.

It has been suggested that the attraction of its silver was the principal reason that brought the Romans to Britain and native Britons certainly did produce silver, apparently from lead, from at least the Iron Age. However, British leads are generally not noted for their high silver contents and most British lead fields are, in fact, silver poor. Only Somerset, Flintshire and the Lake District would have been really worth exploiting for silver and even then the return would have been very much lower than from ores in other countries under Roman control. Whatever the Romans came for, it was not silver which kept them here. That they exploited such silver-poor ores as those of Derbyshire on such a grand scale, implies that they were quite happy to mine lead for the sake of lead alone.

Copper ores are another source of silver and those of both Cornwall and the Lake District contain high silver. Could copper have been the main source of British silver before the Romans came? The Celts of pre-Roman Britain certainly did mine copper for bronze-founding, for the coming of iron did not displace the use of copper alloys. The recovery of silver from copper is more difficult than cupellation from lead, and usually requires an intermediary liquation stage using lead; but it was apparently done, for Gowland (Tylecote, 1962) identified as pre-Roman a cupellation hearth at Hengistbury Head in Hampshire in which some partially cupelled copper still remained. Silver can occur in nature in other forms too. During the oxidation of lead ores the lead sulphide is converted to the carbonate *cerrusite*, which remains more or less in place, but silver released from the lead migrates in solution downwards to concentrate lower in the oxidised zone as the chloride *cerargyrite*, or 'horn silver', or as leaf-like masses of native metal (Fig. 2:4). Such concentrations may sometimes be phenomenally rich, containing many hundreds of ounces of silver per ton of ore, but more usually enrichment ranges from 60 to 150 ounces per ton. Unfortunately, in Britain we are not favoured with such concentrations and the only known silver worked was mined in Linlithgow during the nineteenth century (and there the silver had, in any case, been deposited as a primary mineral in quite another manner) and at Perranzabuloe in Cornwall. Nor has horn-silver been mined except in small amounts, although it may well have been mined mixed with cerussite, which it resembles, and in which case, the smelted lead would have been rather richer in silver than that from primary galena-bearing ores which lay below it.

There is, unfortunately, no direct evidence of lead and silver mining in Ancient Britain. We know it was done but we do not know where. Of the many mines worked by the Romans, many may well have been worked long before, but there is nothing to prove it. Stone hammers, found at many sites, including those in mid-Wales, may be Roman, pre-Roman, or perhaps very much later. We just do not know.

IRON

Iron ores of many different types are ubiquitous in the British Isles. They may consist of one or more of a variety of iron minerals ranging from the oxides *haematite* and *magnetite*, the hydrated oxides collectively termed *limonite*, the carbonate *siderite* (=chaly-bite) and silicates such as *chamosite*. Sulphides such as *pyrite* and *marcassite* cannot be used as iron ore. The largest iron deposits are the huge beds of sedimentary ores of Jurassic age which stretch from the Cleveland Hills of Yorkshire to Lincolnshire, but these ores were probably rather too low in iron content to interest ancient miners. Only during the last century have they come into their own and they are now mined on a massive scale by giant walking draglines in huge open pits. They are in fact the only iron ores now worked in Britain. These ores were precipitated with limey materials in partly enclosed lagoon-like seas where there was restricted circulation of the water. That they were formed in very shallow water is shown by fossil borings from worms which lived close to the shoreline, and occasionally by fossil raindrop imprints. Similar ores, of lesser extent, are found in other parts of Britain too, including Dorset, Wiltshire, Hampshire and Kent.

Historically, the main source of iron was from Carboniferous rocks, either as bands and nodules of carbonate clay-ironstones found in the Coal Measures, or as veins and replacements of haematite in Carboniferous limestone. Clay-ironstones were at one time worked with coal and were one of the mainstays of the Industrial Revolution. The ores in limestone were formed by meteoric waters percolating downwards, leaching iron from above and redepositing it in fractures in the limestone as wide veins of haematitic 'kidney ironstone', or replacing the limestone itself piecemeal to form irregular flatlying bodies of haematite. Clay ironstones and veins of haematite also occur in older rocks, and although these have been of little importance since the Industrial Revolution they were probably of considerable use to the Iron Age miners and their immediate successors who, according to Raistrick (1972) mainly grubbed their iron ores from the surface to satisfy their meagre needs. Not until the Romans did iron mining require deeper workings to produce the ore sufficient for a more metal-using standard of living.

Some of the most important ores of the Iron Age must have been those of the Weald of Kent and Sussex which were widely exploited by the Romans who left abundant evidence of their industry. Most of the ore occurs in the lower 6 metres of the Wadhurst Clay of Cretaceous Age where the ore forms discontinuous horizons of masses and nodules of 'clay-ironstone'. The masses are formed of skins of limonite enclosing a core of siderite and are called 'kernel stones' by local quarrymen. They would have been ideal ores for primitive miners to work, with the nodules and masses embedded in easily excavated clay. Many of the masses would, in fact, be eroded out of the clay to be found strewn over the surface and would merely need collection and breaking before smelting. Nothing would have been easier and it is most unlikely that Iron Age British miners ignored them.

ZINC

Zinc metal was not generally known in Europe until it was imported from China in the sixteenth century, although India claims to have been producing it several hundred years before that; but zinc was, in fact, known to the ancients and Iron Age zinc metal has been found in both Dacia and northern Italy and also as fillings in silver bracelets found at Camirus (Davies, 1935). Again, Strabo talks of 'mock silver' (xiii.1.56) which the Hoovers interpret as zinc and they consider that the secret of zinc smelting was known to the ancients in only a few limited areas (Hoover and Hoover, 1950). If this was so, the secret was never passed on, and was lost for over a thousand years.

Zinc was, however, from an early age used unknowingly in the making of the copper–zinc alloy, *brass*. The oldest brasses known were made in Bithynia in the third century B.C., but very low-zinc copper alloys of even greater age have been found elsewhere, including Mesopotamia. Zinc, in the form of zinc oxide, was also in wide use as a medicament, particularly for the eyes, from at least the first century B.C. The problem with zinc is that though its ores are plentiful, it oxidises easily during smelting and its reduction temperature is higher than its boiling point. Special conditions are needed to produce the metal which primitive smelting furnaces did not provide, for zinc has to be condensed from its vapour in a reducing atmosphere, otherwise only a white smoke of particles of zinc oxide called 'philosopher's wool', or 'tutty' results (from the Persian *dudiya* = smoke). The very name of the zinc sulphide ore mineral *sphalerite* reflects this difficulty, for it is derived from *sphaleros*, Greek for elusive, because it looked so like an ore but produced no metal.

Zinc occurs with lead and sometimes copper ores, and in fact many lead ores are richer in zinc than lead. The medicinal use of zinc oxide possibly arose from observations that workers at lead smelters were healthier at those furnaces where the flues were encrusted with condensed white tutty. Tutty was also in demand in large quantities as a substitute for calamine for brass founding. There is considerable literature on tutty preparation, ranging from Dioscorides, who, in the first century A.D., classified it into several sub-types, to the thirteenth-century Albertus Magnus who often confused it with the natural product *calamine*. Tutty production was, in fact, a well developed industry (Forbes, 1964; Wyckoff, 1967).

The sulphide, sphalerite, is the most important zinc mineral today, but to the ancients it was the carbonate, colloquially called 'calamine' (proper name = smithsonite), which was in demand. Calamine occurs in the oxidation zone of lead–zinc deposits, often as remarkably pure and rich concentrations. It was used in the 'calamine method' of brass-making, a cementation process used from perhaps the third century B.C. until the middle of the last century in Europe, and even later in the East. Calamine, a white 'stone' with at one time no known connection with a metal, was heated with charcoal and granulated copper in a crucible to produce a golden yellow metal, typical of low-zinc brass. Is it surprising that the alchemists came to the conclusion that by finding the right stone they could, in fact, turn base-metal to gold? Albeit, brass came mainly into prominence in the Roman world, during the later part of the first century B.C., although in Britain copper–zinc alloys, too low in zinc to be really called brass, had been in occasional use since the Late Bronze Age. These alloys were probably first made accidentally, but later by design, by smelting zinc-rich copper ore from Cornwall, Wales or Ireland. They needed less tin, or none at all, to improve their castability and hardness, and they were cheaper than bronze too, if not so versatile. Whether the calamine method of brass-making was ever used in Britain before the Romans came is not known, but when they did arrive they certainly brought the method with them, with all its advantages of producing brasses rather than copper–zinc alloys. It presumably gave a better control of the product, although this is not apparent in the analyses of Romano-British alloys given by Tylecote, which show great variations in zinc content, and surprisingly large amounts of tin too (Tylecote, 1962).

The British were not over-endowed with calamine and whether they ever resorted to making tutty from sphalerite as a substitute, as was done elsewhere, is unknown. In fact, we have no evidence of any mining activities associated with zinc at all until the eighteenth century, even though zinc ores abound.

MINING

How did the prehistoric miner set about his business? It would be a mistake to underestimate his prospecting ability though his task was made easier because he had few ores to look for, since few metals were of interest to him. Coghlan and Case (1957) claim of the earliest metallurgists in the British Isles, namely those in Ireland, that '. . . not only could they select the right deposit, hand pick, wash and concentrate the ore; they could control the roasting, smelting, and possibly refining processes in a very competent way, and eventually alloy'. They also had that great ally, time, and probably great patience too. Streams were prospected for gold and tinstone. They may even have very occasionally found native silver. Native copper metal was probably found in streams too, in fragments far larger than the grains of gold and tinstone they were looking for, but this was commoner in the East than in Britain.

Copper was looked for chiefly beneath gossans, those iron-rich surface expressions of sulphide-bearing mineral veins, but not every gossan hides a copper deposit: some overlie lead ores, others tin or even pyritiferous gold veins. Many are formed merely from bodies of barren iron sulphide. Whatever their origin, gossans were also important sources of the iron oxide fluxes used by the ancients to smelt lead and copper ores and it has been suggested that they may even have been the path by which iron smelting itself was discovered (Wertime, 1973).

A leached zone devoid of copper usually lies immediately under the gossan (Fig. 2:4) but Ice Age glaciation largely removed older gossans in Britain so that when found they were usually relatively small compared with those found elsewhere in the world, for they had had only a relatively short time to re-establish themselves. This, together with the high watertable in Britain, also meant that leached zones were thin, so that enrichments of malachite and azurite, the green and blue basic copper carbonates which formed from the oxidation of primary sulphide ores, lay almost directly below the gossan. Sometimes these brightly coloured minerals were even deposited on exposed rock surfaces, giving a clear indication of the presence of copper nearby. Thus the search for copper was not difficult. It was probably made even easier because malachite and azurite were used as pigments long before they were ever used as ores. Metal-using people penetrating into new areas had only to ask the non-metal using natives where they got their pigments, to quickly locate sources of one of their basic raw materials.

Because of the high watertable in the British Isles, oxidised copper ores usually graded rapidly downwards into an enriched zone of secondary copper sulphides (Fig. 2:4). These ores were less easy to smelt than the carbonates, but such difficulties had long been overcome elsewhere. Immigrant metal users had brought this knowledge with them, as can be seen in south-west Ireland where such ores were being mined even in the Early Bronze Age (Jackson, 1968). The secondary copper sulphides passed downwards into primary copper-iron sulphides, abundantly associated with the iron sulphide mineral *pyrite*. These ores required careful hand-sorting, were never as rich as the secondary sulphides and were even more difficult to smelt.

In Britain, many copper ores could be mined at the surface in open pits but most such sites are now obliterated, sometimes by later mining, or sometimes just hidden by later events. Just how easily even comparatively large pits can be lost is illustrated by an Early Bronze Age copper pit 18 metres long, 18 metres deep and $1\frac{1}{4}$ metres wide which was discovered under *4 metres* of bog peat in the early nineteenth century during peat cutting at Derrycarhoon in County Cork (Jackson, 1968). Open pits as deep as 18 metres were probably unusual in the Early Bronze Age of the British Isles for, in most cases, there would be problems with both water and the stability of the pit walls. In fact, there is some indication that in the British Isles, Bronze Age copper miners tended to flit from one shallow surface working to the next and Peak (1937) remarks that in West Wales the earliest miners appeared quite happy to attack small bodies of ore and to ignore larger ones near-by. This would suggest that their needs for metal were so easily satisfied that they could afford to select not only the most accessible ore, but also the most oxidised and therefore most easily smelted. Where ore cropped out on hillsides, there would be in many countries an inducement to drive adits into the more enriched ore a short distance below the surface. In the British Isles, because of the shallower zones of enrichment in copper ores, there was probably less often reason to mine underground, but even here, pre-Roman miners did mine beneath the surface although no extensive workings have ever been found. Sometimes, gently dipping ore bodies in hilly ground made open pit mining unproductive owing to the amount of overburden which had to be removed to get at the ore and then adits were driven in ore directly into the hillside.

Early lead mining in the British Isles did not require deep mining either and in his *Natural History* Pliny the Elder contrasted the difficulty of mining Spanish ores, 200 metres beneath the surface, with those in Britain which were '. . . so abundant in the uppermost part of the earth that the law forbade more than a certain amount to be mined' (Pliny, xxxiv.17.49). This was probably an overstatement of the case, for lead mines believed to be Roman are generally larger than copper mines claimed to be of the same period. The extensive exploitation of lead from the Roman occupation until early in this century makes the survival of pre-Roman lead workings unlikely and the recognition of any which may have survived, almost impossible. Mining methods before the advent of machine mining changed little and although the Romans were better engineers than their predecessors and worked on a grander scale, not all mines in Roman Britain were run by Romans. As in our own time, many mines were small and worked by 'small miners' using inefficient methods. It is only necessary to see some of the mines in the less well developed countries of the world today to see how little progress has been made in some places since the Bronze Age. Quiring (Forbes, 1963) has suggested that miners were conditioned by their dwellings and that any wide low-roofed workings were probably Bronze Age because that was how Bronze Age people lived, whilst tall, narrow workings were made by Roman or later miners. Any miner could tell him he was wrong. The shape of mine workings depends on the shape and attitude of the ore body and the strength and nature of the wall rocks. One has only to compare Grime's Graves with present-day meerschaum workings in Turkey and with the opal mines in Australia. The valuable minerals in all these places are nodule-like and occur in horizontal beds of easily hand-mined rock or gravel some 10 metres or so beneath the surface: in each case, the method of mining is the same, despite the span of over 4000 years. Even many of the basic miners' tools have changed little over thousands of years: just the materials they are made from are better and the shape has been modified a little. Wooden shovels, for instance, persisted from Bronze Age to Middle Ages with little real change except that the edges were later reinforced with iron. Even the present-day miner's single-tanged pick, so like its medieval and Roman forbears, is remarkably similar to the reindeer horn pick of the Bronze Age miner (Fig. 2:5).

Little has been said here about iron mining, but in Britain it was seldom necessary to make more than shallow surface workings to find sufficient ore to satisfy the earlier stages of the Iron Age. Such workings, and indeed even later larger ones, were presumably obliterated by the extensive operations which accompanied the Industrial Revolution for, as far as is known, no really ancient iron mines have ever been found in this country, and very few have been found elsewhere. Roman iron mines have, however, been found in the Forest of Dean. These show a similar approach to exploiting ore to that used by the Romans elsewhere, except that here large shafts were sunk down to the ore to expose it beneath the weathered zone instead of the cavern-like adits used in other places. The ore was hollowed out from the shaft bottom once its attitude and value could be seen.

Underground Methods
Up to the Roman occupation, underground mining was probably limited to adits (mine tunnels driven into a hillside) which seldom penetrated far. What evidence there is, suggests that adit portals (entrances) were low and narrow, broadening out to several metres wide a short distance inside if the ore were flat or, if more steeply inclined, following it in whatever direction it took. Where ore

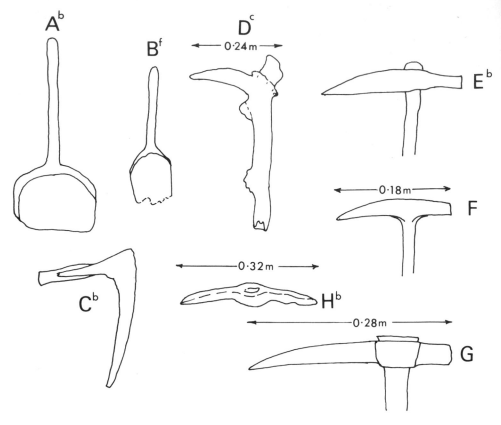

Fig. 2:5 Some tools used by early miners, showing the great similarities to present-day tools. Scales shown where known.

A[b] & B[f] Early Iron Age wooden shovels from mines on the Austrian Alps.
C[b]   Flint axe from the same place.
D[c]   Antler pick from Grime's Graves.
E[b]   Iron pick from mines at Linares, Spain, of 1st or 2nd century A.D.
F   Modern geologist's steel-shafted prospecting pick.
G   Modern metal miner's pick.
H[b]   Pick from Mendips, 1st century A.D.

(After [b]Bromehead, 1940; [c]Cole, 1965; [f]Forbes, 1963)

bodies were wide, pillars of ore were left to support the roof, just as is done today. Some timbering was probably done too and remnants of malachite-encrusted timber have been found at Alderley Edge (Richardson, 1974) but most, especially very early workings, were probably kept small and self-supporting. Cramped quarters did not apparently worry ancient miners and in workings in some countries it is difficult to see how they could have wielded implements with any effect at all, let alone inefficient primitive tools, yet somehow they did manage to mine ore.

Only a child could have entered some workings without becoming wedged, and one must assume that this did in fact happen frequently, and often fatally, for not only were the workings often narrow, they twist and turn to follow every change in direction of the ore, avoiding the removal of unmineralised waste rock wherever possible. Such economy of waste removal was, of course, due to the great difficulty the miners had in breaking rock and its effect on their safety is problematical. Small openings stand well and need less support than larger ones. However, one cannot but feel that accidents were treated with more fatalism than today, and that mine rescue services were rudimentary. Tools were so inefficient that miners trapped even by quite small cave-ins would die before they could be reached and rescued. That mining was hazardous is shown by the frequency with which human remains are found in ancient workings the world over. In one ancient mercury mine in Turkey, more than fifty skeletons were found trapped by an underground cave-in (Barnes and Bailey, 1972).

Fire-setting

Ancient workings in Britain made prior to the Roman occupation seldom appear to penetrate far. Problems due to water and drainage may sometimes explain it, but that cannot always have been the reason because workings in arid countries, such as Iran, where watertables are low, are often just as small. There are some notable exceptions such as the so-called 'King Solomon's' copper mines at Timna in Israel (Rothenberg, 1972), but they are very few indeed. The reason is probably one of ventilation rather than drainage for, in constricted workings, the difficulty would be to disperse the smoke emanating from wooden torches and fat-burning lamps, and especially from fire-setting fires. Fire-setting fires needed constant stoking and this would be quite impossible if miners had to struggle long distances with fuel through dense, choking smoke. Nor would fires burn properly unless there was sufficient air to feed them. In many mining areas, the amount of ore required was small enough to justify opening a new working a little further along the outcrop whenever problems in the current mine became unmanageable.

Where extensive workings are found, the rock was probably soft enough to excavate without fire-setting.

Fire-setting was the main method of rock breaking from the Early Bronze Age until well after the discovery of gunpowder. According to the Hoovers in the copious footnotes they made to their translation of *De Re Metallica*, that great treatise on mining published by Georgius Agricola in 1556 (Hoover and Hoover, 1950), fire-setting continued in use until the end of the nineteenth century A.D. in some German and Norwegian mines, 270 years after explosives had first been introduced into mining. Fire-setting consisted of lighting a fire against the rock face to be broken and feeding it with wood until the rock was thoroughly heated. The rock was then suddenly cooled by quenching it with water, causing it to crack, splinter, flake and spall, after which it could be attacked with wedges and hammers. The Hoovers quote advances of from $1\frac{1}{2}$ to 6 metres a month in the Konigsberg mines of the nineteenth century, an advance which would have been very much less in the Bronze and Iron Ages, but time then probably had less significance than it has today. Water was delivered to the fire presumably in pots, later in buckets and pitch-lined baskets and, as technology developed, by hollowed half tree trunk troughs, joined together to form 'launders'. Some classical reports state that the rock was quenched with vinegar, but this is obviously ridiculous. Apart from any other consideration, the amounts required would be prohibitively expensive. The Hoovers suggest that the original *infosso acuto* of Livy was later rendered as *infuso aceto*, a mistake which Pliny and others perpetuated.

In *De Re Metallica* Agricola gives a first-hand account of how fire-setting was done in his own time. Pliny, from hearsay rather than personal experience, mentions the suffocating fumes and smoke that resulted, and said that battering rams of about 65 kg weight were sometimes used as a cleaner alternative. Fire-setting required adequate ventilation, both to feed air to the fire, to be able to approach and fuel it, and later to quench the rock. In Roman times ventilation became better understood, but before then smoke was obviously a hazard limiting the use of fire-setting, and thus limiting the extent of workings in hard rocks.

Tools

What tools did the ancient miner have to break rock with? The answer is simple – very few! Antler picks could be used in soft ground and for cleaning clay from fissures between rocks so that wedges could be inserted, or they could be used for levering out small blocks already cracked, splintered or spalled by fire-setting. They could have had little other use in hard rock. Large blocks could be displaced by dry wooden wedges hammered into cracks and then wetted to make them swell. For hammers, stone mauls were used. The simplest were merely rounded cobbles collected from river beds or shingle beaches and held in the hand for pounding. Others were 'rilled' by a groove which served to keep a forked stick handle tied into place; or, sometimes, the handle was a flexible root twisted round the maul so that it could be used more effectively, if more dangerously, as a flail. Jackson (1968), in fact, quotes the discovery of a rilled maul dated at 3000–1000 B.C. from the Keweenaw Peninsula of Lake Superior which was found with its cedar root handle still attached. Many stone mauls had a hole drilled through them for attaching the handle and in Wales, Davies (1949) says although rilled mauls were rare, drilled ones were not.

Metal tools were probably little used for mining in the Bronze Age because copper and bronze were not hard or strong enough. Copper chisels were used by Egyptian masons building the pyramids, but there the rock was soft and the chisels were employed to cut grooves for the wooden wedges used to split quarried rock into accurately shaped rectangular blocks. Theirs was a more delicate task and stone tools would have produced less regular blocks. Albeit, no bronze or copper tools have been found in British Bronze Age mines except for bronze axes discovered in Cornwall which were presumably used for cutting timber. As the use of iron increased, iron gads replaced wooden wedges to split rock and some were eyeletted for handles to steady them as they were hammered into place (Forbes, 1963). Bronze hammers have been found in the Tyrolean mines at Mitterberg, which were worked between 1600 and 800 B.C. (Bromehead, 1954), but none are known from British mines of similar ages. Stone hammers were cheaper and more durable and were used in Britain from Bronze Age to Iron Age, throughout Roman times, and well beyond (Peake, 1937), so that although stone mauls are found in abundance at many sites, they are of little use in dating.

Ore was probably transported underground in baskets, and possibly later in leather buckets or dragged in trough-like sledges. Even with the coming of the wheel, it is unlikely that the small British mines used anything else. Sledges were still in use during the Industrial Revolution, and after, for the underground haulage of coal.

Oaken shovels – perhaps only those of oak have survived – were in use from a very early stage in mining and changed little in shape up to the Middle Ages (Fig. 2:5). Presumably wooden ones were cheaper than metal, but it is difficult to see that they were as effective, yet they have been found in Cornwall in both Early Bronze Age and in medieval tin workings, and in Roman galleries at Shelve in Shropshire where 'they were used for shovelling . . . in narrow passages where there was no space . . .' (Roeder, 1901).

Placer Mining

Little is known of placer mining methods in Britain in pre-Roman times. Gold was certainly won from placers in Wicklow in ancient times but there are no signs of any ancient workings to be seen there and any evidence which might have survived was probably destroyed by the Wicklow gold-rush of 1795: Reeves comments (1971) that gold mining was a new experience to the local people and their methods were crude. Gold occurs elsewhere in Ireland, and in Scotland, Cornwall, Devon and Wales, but no ancient placer gold workings have ever been found.

The methods used in early placer mining must be assumed to have been similar to those employed elsewhere. The gold occurred in the sands which filled the interstices between boulders and gravels of the river terraces or of the river bed. The sands and gravels would probably be mined whilst leaving the boulders and larger cobbles in place, and then 'sluiced' (i.e. washed to remove lighter, valueless minerals such as sand and clay) in a dug ditch which was supplied with a controlled flow of water from a nearby stream to recover the gold. Animal skins were pegged to the bottom of the ditch to catch the gold, a process which led to the legend of the Golden Fleece and which survived until relatively modern times; certainly until the Californian gold-rush. The method is in fact still in existence today, except the ditches are now wooden sluice-boxes, or launders, and the fleece has been replaced by corduroy and coconut matting or, to catch the finer gold, coarse canvas. Strabo (xi.2.19), in discussing the origin of the Golden Fleece, states that the present (in the first century A.D.) inhabitants of Colchis still trapped gold with 'fleecy skins' and 'perforated troughs'. The latter were presumably the Colchian equivalent of today's gravel 'dump box', used to screen out the coarser cobbles and gravel, so that only the finer gold-bearing sands reached the sluice.

*

Although it has been mentioned that mining methods throughout the ages have varied little up to the advent of machine mining, this is perhaps not entirely so. In this country, up to the time of the Romans, mines of all sorts appear to have been small, with little penetration underground. Roman mining was more extensive and they apparently took over workings already started by the native inhabitants, destroying the evidence of their predecessors. But even where more ancient mining does still exist, it is probably now impossible to recognise it or to say where one phase ended and another continued, for the tools used were essentially the same, and the miners too, only now they were under Roman direction. Evidence from the mines on the Great Orme and at Llanymynech in Shropshire, suggest that those miners at least were prisoners, and this factor alone would not make for efficient mining, any more than it has done elsewhere. Probably the main difference in mining in Britain before and after the Roman occupation was in magnitude: Romans thought big, the natives did not. They also used a little more thought and one specific distinction in the methods used in this country, noted by a number of writers, is that the Romans started underground operations by driving a large cavern-like opening into the hillside for several metres, unlike the very small portals of the native miners. Perhaps there was a grain of truth in Quiring's ideas, if for the wrong reason. These cavern-like portals allowed the engineers to see fresh unweathered rock and to choose more easily the directions they might follow to the best advantage, and from them they drove out their exploratory drifts (i.e. tunnels and galleries) searching for ore. Such methods can be seen at Ogofau (Dolaucothi), and are also referred to by Roeder (1901). Romans also had more courage in making large stopes or underground working places where ore is mined in bulk. Richardson (1974) quotes a miner who described the Roman workings at Llanymynech as a series of galleries opening into great chambers. Thus any workings which are sizeable are, in this country, probably not pre-Roman and no very ancient mines of any appreciable size are known in the British Isles. Perhaps this country was rather backward in its early mining.

Most early mining in these islands was probably from surface workings which have since been destroyed by later activities, both mining and agricultural. Ireland provides the best evidence of underground mining, where copper ores in several districts were won by numerous small workings driven into hillsides which were abandoned when the going got too difficult. Tin placers were probably mined underground too in parts of Cornwall, but there the evidence is inferential and depends only on the discovery of artefacts found beneath undisturbed beds of oysters and of marine life which is now extinct. That these finds were beneath sea level merely illustrates the fluctuations in levels that quite normally take place over historically long periods of time. Geologically, such periods are insignificant. There is no suggestion that all tin placers in Britain were worked underground, but this does appear to have been a relatively common method for mining alluvial minerals in other parts of the ancient world too. It is logical enough for people with limited earth-moving resources who were seeking gold or tinstone-bearing sands between and beneath boulders lying on stream beds buried by metres of unproductive sands and gravels, especially as many of the boulders were probably very large indeed. The evidence for gold, lead, silver and iron mining is even more inferential and depends largely on the fact that products of these metals were made in this country and often exported to other parts of Europe, sometimes to places a considerable distance away. Occasionally smelting sites have been found, notably those for iron, and where iron ores do occur near ancient hearths, it must be a reasonable assumption that the ore was mined there too.

The British Isles were late in entering both the Bronze Age and the Iron Age, although not as late as more northerly European countries, and we never seem to have mined on the scale found in more eastern countries where quite extensive underground work-ings have been found occasionally, such as those of Timna, in Israel. In general our markets were more domestic and smaller. Even that first British mineral export, tin, was traded only in relatively small quantities: a few tonnes of tinstone were probably sufficient to satisfy the annual needs of the whole world in those days. In the East there were also many small mines and some were remarkably similar to those in Ireland because the problems of working and the tools available were much the same (Holzer and Momenzadeh, 1971). But there were some very large mining areas too, such as copper workings at Ergani Maden on the Tigris in eastern Turkey which supplied copper to Sumer via the Euphrates, their 'Copper River'. Maden, in fact, supplied copper to many of the people of the Fertile Crescent from as early as 7000 B.C., and it is still a major copper producer today. Despite this intensive activity spanning 9000 years of mining, no evidence of ancient workings can be seen now except for slags from smelting. Perhaps, therefore, it is not surprising that little evidence of pre-Roman mining can be found even at Parys Mountain. We can judge ourselves lucky that we have any evidence of mining at all.

BIBLIOGRAPHY

AGRICOLA, GEORGIUS *De Re Metallica* trans. Hoover, H. C. and Hoover, L.H., Dover Publications, New York 1950, 638 pp.

Anon. 'Gold mining gallery discovered in Thrace, probably world's first placer operation' *Northern Miner* 1972, no. 730, 18 pp.

BARNES, J.W. and BAILEY, E.H. 'Turkey's major mercury mine – how it was mined 8000 years ago' *World Mining* 1972, vol. 25(4), European edn pp. 49–55.

BICK, D.E. *The Old Metal Mines of Mid-Wales* Poundhouse Press, Newent, Glos. 1977, Part 4, 64 pp.

BOWEN, E. G. and GRESHAM, C.A. *History of Merioneth* Merioneth Historical and Record Society, Dolgellau 1967, vol. 1.

BRIGGS, S., BRENNAN, J. and FREEBURN, G. 'Irish Prehistoric goldworking: some geological and metallurgical considerations' *Bull. Hist. Metallurgy Group* 1973, vol. 7(2), pp. 18–26.

BROMEHEAD, C.E.N. 'The evidence for ancient mining' *Geogr. Journal* 1940, vol. 96, pp. 101–20.

'Mining and Quarrying' in *A History of Technology* ed. Singer, C., Holmyard, E.J., Hall, A.R. and Williams, T. I. Clarendon Press 1954, vol. 1, pp. 558–71.

CHARLES, J. A. 'Where is the tin?' *Antiquity* 1975, vol. 49(193), pp. 19–24.

COGHLAN, H.H. and CASE, H. 'Early metallurgy of copper in Ireland and Britain' *Proc. Prehist. Soc.* New Series 1957, vol. 23, pp. 91–123.

DAVIES, O. *Roman Mines in Europe* Clarendon Press, Cambridge 1935, 291 pp.

'The copper mines on Great Orme's Head, Caernarvonshire' *Archaeologia Cambrensis* 1949, vol. 100, pp. 61–6.

FORBES, R. J. *Studies in Ancient Technology* Brill, Leiden 1963, vol. 7, p. 253, vol. 8 (1964), 288 pp.

FORD, D.T. and RIEUWERTS, J.H. *Lead Mining in the Peak District* Peak Park Planning Board 1968, 124 pp.

FRERE, S. *Britannia, a history of Roman Britain* Sphere Books 1974, 487 pp.

GOWLAND, W. 'Silver in Roman and earlier times' *Archaeology* 1917–18, vol. 69, pp. 121–60.

HARBISON, P. 'Hartmann's gold analyses: a comment' *Jnl. Royal Soc. Antiquaries, Ireland* 1971, vol. 101, pp. 159–60.

HARTMANN, A. *Goldfunde aus Europa* Gebr. Mann Verlag, Berlin 1970.

HAWKES, J. and WOOLLEY, Sir L. *The History of Mankind* Allen and Unwin 1963, 873 pp.

HOLZER, H.F. and MOMENZADEH, M. 'Ancient copper mines in the Veshnoveh area, Kuhestan-e-Qom, West-Central Iran' *Archaeologia Austriaca* 1971, vol. 49, pp. 1–22.

HOMER *The Iliad*, trans. Rieu, E.V., Penguin, London 1972.

HOOVER, H.C. and HOOVER, L.H. in *De Re Metallica*. Footnotes to the Hoover and Hoover translation, Dover Publications, New York 1950, 638 pp.

JACKSON, J. S. 'Bronze Age copper mines on Mount Gabriel, west County Cork, Ireland' *Archaeologia Austriaca* 1968, vol. 43, pp. 92–114.

'Mining in Ireland, some guidelines from the past' *Technology Ireland* Institute for Industrial Research and Standards, Dublin 1971, vol. 3(7), pp. 30–4.

LLEWELLYN, A. in discussion of paper by Davies, O. 'Roman and Medieval mining technique' *Trans. Inst. Mining and Metallurgy* 1933, vol. 33, pp. 49–53.

MACLAREN, J.M. 'The occurrence of gold in Great Britain and Ireland' *Trans. Inst. Mining and Metallurgy* 1903, vol. 25, pp. 435–508.

MUHLY, J. D. 'Copper and tin. The distribution of mineral resources and the nature of the metal trade in the Bronze Age' *Trans. Connecticut Acad. Arts and Sciences* 1973, vol. 43(4), pp. 155–535.

PEAKE, H.J.E. (Chairman) Report of the committee appointed to investigate ancient mining in Wales. In *Report of the British Assoc. for Advancement of Science for 1937*, pp. 301–3.

PLINY, the Elder *Natural Science* Heinemann, London.

POSS, J.R. *Stones of Destiny* Houghton, Mich. 1975, 253 pp.

RAFTERY, J. 'Irish Prehistoric gold objects: new light on the source of the metal' *Jnl. Royal Soc. Antiquaries, Ireland* 1971, vol. 101, pp. 101–5.

RAISTRICK, A. *Industrial Archaeology* Methuen, London 1972, 314 pp.

REEVES, T.J. 'Gold in Ireland' *Geol. Surv. Ireland Bull.* 1. 1971, pp. 73–85.

RICHARDSON, J.B. *Metal Mining*. Industrial Archaeology Series No. 12, Allen Lane 1974, 207 pp.

RICHMOND, I.A. *The Pelican History of England: I Roman Britain* Penguin Books, 240 pp.

ROEDER, C. 'Prehistoric and subsequent mining at Alderley Edge' *Trans. Lancs and Cheshire Ant. Soc.* 1901, vol. 19, 1909, pp. 77–118.
and GRAVES, F.S. 'Recent archaeological discoveries at Alderley Edge' *Trans. Lancs and Cheshire Ant. Soc.* vol. 23, 1909, pp. 17–29.

ROTHENBERG, B. *Timna: valley of the biblical copper mines* Thames and Hudson, London 1972, 248 pp.

SHAW, W.T. *Mining in the Lake Countries* Dalesman Publg. Co. Yorks 1970, 128 pp.

STRABO *The geography of Strabo* Trans. Jones, H.L., Heinemann 1929, vol. 5.

TYLECOTE, R.F. *Metallurgy in Archaeology* Arnold 1962, 368 pp.

WARRINGTON, G. 'The metalliferous mining district of Alderley Edge, Cheshire' *Mercian Geologist* 1964–66, pp. 111–29.

WERTIME, T.A. 'The beginnings of metallurgy: a new look' *Science*, vol. 182 (4115) 1973, pp. 875–87.

WILLIAMS, H.V. *Cornwall's Old Mines* Tor Mark Press, Truro *c*. 1970, 46 pp.

WYCKOFF, D. *Albertus Magnus – book of minerals* Trans. and annotated by D. Wyckoff, Oxford 1967, 309 pp.

3

The Roman Evidence

G. D. B. JONES

Caves are, of course, well known as habitation sites; but habitation sites that have attracted men and animals almost to the present day. This means that caves are archaeological sites that may produce evidence from the Palaeolithic to the modern. Some, such as Ogof Pant-y-Wennol near Llandudno in Gwynedd, have even had such a lifespan that they contain what are thought to be inter-glacial deposits. Accordingly, the range of animals and other species attested at that particular site range from rhinoceros, horse and reindeer to pigs, fish and birds as well as humans in the later levels. Caves are natural phenomena, used by humans and animals which can be dated by careful stratigraphic excavation. By way of contrast, mining galleries and adits are artificial creations formed by the destructive processes of mineral extraction. Just as caves were re-used they tend to be reworked as mining techniques improve.

THE INDUSTRIAL EVIDENCE

It is no surprise, therefore, to find that any precise dating of mines often defies the investigator, archaeologist or otherwise. Typical of this problem is some of the evidence for early copper mines at Great Orme's Head, Llandudno. At Bryniau Poethion, for instance, early in 1976 various shafts last located in the late nineteenth-century reworkings were re-located. Stone and bone tools were discovered both in undisturbed locations as well as with demonstrably modern equipment. Chisels and gouges made from ox and deer bones were found, impregnated greeny-blue in colour by mineral salts, while the stone tools included mortars and pounders. The difficulty lies

A select bibliography is printed on p. 99.

in assigning the early evidence specifically to one period. Relatively primitive tools remained in use into the medieval period. On the other hand stalagmite deposits up to 28 cm thick would militate against a late date and suggest at least a Bronze Age context, if not earlier. Barring the discovery of diagnostic pottery or the availability of a Radiocarbon date, further precision is difficult. Although this example is probably earlier than the Roman period with which this chapter is principally concerned, it illustrates the methodological problem aptly enough. Accordingly, in discussing the important evidence from mining sites the approach is selective, rather than comprehensive, involving only those sites that actively forward the argument.

None the less there is a certain inherent logic to the sequence of development within mines above a certain size. Normally the first steps in exploitation do not survive subsequent events but would have involved trenching and/or pitting of a promising metalliferous ore body found by prospection. In the case of Roman gold mines such as Dolaucothi or many of those known in north-western Spain prospection was partly carried out by hydraulic means. The next steps towards a larger scale of exploitation usually took the form of the excavation of adits and galleries into the more accessible veins (Fig. 3:1). There are limits to the efficiency of such galleries, however, depending on the quality of the mineral deposit and the overburden involved. It is normal to find therefore that the next stage takes the form of the development of an opencast of modest proportions, in the more promising areas, like Area C at Dolaucothi. As opencasts develop, the problem of operation increasingly centres on the difficulties of removing useless overburden. If mining continues, therefore, it generally takes the form of deep galleries, or stopes, connected to a minehead shaft or driven direct from the floor of the opencast. These deep stopes in turn brought their own problems. First there was the difficulty of disposing of the useless rock debris which was normally of such quantity as to make its complete removal impossible. Second was the question of drainage. Water seepage must always have made working conditions difficult. To prevent them becoming impossible the normal Roman solution appears to have been the provision of water drainage wheels such as the famous examples from the copper mines at Rio Tinto in southern Spain. A very fragmentary example from the Dolaucothi mine confirms the existence of similar devices in Roman Britain. Eventually the continued exploitation of a deep vein system became technically impossible or simply

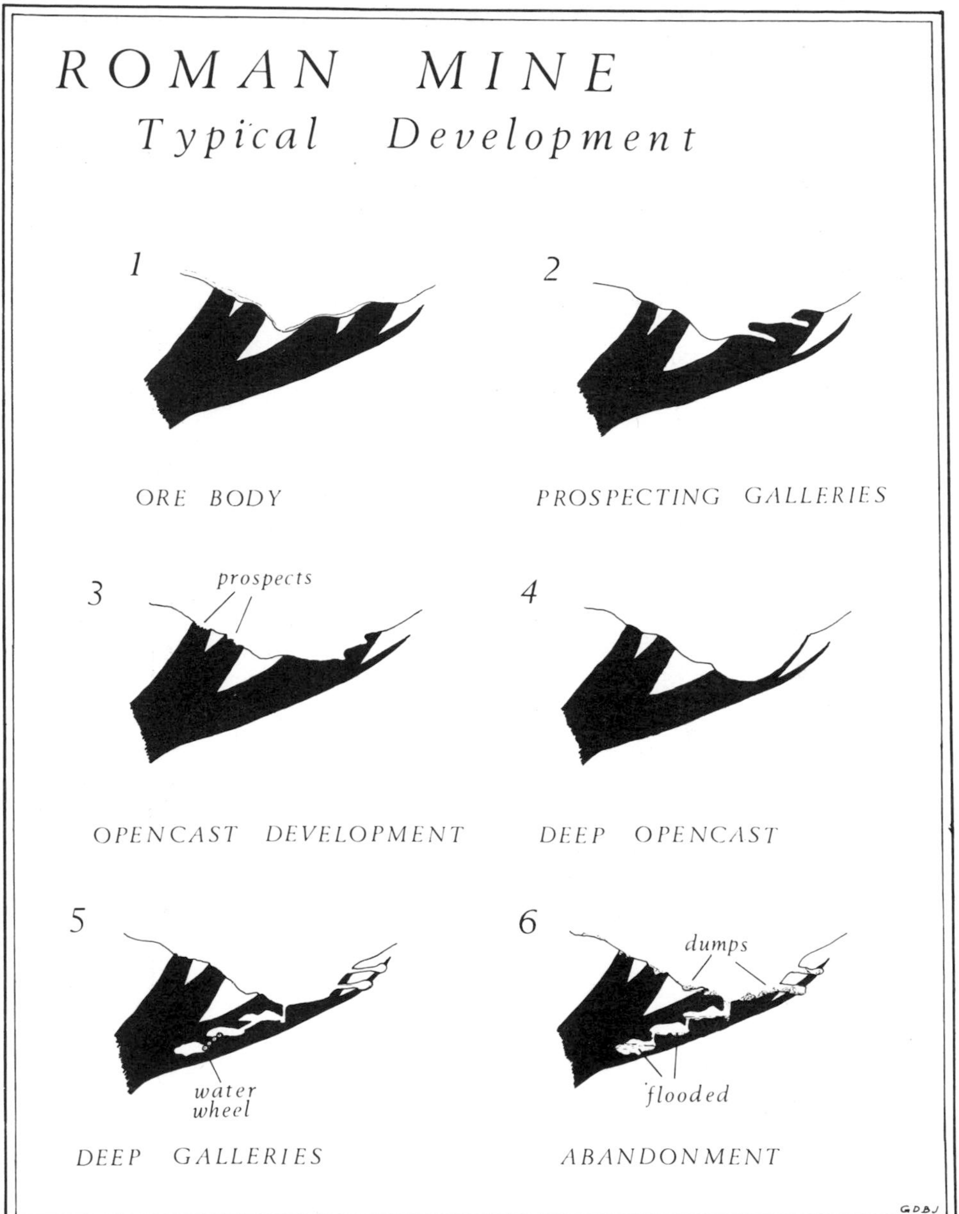

ROMAN MINE
Typical Development

1 ORE BODY

2 PROSPECTING GALLERIES

3 OPENCAST DEVELOPMENT
prospects

4 DEEP OPENCAST

5 DEEP GALLERIES
water wheel

6 ABANDONMENT
dumps
flooded

GDBJ

Fig. 3:1

uneconomic. At that stage the mine entered a state of abandonment with the deep galleries flooded, although, of course, as techniques improved, miners of the early modern period often felt it worthwhile either reworking the remains of ore systems or, as at Charterhouse-on-Mendip, re-processing many of the Roman slag dumps.

Much of the most important evidence of mining in Britain comes not from deep underground workings but from relatively superficial working of veins close to the surface. Indeed, one can argue, particularly in places like the Roman gold mines at Dolaucothi where there are surface indications of an elaborate aqueduct system, that the surface indications are archaeologically more important than the evidence of deep exploitation. This is largely because, in relatively extensive mining areas or those that saw relatively restricted reworking, such as Halkyn Mountain or Charterhouse-on-Mendip, such superficial remains are often capable of analysis to discover the sequence of mining development. Indeed, once extensive mining occurs in the same spot, involving a wide time-span, it is extremely difficult to unravel the development sequence.

The development of opencast workings, as mentioned above, contains its own inherent logic. Most mining developments of any scale follow a relatively predetermined pattern. Surface workings in the form of pitting or trenching are superseded by the creation of underground adits or galleries from which the overburden was often ultimately removed to form the beginnings of a small opencast. From this stage opencasts expanded to the limits allowed by the manpower available, the volume of rock debris and difficulties of drainage. Occasionally, as at Dolaucothi, it proved possible in the final phase of exploitation to create extensive galleries below the bottom of the major opencast, but these were only won at the expense of considerable difficulties with drainage and the disposal of waste. Economically, the mine may have been at its least efficient in this final stage. In archaeological terms it is more common to have to deal with an opencast pure and simple. Because the extraction of minerals normally involves the destruction of evidence by the very processes of mining, then it is extremely difficult to demonstrate the age of any particular working. Take the famous copper mines at Parys Mountain as an instance. There it is not possible to show that the great opencast system cut along the axis of the mountain originated in the Roman period or earlier. The earlier evidence has been obliterated by the copper boom of the late-eighteenth century which made the site the largest mine of its kind in the world. And yet the trail of copper ingots leading from Parys Mountain to the Menai Straits attests the antiquity of mineral exploitation on the site.

These considerations show the way in which we have to appreciate that the evidence for ancient, and particularly Roman, mining comes down to us at various information levels and it is worth emphasising that the relatively superficial is often more informative than a deep working. For instance, the top of the High Mendip is an excellent area for us to appreciate the effects of large-scale pitting and trenching, much of which is of Roman origin. The major point of exploitation lay around the mining town of Charterhouse-on-Mendip, but further areas of Roman exploitation have now been identified close to Stock Hill and St Cuthberts some six kilometres to the south-east. The best surviving examples of this kind of work are probably those still at Charterhouse. There the lead veins close to the Roman fort reached the surface near vertically, and have been quarried away leaving side walls of limestone. The top of Halkyn Mountain in Clwyd is roughly comparable and is capable of the same kind of analysis. The ancient extraction areas were less concentrated because the dressed ore was removed down the mountain for processing to the associated Roman settlement at Pentre, near Flint. Some parts of the mountain, like parts of the High Mendip, reveal areas that appear to have remained intact since antiquity. Areas survive in which both ancient pitting and trenching are clearly recognisable – a point best appreciated from aerial photography. Indeed the value of air photography, in this instance for examining the ancient workings, lies in the way in which it helps bring out the original structure of the mineral lodes. Yet it is important to realise that neither pitting, a shaft sunk into the ground, nor trenching, a linear extraction of the vein system, is by itself an absolute indicator of date. Pitting, the most primitive method involved, is typical of late medieval mining at Shipham on the western edge of Mendip. Likewise, one of the best examples of trench mining occurs in the copper ores of Alderley Edge in Cheshire where the Engine Vein is often said to be of ancient origin. The vein is a fine example of trenching but there is nothing to support the commonly held belief in its ancient origin. [For another view cf. Chapter 2, p. 57.] Similarly, the mine at Penpark in south Gloucestershire, while of greater antiquity, appears to have been exploited over a lengthy period.

In an ascending order of complexity one might next cite the

extraction area associated with the Roman site at Prestatyn. Behind the Roman fort and settlement there towers the limestone wall of Craig Fawr rising some 200 metres from the coastal plain. Lead outcropped there as an outlier of the mineral system further south on Halkyn Mountain. Around Tan-yr-allt the veins were attacked in the Roman period by galleries and trenching, of which the latter is best exemplified by the deep trench on Craig Fawr, the spur overlooking Meliden. The deep trench excavated there leaves a clear impression in the present configuration of the bedrock and it is possible to reconstruct the points where the miners gained deepest access into the ore body.

The difficulty with remains of this kind is to be certain of their date. In many sites one has to argue largely *a priori* from the presence of an adjacent site of Roman date, as at Prestatyn; and in nearly all cases there has been subsequent reworking to a larger or smaller extent. This is not the case, however, in one little known example which is of particular importance in the present context. Llanymynech Mountain, standing on the edge of the Welsh mountain massif, overlooking the Shropshire Plain, is a Carboniferous limestone mass containing many malachite deposits. Much of the eastern face of the mountain has been removed by relatively modern limestone quarrying. The golf course on the summit, however, contains widespread vestiges of much earlier mineral extraction. Amongst these lies the best preserved example of a small-scale mine in Roman Britain, controlled perhaps by a freedman or other entrepreneur. The workings are approached down a ramp leading into the main entrance and working chambers, and form an excellent example of a cave and gallery mine. Two of these were perhaps prospecting adits, while the main gallery followed the principal lode for a considerable distance. In its final stages the adit divides repeatedly with even smaller galleries exploiting the diminishing ore-shoots. Closer to the main working area a vertical shaft was sunk down to the workings both for ventilation and perhaps the extraction of ore, an operation that was at least partly carried out in front of the workings. This gallery was flanked by two benches and the floor content suggests ore-dressing on the site. In two of the galleries human bones (presumed to have belonged to miners) were found buried along with some coins. This enables us to date the mine to the third quarter of the second century A.D. There is no evidence of later exploitation, and with the lead mine at Draethen, it forms an early example of its kind in this country.

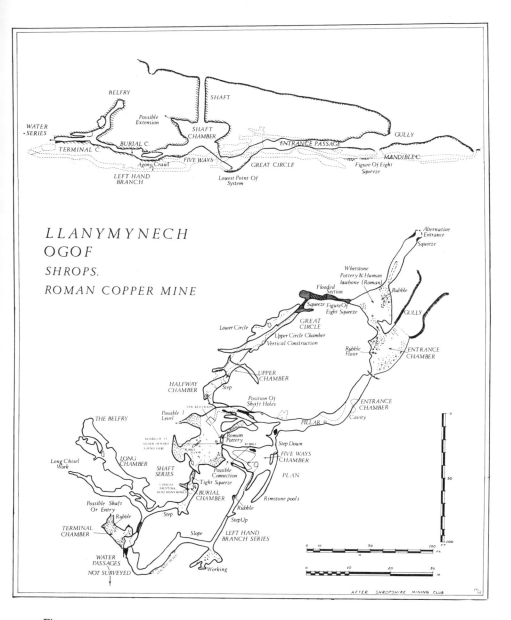

LLANYMYNECH
OGOF
SHROPS.
ROMAN COPPER MINE

Fig. 3:2

91

Fig. 3:3 Llanymynech copper mine: Roman galleries radiating from the foot of the vertical shaft.

The internal details of the Llanymynech gallery mine were recently surveyed by the Shropshire Mining Club (Fig. 3:2) and are of very considerable interest. The front entrance chamber has been considerably infilled in recent years and the limestone rubble which originally suggested the presence of side benches is now obscured (Fig. 3:3). A small passage provides the access to the main gallery which bends past a pillar of unquarried limestone towards the lowest point in the system (Fig. 3:4). From there the adit divides. One gallery leads into Five Ways Chamber while two continue ahead, the principal passage climbing steeply towards the Shaft Chamber. This chamber, palely lit by the light from the vertical shaft driven from the hillside above, functioned (not necessarily contemporaneously) at two different levels. The Upper Chamber to the west follows a tight bend to the north and is distinguished by the stacked deads overlooking the lower floor of the chamber. This area below is the most important in the whole complex because of the Roman finds made in the vicinity. A hoard of thirty-three

Fig. 3:4 Llanymynech copper mine: part of the main gallery with a column of limestone left as a roof support.

denarii was found beside the rubble-choked mouth of one side chamber. Two further side chambers lead to dead ends but a third passage leads through to an extensive set of workings, the final stages of which are known as the Long Chamber and the Belfry. A southern branch within the system was water-filled and incapable of complete examination. Close to the start of this system a coin of the Antonine empress Faustina was recovered, along with human bones probably representing more than a single burial.

The extensive gallery was only one of three such systems. The second, as mentioned above, led into Five Ways Chamber, whence a straight gallery continued through a very narrow passage to a medium-small stope. In turn, a branch passage led through an S-shaped bend to a larger working area at Terminal Chamber. The third passageway, the Great Circle, leads from the lowest point in the main gallery round and back towards the original entrance chamber, although part of the link is currently flooded close to the working area of the Upper Circle Chamber. The final link in this route is formed by a large sub-rectangular gallery to the entrance chamber; it may have had its own gallery adjacent to the entrance leading down from the hillside above but this is obscured by rockfall. Certainly the presence of Roman pottery and bones suggests that this working area was abandoned at a time when other parts of the mine were still in operation.

The only comparable site to Llanymynech in Britain is a recent discovery from Gwent. The mine at Draethen was located by chance in the 1960s when caving enthusiasts from the Bristol Mining Club discovered its vertical entrance on the Tredegar Estate. The over-all system, so far as known, extends nearly 120 metres underground. The entrance leads directly into a large entrance chamber, from the upper wall of which the main gallery leads through to the enlarged gallery in which the remains of a Roman counterfeiting operation (discussed below) were found. This enlarged area continues down and round to a junction with subsidiary passages of small size running roughly parallel to the main adit. The main line of the exploitation continued along Potsherd Passage as far as Comb Rift, where rockfalls prevent further exploration. Like the more complex surviving evidence at Llanymynech, Draethen claims its importance through being one of the only two small gallery mines that are positively datable to the Roman period by internal artefactual evidence and appear to be preserved in practically their pristine state.

The Llanymynech and Draethen mines are unfortunately isolated examples of their kind in this country and for close parallels one must turn abroad. The Roman gold mines at Dolaucothi between Llandovery and Lampeter in Dyfed, however, offer comparable evidence on an altogether larger scale. When modern exploitation broke into the Roman galleries in the late 1930s the activities of the ancient miners were found to reach to a depth of approximately 220 metres below the present floor of the main opencast.

Attention focussed almost entirely, and rather unfortunately, on the more obviously newsworthy aspects of what was found. This included a fragment of a drainage wheel and several examples of miners' implements as well as a slave manacle, all items that might have been inferred in the particular context of a mine. What was lost was the chance to record an intact mining gallery of the Roman period. Cross-examination of several eye-witnesses, however, has established some valuable facts, notably in relation to the disposal of waste rubble. This was found carefully stacked to the ceiling of

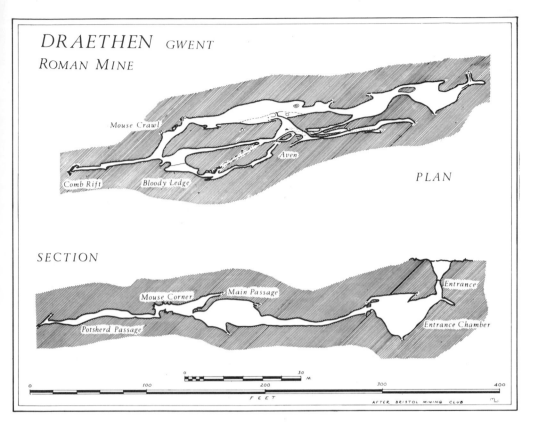

DRAETHEN GWENT
ROMAN MINE

Mouse Crawl

Aven

Comb Rift
Bloody Ledge

PLAN

SECTION

Mouse Corner
Main Passage

Entrance

Potsherd Passage

Entrance Chamber

0   30
M

0   100   200   300   400

FEET

AFTER BRISTOL MINING CLUB

Fig. 3:5

the galleries to act as solid roof supports. Moreoever, to give additional rigidity the waste stacks were evidently held together with horizontal layers of brushwood set within the conical heaps. The full extent of the Roman mining galleries was not recovered and exploration is currently ruled out by the flooding of the modern workings.

None the less, the mining plans of 1934 enable us to reconstruct something of one stope of a large gallery encountered close to the modern minehead at roughly the 48 metre level, i.e. approximately 98 metres above Ordnance Datum at the upper (eastern) end of the stope. The modern workings broke into a major stope aligned north-east south-west and measuring some 75 metres long. Its width at the widest known point measured at least 22 metres but

95

this is only a minimum measurement because the full extent of the stope could not be examined. The south-western end comprised a large chamber following the auriferous quartz veins. At the other end, close to the modern mineshaft, a narrow passage led up from the main gallery while a small prospect immediately alongside it ran backwards and upwards over the main gallery. This is the tantalising limit of certain knowledge of the extensive evidence that was re-located in 1934 and subsequent years.

While the adits and galleries below the main opencast are by far the most extensive on the site, there are other features of particular interest above the opencast and in broad terms belonging to the earlier phases of the mine's development. Several adits of probable ancient origin ring the opencast area. Galleries are good examples of adits following down the auriferous quartz veins which dip at an angle of approximately 45° in this area. Across the narrow col to the south, in the area of Allt Cwmhenog, a large trench of nineteenth-century origin marks the pattern of the mineral extraction and also runs close to a well-cut gallery driven approximately north-south into the slope of Allt Cwmhenog. It has been claimed as being Roman in date, principally on the evidence of the neat pick marks along the side walls, but this is clearly far too simplistic a diagnostic of antiquity to carry conviction and very similar pick work has been observed in nineteenth-century lead workings a few miles away at the head of the Towy valley. The mining gallery sealed by a late third-century hut floor at Lydney Park appears to be almost the only *isolated* adit one can date to the Roman period with confidence.

Such doubts do not, however, extend to the medium sized gallery and shaft system known as Opencast C. This particular opencast is directly associated with the development of the aqueduct system that supplied the minehead with between 9 and $13\frac{1}{2}$ million litres of water a day. Initial hydraulic prospection evidently discovered the presence of an ore body at this point. It was extracted first, presumably by means of trenching or pitting, and then developed as an opencast. In the next stage the miners evidently thought that the task of removing further overburden in its entirety was excessive, and the third and final stage of extraction saw a return to an adit and gallery system. Fortunately this has survived extensively although evidence of shot-holes indicates that the adit was partly reworked in the period of the so-called Mitchell Mine when an Australian mining engineer embarked on a programme of reworking the deposits. So much was apparently evident from the visible remains. It was a far more difficult task to confirm this supposition in archaeological terms; yet it proved possible in 1968 when a section was cut across the floor of the more northerly of the two galleries that give access to the main ore body which drops near vertically at this point towards the head of the main opencast. Beneath the obviously modern accumulation lay a series of strati-graphic levels, albeit levels compacted principally of mud and debris. Amongst the upper levels one contained the remains of a nineteenth-century whisky bottle to link the level with the period of exploitation by the Mitchell Mine. The second level from the bedrock contained what we might perhaps see as the equivalent of the whisky bottle, namely a fragment of a Roman square bottle. Its precise date lies in the first–third century A.D. and although it is thus difficult to be precise, its chronological implications are basically not in doubt. One cannot normally expect to discover artefacts by what is random trenching within a mining gallery. So the recovery of Roman material corroborating the presumed origin of this particular adit can be regarded as a fortunate discovery.

DOMESTIC AND CLANDESTINE USAGE

While it is commonplace to find that prehistoric man lived in caves, cave dwellings are less well known in the late Iron Age–Romano–British period. Once again, as we have seen to be the case with mining galleries, the archaeological problem centres on estab-lishing relatively precise dates for human occupation or other use. Caves tended to be inhabited from pre-historic times and it is often difficult to assess the relative importance of random finds made within a cave. Two areas, however, demand our attention in this context; the Mendips and the Peak District of Derbyshire.

In the Mendips particular attention centres on Gough's Cave, opened up in 1877. In making the cave accessible to the public considerable archaeological material was uncovered, notably from the late Roman period. The material comprised iron spear-heads, Roman coins and pottery, together with bronze implements and a wide collection of animal bones. In a small gallery extending up from Gough's Cave to the so-called Long Hole a further interesting numismatic discovery was made. It comprised a collection of more than three hundred Roman coins. The deposit was principally of the later empire and a *terminus post quem* for the group is provided by two rare coins. They were a silver *denarius* of Julian the Apostate (A.D. 355–365) and more remarkably a gold *aureus* of Valentinian II (A.D. 375–392). Curiously, the coins were found standing in heaps on a rock ledge as though the inhabitants of the cave, unless we are dealing with some kind of discontinuous religious use, arranged the money in piles. Whatever the interpretation, the evidence attests use of the cave at the transition from the Roman into the early Migration period about which we can only speculate. At the other end of the time scale, to broaden the perspective, in 1903 remains of a human skeleton often called Cheddar Man and now dated by Radiocarbon to 9080 ± 150 B.P. (c. 7130 B.C.) were found between two large blocks of stone and covered with an unbroken layer of stalagmite. In associated, or still earlier layers (the strict stratigraphy demanded by modern excavation was not developed at the time), occurred flint and bone implements and the bones of cave bear, elk, horse, reindeer, red deer, giant Irish deer, bison, bear, fox, wolf and lynx.

Gough's Cave, therefore, is probably the most informative of the Mendip sites with its broad range of occupation. But other sites used for habitation also characterise one aspect of the later Roman period. Wookey Hole cave, Read's and Rowberrow Caverns and Aveline's Hole were all used in this way. Wookey Hole is notable for finds of bronze artefacts spanning a lengthy period and coins of Valentinian I and Gratian. Dramatically, part of Read's Cavern collapsed entombing several of the occupants and in this way preserving for posterity much metalwork including a fine set of shackles and four bronze bands from a tankard of late Iron Age date. Aveline's Hole at the foot of the east side of Burrington Coombe was perhaps not occupied quite so late, but it would be a mistake to regard cave dwellings as necessarily primitive and poor. At the time, in the area, they were probably an acceptable alternative to a round timber hut on one of the more exposed hillforts of the High Mendip. Indeed, finds from some caves probably reflect late pre-Roman lead exploitation from the High Mendip above.

The most clearly attested home industry is known from the Roman period. White Woman's Hole near Leighton in Eastern Mendip proved on systematic excavation to have been used as a Roman counterfeiter's workshop. The cave entrance was small but expanded into a larger passage. The stratification was much affected by previous grubbing and animal disturbance which in places inverted the occurrence of ancient and modern material, accounting for the presence of medieval-early modern material below the coining material. The latter comprised coins, flans and rods; a hoard of seventy coins was found at one point. These formed part of two groups of die-linked counterfeit coins, namely 76 counterfeit *antoniniani* and 45 Constantinian counterfeits that comprised the bulk of the numismatic material. The date of occupation is not yet paralleled at other Mendip sites but, despite the cave's isolation, the absence of slag, dies, moulds and crucibles indicates that the site may only have been used for the storage rather than the manufacture of the counterfeit material. Whatever the precise details a roughly similar counterfeiting den was operating in the late third century some 45 metres inside the (then) abandoned Roman lead mine at Draethen near Machen on the Glamorgan–Gwent border.

The occupation of caves is attested elsewhere (at Devonshire Kent's Hole, for instance, near Torquay and as far north as Kirkcudbrightshire and East Lothian). Ancient man's use of these natural phenomena is otherwise mainly limited to those areas most similar to the limestone of Mendip, namely, certain parts of Yorkshire, Derbyshire and North Staffordshire. The Victoria and Dowkerbottom caves, the principal Yorkshire examples, produced evidence of first–fourth century occupation notable for a fine range of silver and enamelled brooches. In Derbyshire, excavations in Poole's Hole, Thirst House, Cresswell Crags and Bat House yielded pottery, metalwork and coins principally of first–second century date, likewise Thor's Cave in Staffordshire. By and large these cave sites should not be treated as remote refuges; extensive field systems associated with some of them show that they can better be regarded as natural shelters preferred to usual native huts and linked with otherwise normal agricultural units exhibiting wide cultural and economic contacts.

BIBLIOGRAPHY

DAVIES, O. *Roman Mines in Europe* Oxford 1935.

Derbyshire, *Victoria County History* 236 f. etc. References to cave sites occur frequently in the *Derbyshire Archaeological Journal*.

GOUGH, J. W. *The Miner of Mendip* Oxford 1930.

JONES, G.D.B. and LEWIS, P.R. 'The Roman Mines at Dolaucothi' *Antiquaries Journal* vol. LXIX, 1969, 244ff.

KNIGHT, F.A. *The Heart of Mendip* Bristol 1971.

The Future of Non-Ferrous Metals in Great Britain and Ireland: A Symposium Institution of Mining and Metallurgy, London 1959.

4

The Irish Souterrains and their Background

RICHARD WARNER

Ireland is one of the richest countries in the world in its store of surviving monuments from the Neolithic to the present day. This may be partly due to the superstitious awe in which they were once held, and partly because of the emphasis, until recently, on pastoral rather than arable agriculture. Ironically the change in farming methods, and the increasing use of heavy machinery and 'rational-isation' of the landscape both create a distinct threat to the known monuments, *and* bring to attention a class of monument which has too often been ignored.

The souterrain is, at the one time an 'invisible' site (thus seemingly ruling out any status as a surviving monument), and the most perfectly preserved structure which can be uncovered today. It is a feeling which few can imagine to enter an ancient structure which is now in precisely the same state of preservation as when it was abandoned one thousand years ago. Yet, despite the fact that several hundred souterrains are known, and new ones come to archaeological attention at the rate of about a dozen a year, few have been properly excavated and only one has been made into a National Monument in its own right (several others are *parts* of monuments).

Souterrains have been (and still are) described as mysterious and enigmatic structures. I hope to show that this is far from the case, that they are easily explained in terms of the known history and archaeology of later Iron Age Ireland.

Bibliographical notes are printed on page 144.

DESCRIPTION

An Irish souterrain can be defined as an artificial, subterranean (or semi-subterranean) structure built to allow access and associated with habitation. The following basic construction techniques are found.

(1) Tunnelling into rock or highly cohesive boulder-clay.
(2) Dry-stone building within an open topped trench.
(3) Use of a natural rock-cave, cleft or fissure.
(4) Wooden construction in an open topped trench.
(5) Incorporating the souterrain within the rampart or wall of a Ringfort or other enclosure.

Tunnelled Souterrains

These are found in all parts of the country, wherever the surface rock or clay is of the right consistency to be tunnelled, but are particularly common and sophisticated in Co. Cork. The advantages of a pure rock souterrain would have been the difficulty of digging out the occupants or of finding the course by ground thumping or probing. Disadvantages would have included the

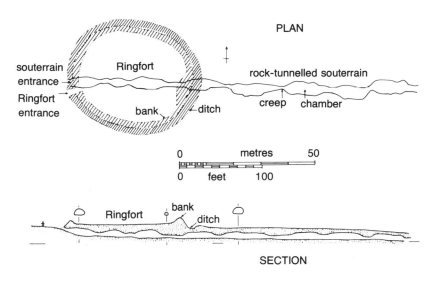

Fig. 4:1 An 1838 plan and profile of the enormous rock-tunnelled souterrain at Rathmore, Co. Antrim (after Boyle), now closed.

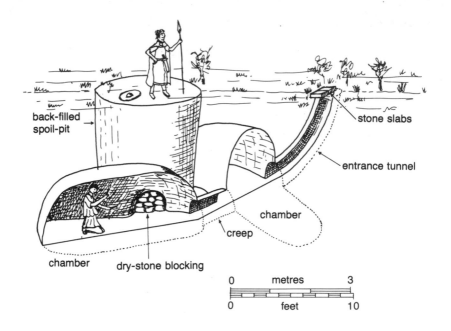

back-filled
spoil-pit

stone slabs

entrance tunnel

chamber

creep

chamber   dry-stone blocking

| 0 | metres | 3 |
| 0 | feet | 10 |

Fig. 4:2 Schematic view of a tunnelled souterrain with spoil-pit. It should be noted that the spoil-pit was backfilled immediately after construction.

difficulty of air supply and drainage, and in constructing complex internal impediments. In the case of the clay-cut souterrains instability and the ease of unwanted entry by digging from above would have been a disadvantage. Construction of the simpler tunnelled souterrains would probably have been within the technical capabilities of anyone with available labour and a minimum of expert advice. The rock-cut souterrains are the least likely to be discovered today by accident, for instance during casual farming activities, but upon discovery have a very good chance of survival. The clay-cut class, on the other hand, have a high chance of discovery, by collapse of the roof, and a poor chance of subsequent survival.

The simpler tunnelled souterrains, such as most of those in the north, seem to have been hollowed into the rock or clay in straightforward fashion, the spoil being removed through the entrance. The resultant meandering cave typically has few chambers and passages, and impediments are uncommon. The longest souterrain known is of this type; it runs under the Ringfort of Rathmore, Co. Antrim (a royal site since the seventh century A.D.) and is at least 130 metres long with eight known chambers (Fig. 4:1). The more complex structures, particularly the clay-cut Co. Cork souterrains, were constructed in an altogether different fashion. One or more large, deep 'spoil-pits' were dug to what would be the level of the bottom of the souterrain. The chambers and passages were dug into the lower walls of these (Figs. 4:2 and 4:3). Finally the pits were filled with spoil and rubbish, the loose soil being prevented from filling the chambers by dry-stone revetment walls. Occasionally *air vents* were left in the sides of the pit as it was back-filled. The entrance seems to have been invariably a narrow, near vertical or steep shaft whose mouth was sealed by several stone slabs or lintels. This led to the complex of low, irregular but roughly oval chambers, from $1\frac{1}{2}$–6 metres long, about $1\frac{1}{2}$ metres wide and 1–$1\frac{1}{2}$ metres high, with flat floors and evenly domed walls and roof, joined by very narrow, usually short, passages (creeps) some 30–60 cm wide and high. The whole complex, which could amount to seven or more chambers, may be in an irregular, zig-zagging line (as Curraghcrowly, Co. Cork), a circle of chambers, rather like a bracelet, served by a single 'spoil pit' (as at Ballintemple, Co. Derry) or an irregular pattern (as most of the Co. Cork structures). Drainage was not usually a problem, but at least one had a well-built stone drain leading away from it (Ahakeera, Co. Cork).

It is not at all uncommon for stretches of rock-tunnelled or clay-tunnelled souterrain, both chambers and passages, to be incorporated in an otherwise dry-stone construction, but these are invariably of the simple tunnelled variety, without spoil-pits. Good examples of mixed construction are to be found in Co. Antrim.

Dry-stone Souterrains

This class of souterrain construction, involving the skilled use of undressed, unmortared stone, results in some of the most spectacular specimens of ancient masonry. Souterrains built in this fashion have the advantages of stability and strength, and a potential versatility of constructional complexity. The disadvantages would have been the ease with which they could be traced by probing or thumping, and the fact that any but the simplest could only have been built with the advice of a highly skilled souterrain-engineer, and skilled masons and artisans to supplement available local unskilled labour. A plentiful supply of suitable stone would also

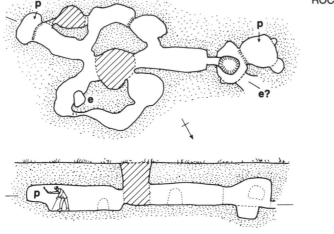

ROCK-TUNNELLED

e = entrance   **p** = platform

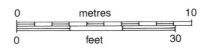

spoil-pit

dry-stone walling

CLAY-TUNNELLED

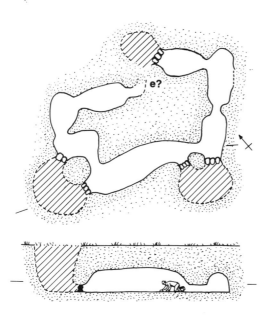

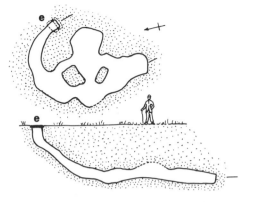

Fig. 4:3 *Upper left* Rock-tunnelled souterrain with spoil-pits (the southern one may be a ventilation shaft) at Ballintemple, Co. Derry (after May and Cooper).

Lower left Clay-tunnelled souterrain at Lisheen, Co. Cork (after Fahy). The entrance was not found.

Above Clay-tunnelled souterrain, apparently without spoil-pit, at Ballyrisode, Co. Cork (after Twohig). Note the slabs sealing the entrance tunnel and the extremely confined nature of the chambers.

have been necessary, either from the boulder-clay, or quarried. Discovery is usually by the movement of a roofing stone during ploughing, and subsequent preservation is very variable, and dependent on the whim of the owner.

The first stage of construction was to dig a deep straight-sided trench more than large enough to contain the final souterrain (Fig. 4:4). Where rock was close to the surface a natural cleft was often used, and enlarged, as the trench (particularly in Co. Clare). In cases where no such clefts were available and the rock was too hard to dig, or where drainage was a severe problem, the souterrain could be partly or wholly above ground, in a mound of soil, or in the rampart of a fortification (below). Within the trench the dry-stone walls of the souterrain were built up, using boulders, soil, or wood as the temporary centering and packing rubble and clay into the back-space between the wall and the trench sides. The wall stones were usually laid with their long axes at right angles to the wall-face (as 'leaders'), their broad axes horizontal. Occasionally, if large stones were still plentiful after those for roofing had been put aside, they were placed as grounders in a 'stretcher' position, usually face down rather than face out (as in Scotland and Cornwall). Where the wall stones were rough, uneven, unsorted

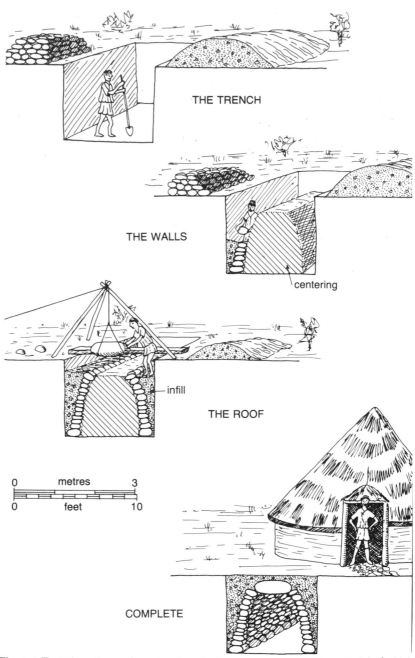

THE TRENCH

THE WALLS

centering

infill

THE ROOF

0 ____ metres ____ 3
0 ____ feet ____ 10

COMPLETE

Fig. 4:4 Tentative scheme of construction of a dry-stone souterrain. The material of which the centering was made is unclear.

boulders (sizes varying from less than 30 cm to 60 cm greatest dimension) the walling is truly random and has an appearance (unjustified) of instability. This is typical of the basalt-built souterrains of Co. Antrim (Fig. 4:5). Where quarried, or at least more regular, stone was used (such as slate) there may be an appearance of coursing (Fig. 4:6). When the required height had been reached the roof gap was bridged by long lintel slabs, contiguous when plentiful but laid with gaps between, bridged by smaller stones, when scarce. Where the lintels were appreciably shorter than the required base width of the souterrain a pronounced inward batter to the walls, almost a corbelling, was used. In cases where long lintels were available the walls were often vertical or battered outward. Forces from the heavy roof and walls tend to dissipate into the trench sides and floor, and it is a credit to the builders that these souterrains can support extreme weights without collapsing.

Finally, the gap between the top of the roof lintels and the surface was filled with stones and soil, and the internal centering was removed. Buildings could be placed over the structure and every trace of the trench quickly eradicated.

In a very basic sense – the provision of underground chambers with restricted access – all souterrains are the same. But the ways in which the basic structural features (which we shall now describe) can be deployed can create an almost infinite variety of souterrains. Where original entrances have been found they are usually vertical or steeply sloping shafts, not always stone-lined. Occasionally they may be stepped, or have a shallow slope, but in such cases it is usual for an impediment to appear very soon. The entrance may lead straight to a chamber, usually via a 'creep' impediment, or into a passage, which itself will usually lead to one or more chambers.

Two types of passages are common. The 'restricted' passage can be long, meandering, and is typically 60–90 cm wide and high (for instance at Knowth, Co. Meath). This type of passage will almost always lead to one or more chambers (not infrequently of the 'beehive' type) and to other passages. It is unusual for 'restricted' passages to contain further impediments. The second class of passage is more roomy, can be as high as a chamber, that is about $1\frac{1}{2}$ metres, up to over 1 metre wide, and very long (for instance, 15 metres in one stretch) and is not uncommonly curved or angled. This type can be divided into a series of shorter lengths by impediments, or can join other passages through creeps, a change in direction often happening at this point. Such passages may lead to chambers, but are often of sufficient dimensions to have been

Fig. 4:5 Interior of a souterrain at Drumnakeel, Co. Antrim showing the unstable-looking stonework typical of basalt boulders from the glacial 'till'. Note the simple creep, little more than a half metre square. *Photo. A. E. P. Collins, Historic Monuments Branch, Belfast. Crown Copyright reserved.*

chambers themselves, or may widen out at their far ends to chamber dimensions. Passages were always constructed in the normal lintelled manner already described.

The chambers are usually oval or sub-rectangular, 3–9 metres long, about $1\frac{1}{2}$ metres high. The width is governed by the length of available lintels, single spanning being the norm giving about $1\frac{1}{2}$ metres base width, although heavy inward battering of the wall, almost to the extent of corbelling, may increase the base width to up to 2 metres. True corbelling, using medium sized stones but no true lintels, to create a domed, or 'beehive' shaped circular chamber is not at all rare, particularly in Cos. Louth and Meath. The use of pillars to support the roof, allowing a greater chamber width (as in the northern Scottish Islands) is unknown, but in Co. Waterford some wide lintelled chambers have corbelling semi-lintels to increase the width.

Impediments take several forms, and are usually of one build with the whole structure. I shall call them all 'creeps' (Fig. 4:7). The 'simple creep' is a short lintelled tunnel, perhaps 60–90 cm high and wide, and little more than 1 metre long, between chambers, between entrance and chamber, or in the 'roomy' class of passage (Fig. 4:5). The 'drop hole' creep is a small square opening, again about 60–90 cm square (sometimes less), in the floor of one chamber (or passage) and the roof of the next chamber (or passage) which is consequently below the first. According to how the land falls one might drop or rise on moving inwards through such a creep. At Rathmullan, Co. Down, 'drop hole' creeps have been created without change of level by building a cross wall just in front of a 'simple' creep. Here the combination of 'drop hole' and the following restriction of height makes ingress very difficult indeed. At Channonrock, and Donaghmore (Fig. 4:8), both in Co. Louth, an upward 'drop-hole creep' into a short passage, followed immediately by a downward 'drop-hole creep' creates a complex obstruction involving a short bridging passage at a higher level.

The list of structural features could go on, but I think a few more would suffice. Air vents, usually stone built, leading up from an upper corner of a chamber or passage are common (Fig. 4:6). Drains leading from a souterrain are much less common, probably because, as inspection has shown, most souterrains are exceptionally well drained by natural means. Platforms are found in some rock-tunnelled souterrains liable to flooding, such as Curraghcrowly and Ballintemple (Fig. 4:3). The latter also has a sump-pit which could have served as a well and as an obstacle. 'Cubby holes', and

Fig. 4:6 Interior of a souterrain at Sheepland More, Co. Down. The stonework, of slate, is more even than in Fig. 4:5. Note the beginning of a ventilation shaft at the upper far wall, below the last lintel. *Photo. A. E. P. Collins. Historic Monuments Branch, Belfast. Crown Copyright reserved.*

small wall cupboards have frequently been recorded, and, less commonly, full height recesses behind a creep which could be interpreted as guard-chambers (particularly with the 'drop-hole' creep type). Shelves and benches have also, rarely, been encountered. At Rathnew, Co. Westmeath, the post-holes of wooden doors were found against two creeps (Fig. 4:15). Finally, 'escape passages' can be found, leading from an inner chamber to the steep side of a valley or the ditch of the fort (see below) (for instance, Rathmulcah, Co. Sligo; Cahercommaun, Co. Clare. Fig. 4:12).

The size of a souterrain is really a measure not of the size, but of the number, of these features. Thus stone-built souterrains can range in complexity from the single chamber, single 'simple creep' type, to the multi-chamber/passage, multi-creep monsters of up to

60 metres in total length (for example, Knockdhu, Co. Antrim (Fig. 4:9) and Donaghmore, Co. Louth (Fig. 4:8)). Yet the simple are built identically to the complex, and in many cases it can be difficult to know if one is exploring a single-chamber souterrain, or the single chamber of an otherwise destroyed multi-chamber structure.

The layout of the simple souterrain is roughly the same wherever it occurs, little variation being possible unless a long 'restrictive' type of passage is present, in which case it can meander unpredictably. The layout of the complex souterrain is very variable, but even so certain regional preferences can be seen. In the case of the multi-chamber souterrains with mostly simple creeps and short, or no, passages the chambers can be placed in any position: end to end, end to side, side by side. The resultant pattern is totally unpredictable from the surface. This class was preferred in Co. Antrim (for instance, Knockdhu). The roomy-passage souterrains, commonly with 'drop-hole' creeps, short chambers at right-angles to the passage and a major chamber at its end, were the type favoured in Cos. Down, Louth and Meath (but it must be stressed that all variants can be found anywhere).

The *rock-cleft* souterrains were generally built in the same way as the rest of the dry-stone type, except that the direction, extent and shape of the passages and chambers were predetermined by the cleft. Creeps are usually simple.

Wooden Souterrains

Excavation has revealed a number of simple souterrains with stone walls and post-holes, but without stone roof lintels (for instance at Ballycatteen, Co. Cork (Fig. 4:10) and Raheenamadra, Co. Limerick), or without even the stone walls (Letterkeen, Co. Mayo), and it seems an inescapable conclusion that these were roofed with, or even completely constructed of wood. That these would have been easy to build is hardly questionable, but their effectiveness would have been short-lived, and one at Ballycatteen appeared to have been burned.

Rampart Souterrains

A number of souterrains have been found partly or wholly built within the earth rampart of a Ringfort. In some cases they have been inserted after construction of the rampart (as at Shanes Castle, Co. Antrim), in others (such as Ballywillwill, Co. Down) they were original features. At Stranocum, Co. Antrim and Rathmulcah, Co.

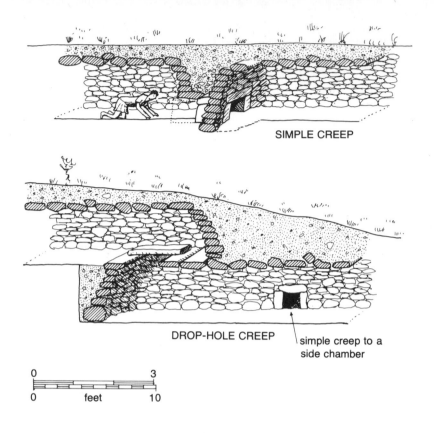

SIMPLE CREEP

DROP-HOLE CREEP

simple creep to a side chamber

0   3

0   feet   10

Fig. 4:7 Basic creeps in dry-stone souterrains.

Sligo, and elsewhere, a single chamber of a complex souterrain was incorporated within the rampart, and at Leacanabuaile, Co. Kerry, for instance, a small chamber within the *stone* rampart of the fort was connected by a subterranean 'restricted' passage with a house within the fort (Fig. 4:11). Finally, some stone Ringforts (and monastic enclosures) on the west and north coasts and islands have been found to contain, within the defensive wall, small chambers, or simple, but extensive passages, entered through small 'simple creeps' from the interior of the fort. Similar structures are found in the west of Scotland. A remarkable site is the stone promontory fort at Dunbeg, Co. Kerry, where the stone rampart contains, near its

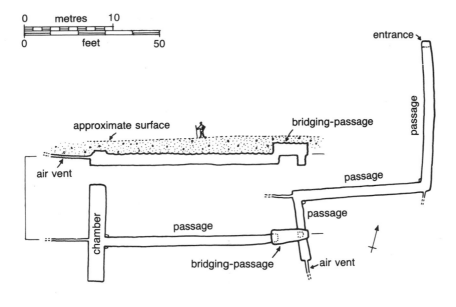

Fig. 4:8 The massive Donaghmore souterrain, Co. Louth (after Rynne). The stone-built passages and chambers lack simple creeps, but the bridging passage was an effective obstruction.

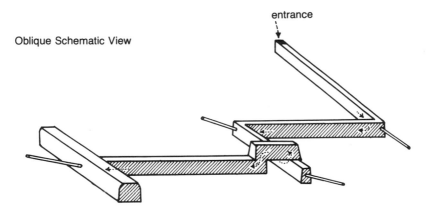

Oblique Schematic View

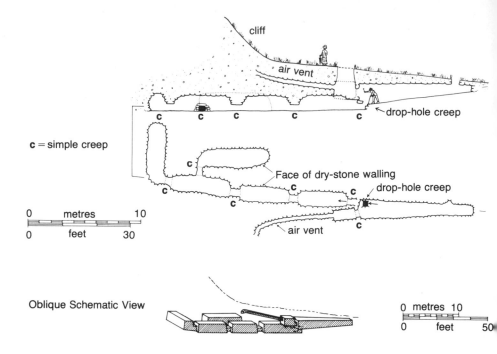

cliff

air vent

drop-hole creep

c = simple creep

Face of dry-stone walling

drop-hole creep

air vent

0 metres 10

0 feet 30

Oblique Schematic View

0 metres 10

0 feet 50

Fig. 4:9 Stone-built souterrain at Knockdhu, Co. Antrim (after Lawlor). It contains a passage-chamber, five other chambers, six simple creeps and one drop-hole creep, and an air-vent which might also have served as an escape passage. The position of the original entrance is not clear.

top, a passage-gallery of souterrain-like appearance, and underneath the main entrance passage of the fort, leading from outside the gate to just inside, a normal dry-stone 'roomy'-passage souterrain.

CONTEXT

By far the greatest number of recorded souterrains have been found in, apparently, isolated positions unconnected with any obvious traces of habitation. Yet from the siting of these (in the same hill-slope, or knoll situation as habitations of the period); from the frequent scraps of occupation material which have filtered into them, and from those cases where careful excavation has taken place and invariably produced the remains of surface houses (such

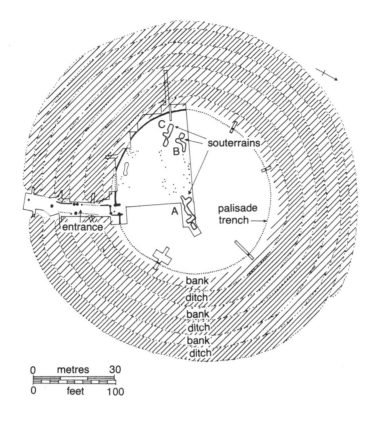

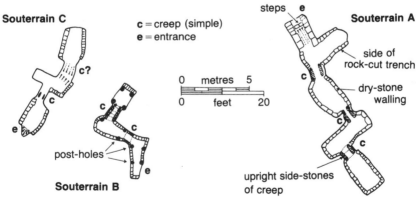

Fig. 4:10 The multivallate earthen Ringfort at Ballycatteen, Co. Cork (after Hartnett and ÓRíordáin), with three souterrains in the excavated quadrant. One is stone-walled throughout and was probably stone-roofed, another had posts for a wooden roof and two stretches of clay wall are left unlined.

as Craig Hill and Antiville, both in Co. Antrim), it can confidently be proposed that all souterrains were adjuncts to normal habitation sites. Indeed, the presence of a souterrain is probably a reliable indication of the existence of an otherwise invisible settlement or farm.

Extensive settlements may be implied by the multi-chamber souterrains and by reports of clusters of souterrains (although these may sometimes be multi-chambered examples in which the connecting passages have become obscured). At Ballywee, Co. Antrim, excavation showed the presence of several souterrains and surface buildings (one of the souterrains ran from the finest house) in a settlement of about 2000 square metres in extent (Fig. 4:13).

Ringforts, perhaps the most distinctive monument of the Irish later Iron Age (below), being farms or settlements defended by one or more earth or stone ramparts, have frequently contained souterrains. At Whitefort, Co. Down, an unfinished trench to take a small souterrain ran out from the central main house of the fort. At Raheenamadra, Co. Limerick, a simple stone and wood souterrain was entered from within the central house, ran through two simple chambers, and exited as an 'escape' passage through the bank of the fort (Fig. 4:12). At Cush, Co. Limerick, a closely set complex of earth Ringforts each contained a souterrain, most of them running from a wooden house. At Rathmulcah, Co. Sligo, a multi-chamber souterrain began in the centre of the Ringfort and ran in a zig-zag path to exit, as a narrow vent, in the outer face of the bank. At the large Ringfort of Ballycatteen, Co. Cork, in the single quadrant excavated, three souterrains were uncovered, one exiting from the central house (Fig. 4:10). At Oldcourt, Co. Cork, the souterrain opened just against the inner revetment of the bank and was partly placed within the bank. No more examples are needed, the association of souterrain and Ringfort being well established.

Souterrains have also been commonly found in, or near, monastic settlements, both of the defended and undefended kind. Indeed there is a strong association with later Iron Age church sites.

The association of souterrain and house has already been described. This has been very clearly established in three careful excavations in Co. Antrim. At Ballywee, one of the souterrains ran from the back wall of a paved rectangular house, the very small creep entrance being above ground level due to a high local water table (Fig. 4:13). At Craig Hill, the souterrain again opened from the back wall of a rectangular house through an above-ground creep, but immediately descended, turned sharp right and entered

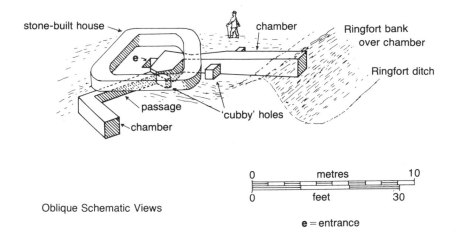

stone-built house

chamber

Ringfort bank
over chamber

Ringfort ditch

e

passage

'cubby' holes

chamber

0   metres   10

0   feet   30

Oblique Schematic Views

e = entrance

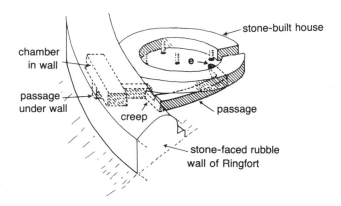

stone-built house

chamber
in wall

passage
under wall

creep

passage

stone-faced rubble
wall of Ringfort

e

Fig. 4:11 *Upper* The 'western house' in the annexe to the Rathnew Ringfort, Co. Westmeath (based on Macalister and Praeger).
Lower The circular house in the stone Ringfort at Leacanabuaile, Co. Kerry (based on ÓRíordáin and Foy). The stone-built souterrain ran from the interior of the stone-house to a chamber in the Ringfort wall.

a second simple creep, into the first passage (Fig. 4:14). Entry was thus extremely difficult and it seems that the internal wooden structure of the house might have been so placed to allow access to the souterrain, but at the same time to hide it. At Antiville, the tiny entrance creep of the souterrain was in the base of the wall of the

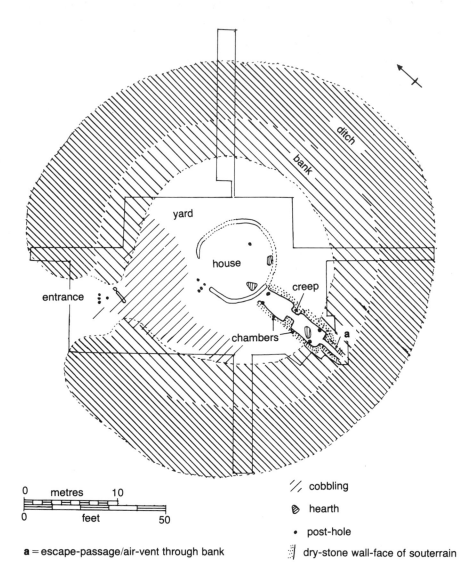

ditch

bank

yard

house

creep

entrance

chambers

a

| 0 | metres | 10 |
| 0 | feet | 50 |

⁄⁄ cobbling

🐚 hearth

• post-hole

▯ dry-stone wall-face of souterrain

a = escape-passage/air-vent through bank

Fig. 4:12 The earthern Ringfort at Raheenamadra, Co. Limerick (after Stenberger). The wooden-roofed, two chamber souterrain runs from the central house.

rectangular house and the 'restricted' passage of the souterrain turned to run along the house wall which formed its upper side, before turning away to widen into a passage/chamber. At Rathnew, Co. Westmeath, a complex souterrain was entered straight down into a central chamber from the centre of a 'house'. The souterrain then ran under the wall of the house in opposite directions (Fig. 4:11). In the same Ringfort a rectangular stone house gave access through creeps in its wall to a number of interconnected souterrain chambers contained within the much thickened wall of the house, and dug down into the clay (Fig. 4:15).

DISTRIBUTION

Souterrains have been found in almost every part of Ireland, over a thousand examples being recorded, or known. But unlike the distribution of the contemporary Ringforts, which are a fairly good indicator of the extent and density of later Iron Age settlement, the distribution of souterrains is uneven. In some areas, such as north and mid-Co. Antrim and Co. Louth, they are so common as to be a positive hazard to ploughing (in Co. Antrim over 600 souterrains have been recorded). In other areas, such as north Co. Down, or the fertile Clogher Valley in Co. Tyrone, where contemporary settlement was heavy, souterrains are almost unknown. Some reasons for this imbalance are given later, to which must be added that the chance of discovery is unlikely to be a satisfactory explanation. In those areas in which souterrains are not found, excavation of Ringforts, in which they might be expected, has failed to uncover them, while in those areas in which souterrains are found, Ringforts can be expected to contain them. It should be added that the topographical restrictions on settlement in the later Iron Age, such as strong avoidance of land of over 180 metres altitude, applies equally to souterrains.

An example of the uneven distribution is found in the area around Belfast. Some miles to the north an area almost devoid of Ringforts contains a very large number of souterrains, until a small river (the 'Six-mile Water') is crossed when Ringforts, souterrains and Ringforts with souterrains are found. This situation is maintained until another small river (the Farsett) is encountered, south of which souterrains are unknown for several miles, although Ringforts are still common.

Fig. 4:13 View of a house at Ballywee, Co. Antrim. On the right, just outside the paving, is one side wall, while the other is on the extreme left. The hearth is in the centre of the photograph (and of the house). The entrance to the souterrain, and the first lintel, is seen at the back, beyond the hearth. *Photo. C. J. Lynn*

CHRONOLOGY

Problems

Any discussion of the chronology of Irish souterrains must take cognisance of three main factors. The vast majority of discovered or explored souterrains have produced no dating evidence of any kind; the finds of artifacts in souterrains have, in many if not most cases, been inadequately recorded; souterrains have often made useful hide-holes at many times since their construction, even to the present day. Thus, although there are reports of objects of all dates from prehistoric to modern times being found in souterrains, serious chronological discussion can only be based on those cases where the record is of sufficient detail and reliability to leave no room for ambiguity or doubt, and these are, unfortunately, rare in

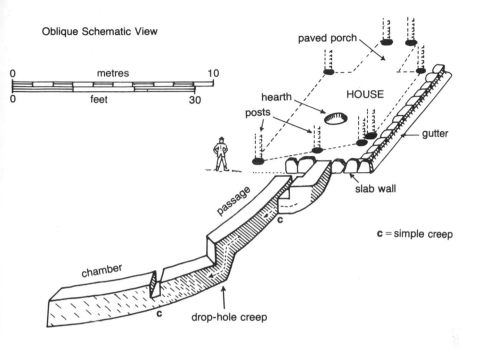

Oblique Schematic View

paved porch

0 metres 10
0 feet 30

hearth

posts

HOUSE

gutter

c = simple creep

passage

c

slab wall

chamber

c

drop-hole creep

Fig. 4:14 The house and souterrain at Craig Hill, Co. Antrim (based on Waterman).

comparison with the number of souterrains which are known to have existed.

Two extreme examples will serve to illustrate the problem. A long and complex souterrain in Co. Antrim (Donegore) reportedly produced, in the last century, some Neolithic stone and flint implements and a late Neolithic bowl. There is also, in museum collections, a quantity of pottery of later Iron Age date, the so-called 'souterrain' ware, reportedly from the same structure. This last is, as we shall see, perfectly consistent with other evidence for the date of souterrains, and the fine, complete, condition of one of the pots fully supports its reported provenance. On the other hand the Neolithic material would seem to be at odds with all the other evidence. However, its reported association with the souterrain is no weaker than that of the other pottery, and we are only justified in dismissing it if we are able to find a reasonable alternative explanation. Very close to the souterrain is a large mound which archaeologists agree is very likely to be a medieval motte re-using a late Neolithic passage-grave mound, and it is not at all improbable that either the souterrain intersected and utilised the passage and burial chamber of the passage-grave, or finds from the separate but similar structures were confused. In support of this, and in further illustration of the problem, the great double-passage-grave mound at Knowth, Co. Meath, (incidentally re-used as a medieval motte) produced, during intensive modern excavation, a number of souterrains associated with a settlement of tenth-to twelfth-century A.D. date. Both prehistoric passages, and thus their burial chambers, were incorporated into the souterrain system, and had they been explored in a less careful age would most certainly have produced, to be reported without distinction of stratification, objects of very different dates. At the other extreme, the author has explored a souterrain that was re-used in the last century as the store for an illicit drinking house, and they can, today, make useful hiding places for *poitin* (an illicit form of whiskey) and, unfortunately, arms.

The Evidence
It is obvious that the date of construction of a souterrain will post-date any objects incorporated in it. Unfortunately, few souterrains have been systematically and carefully demolished by excavation, and the number of objects definitely from a constructional context is small. The upcast from a Co. Mayo example (Letterkeen, apparently made completely of wood) was found to cover a bronze pin with a spiral ring through its head, which should date between the seventh and ninth centuries A.D. Similarly, upcast from a Co. Antrim souterrain covered 'souterrain' pottery dating somewhere between the eighth and twelfth centuries A.D., and other north-eastern souterrains have occasionally been shown to cut into occupation layers containing pottery and finds of the same general date range. A number of souterrains, (in Cos. Waterford, Cork and Kerry in the extreme south; Co. Louth in the east; Cos. Antrim and Derry in the north and Co. Roscommon in the west), have contained, as walling stones and as roof lintels, re-used pillar-stones carved, in Ogham characters, with memorial inscriptions in the 'primitive' form of the Irish language. In some cases several have been found, up to fifteen, in a single souterrain. It is generally accepted that the major period of popularity of the Ogham memorial inscriptions was roughly between the third or fourth centuries and the sixth or seventh centuries A.D., their often pagan formulae being unlikely to have continued after the consolidation of

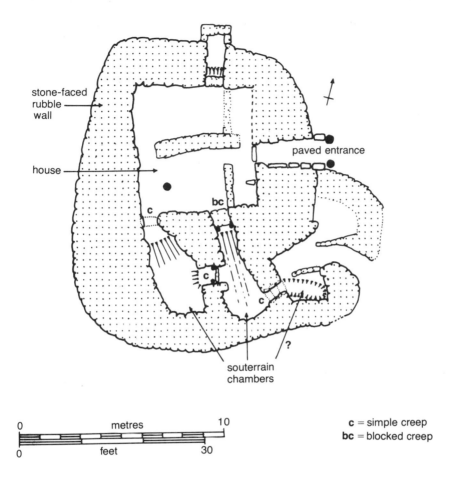

stone-faced
rubble
wall

house

paved entrance

bc

c

c

c

?

souterrain
chambers

0   metres   10

0   feet   30

c = simple creep
bc = blocked creep

Fig. 4:15 The 'eastern house' and souterrain with shared wall in the main Ringfort at Rathnew, Co. Westmeath (after Macalister and Praeger). Note the wooden door posts at two of the creeps.

Christianity as the major Irish religion in the seventh century. It would be expected, on the other hand, that the desecration of pagan cemeteries or graves in a widespread fashion for the obtaining of building material (it is a fact that in the north-east of the country most of the known Ogham inscriptions come from souterrains) would be unlikely to have happened *before* this consolidation, when Christian confidence was equal to the action. Rather surprisingly, however, there are at least four cases (Dunloe, Co. Kerry; Glencolumkille, Co. Donegal; Drumeeny, Co. Antrim; Seaforde, Co. Down) of Christian memorial slabs, or cross-inscribed slabs, used in the construction of souterrains. As far as these slabs can be dated they would seem to belong to the seventh to ninth centuries A.D., and we must surely suppose that they were taken from their original place well after the demise of the monasteries or other ecclesiastical sites, to whose cemeteries the slabs belonged. There seems to be reason to believe that many ecclesiastical foundations became uninhabited at all periods from the sixth century onwards, for a variety of possible reasons (sacking, plague etc.).

Clearly the loss or deposition, though not necessarily the manufacture, of an object found *in* a souterrain will post-date its construction. Unfortunately, as has been indicated, the continued use of these structures for concealment, or as rubbish pits, will complicate this rule, especially as it is not unusual for there to be only the tiniest amount of silt on the floor, thus ruling out stratigraphic analysis. For reasons of unreliability of record we must dismiss the reported finds of Neolithic material (Co. Antrim, above) and Bronze Age objects (one souterrain each in Cos. Cork and Wexford). We should be equally harsh in our treatment of the inadequately recorded find of a fine 'Teutonic' glass beaker of about ninth-century date from a souterrain in Co. Sligo (Fig. 4:16), and of two mid-tenth-century Anglo-Saxon coins from one in Co. Cork. However, not only are both perfectly consistent with other evidence, but in the former case the vessel is unlikely to have survived so well, and to have been casually discovered without further damage, in any other situation than the protective conditions of a souterrain. The second case is strikingly similar to the find of two mid-tenth-century Anglo-Saxon silver pennies in one of the souterrains at Knowth, Co. Meath. These carefully excavated souterrains were associated with the settlement of a well-off farming community in at least the tenth to twelfth centuries, and were apparently the focus of unwelcome attention from raiders in the ninth and tenth centuries, as the literary evidence shown below reveals. One of the souterrains in the stone Ringfort of Cahercommaun, Co. Clare, produced an eighth- or early ninth-century silver penannular brooch, of an Irish type, at the bottom of a thick layer of ashes which had subsequently filled the structure (Fig. 4:17). It can hardly be doubted that the object had been hidden in the souterrain for safety not too long after the construction of the structure, and, due perhaps to the death of the owner, never recovered. The smallest drift of occupation ash into the souterrain

Fig. 4:16 Glass flask of Continental origin, approximately ninth century A.D., from a souterrain at Mullaghroe, Co. Sligo. (Approx. 5 cm high.) *Photo. National Museum of Ireland*

Fig. 4:17 Silver brooch, of about the ninth century A.D., found hidden on the floor of a souterrain in a Ringfort at Cahercommaun, Co. Clare. (Approx. 14 cm long.) *Photo. National Museum of Ireland*

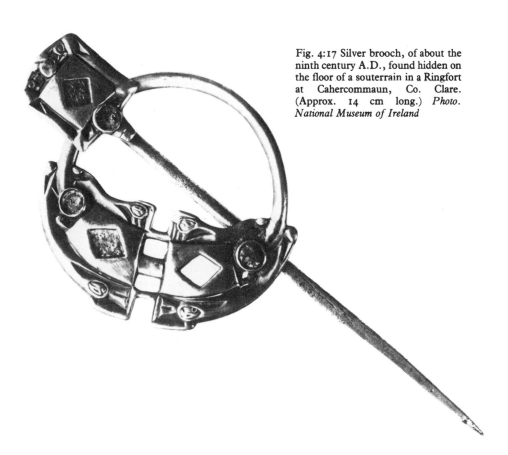

would have been sufficient to conceal the object from later occupants of the Ringfort. A fair number of souterrains have produced material (occasionally well recorded as being in primary silt) which is difficult to date precisely but which belongs to what is popularly called the 'Early Christian Period' (but which we are calling the later Iron Age), roughly between the sixth and twelfth centuries A.D. Later material, such as medieval and post-medieval pottery, and sixteenth- (Co. Derry) and seventeenth-century (Co. Offaly) coin hoards, has, as indicated, frequently been reported to have been found in souterrains, but in the few cases where a stratigraphic analysis has been possible this later material has been found to be in a secondary position, not associated with the original builders and users of the structure.

The third line of evidence for the date of souterrains is context, and, as has already been seen, in those cases where a context can be found by excavation, or is obvious without excavation, they are invariably associated with stone or earth Ringforts, ecclesiastical sites usually of a monastic sort, or apparently undefended secular settlements. Where these have been dated by excavation those contexts in which souterrains are present have invariably belonged to the later Iron Age (as previously stated, between the sixth and twelfth centuries A.D.). In those cases where excavation has not been undertaken or where datable material was not found the apparent contexts are nearly always of a type usually placed into this same period. Of course, other contexts have been reported which would, on the surface, seem to clash with this generalisation. For instance, souterrains have been recorded from a number of medieval or post-medieval earthworks (such as mottes) and castles. But in no case known to the writer has excavation shown that the souterrain belongs to the apparent late context, and in some cases the souterrain has been shown to be earlier (for instance, at Dunluce, Co. Antrim, where a souterrain containing later Iron Age 'souterrain' pottery was clearly sealed by the fourteenth-century castle tower). A particularly contentious excavation result came from one of the Ringforts in an earthwork complex at Cush, Co. Limerick. The excavator claimed that the souterrain within the earthen Ringfort was earlier than a number of Bronze Age burials which, he believed, were dug into its collapsed roof. However, the consequent necessity to view as, at latest, Bronze Age, domestic material which almost every archaeologist would now place *after* the sixth century A.D., has led most scholars to reject completely this controversial claim for an early souterrain.

A direct date for a souterrain has been obtained from the Ringfort at Raheenamadra, Co. Limerick, by the so-called 'Radiocarbon' method. Measurements from what were probably timber uprights for the wooden roof, and from hearths associated with the souterrain, showed that it was constructed sometime between the sixth and ninth centuries A.D. Unfortunately the Radiocarbon method does not often allow a more accurate assessment to be made, but the result is perfectly consistent with the other evidence that has been outlined.

There is a certain amount of early literary evidence relevant to this discussion, some of which is explored more fully in other sections. A number of stories and Saints' lives, mostly written down after the tenth century, contain direct and indirect references to underground structures usually called, in Old Irish, *Uaim* (or a derivative of this word), and translated as 'cave'. That these structures were souterrains is quite clear from the contexts and descriptions, but because of the way details attached themselves to popular stories during their often long verbal lifetime, before fossilisation in one of the monastic scriptoria, it is not often possible to date the period of the individual references accurately. It is, however, clear that the general period to which the majority of these references belong, or during which the accretions were made, was between the eighth and thirteenth centuries. Rather more usefully, the contemporary recording of events in Ireland was well established by the seventh century (although the records go back, with decreasing reliability, well before then). Although the annalistic compilations which have come down to us are mostly copies of the eleventh century or later, there is no reason to doubt the detailed accuracy of the annalistic records back to the eighth century or earlier. They tell us (and again the word 'cave' is a translation of *Uaim*, to be almost always regarded as a souterrain, or allied structure) that:

some time after A.D. 853 one 'Muchdaighren, son of Reachtabrat, was suffocated in a "cave"' by Scandinavian ("Viking") raiders, probably in what is now north Co. Tipperary;

in A.D. 862 many 'caves' in the territory called Brega (roughly Cos. Meath and north Dublin), including Knowth, were plundered by Scandinavians and Irish jointly;

in A.D. 866 the Scandinavians of Dublin plundered the 'caves' of north Co. Kerry;

in A.D. 964 the Scandinavian king of Dublin plundered the 'cave' of Knowth;

in A.D. 999 the Scandinavians were described as plundering the 'caves' of Ireland;

in A.D. 1006 a Bishop, one Muiredhach, was 'suffocated in a cave' in what is now Co. Sligo by Ua Ruairc, a powerful local king;

in A.D. 1059 'Mael-Sechlainn Ua Bric was smothered in a cave by Mael-Sechlainn Ua Faeláin'. These namesakes were kinsmen, and chiefs in what is now Co. Waterford, where presumably the murder took place;

in A.D. 1135 'Echri Ua Taidhg, king of Feara-Lí, with his brother, and with his wife, was smothered in a cave by the Ui-Tuirtre'. The Fir-Lí were a tribe in north Co. Antrim at this time, and the Uí Thuirtre their powerful southern neighbours. North Co. Antrim is an area rich in souterrains.

Summary

Having outlined the archaeological and historical evidence, it is clear that the major period of currency for Irish souterrains, indeed the only period for which positive evidence of their construction and original use has been found, is the later Iron Age, roughly between the sixth and the twelfth centuries A.D. Material information for the period before this, and material and documentary evidence for that following is not lacking and it can hardly be chance that souterrains cannot in any cases be demonstrated to fall outside our bracket. It might be said that souterrains would not be the only thing to belong specifically to this period, for it has been found that the general material culture of the Irish later Iron Age, to which we shall return, bears surprisingly little provable relationship to the Irish earlier Iron Age (before the fifth century A.D.) or the medieval period (after the twelfth century A.D.).

PURPOSE

Ever since souterrains first came to the attention of scholars, their purpose has been the subject of much debate, during which a number of possibilities have been advanced. The two most popular views have always been that they were primarily for refuge (this is the view that used to be most widely held, now out of fashion) or for storage (the view held, erroneously, by most writers today).

Storage

Careful excavation of some of the roomy, paved, easily accessible south-east Scottish souterrains convinced their greatest authority that they were primarily constructed for storage, and perhaps even for temporary habitation. The evidence, including paved floors and drains, makes this an acceptable conclusion, and the construction of wholly, or semi-, underground structures for storage in more recent times (such as the 'hulls' of Cornwall) seems to add support. In Ireland occupation debris, albeit on a small scale, and the finding of the staves of wooden vessels and complete ceramic pots, has been taken to confirm this conclusion in its Irish application. There are a number of roughly contemporary historical anecdotes and annalistic entries which *can* be interpreted as referring to use for normal storage (the historical material, while not always as early as the events it records, is contemporary with the general cultural background).

> 'Caves' in the east Midlands were searched (plundered according to another text) by 'Vikings' and Irish in A.D. 862.
>
> 'Caves' in north Co. Kerry were plundered in A.D. 866 by 'Vikings' from Dublin.
>
> A saint's life tells how a man was doing penance for digging 'under the houses of the Church and carrying away treasures out of them'.

The Scottish excavator who was the main proponent of the storage view was careful to stress that this interpretation was only immediately valid for that restricted class of souterrains on which it was based. This warning has been ignored by most modern writers (though not usually, one would add, by those Irish workers who have explored souterrains) and the following discussion should show that storage is an inadequate explanation of the Irish (and most of the British) souterrains.

The majority of Irish souterrains are the antithesis of the roomy, comfortable south-east Scottish group. As the descriptions and plans will have shown, entry into the souterrain is (in those cases where details of the original entry are clear) extremely difficult, almost without exception. In a majority of well preserved souterrains further movement to the extremities is awkward, if not hazardous, for the average inter-chamber 'creep' (and not infrequently the complete passage) is scarcely large enough for a thin person to squeeze through, without the encumbrance of stores. Furthermore, it is usual for the main chamber(s) to be separated from the entrance by impediments, and twists and turns (with what extra cost to construct one can hardly guess) that seem to make such a telling case against the storage interpretation that it is scarcely credible the theory survives. When occupation debris has been found careful study has usually shown that it trickled in from the entrance, or was incorporated in destructive infill, and its otherwise general scarcity, and the undamaged condition of those whole vessels and large sherds which have been found, tell strongly against frequent entry of the structures.

The historical evidence is more revealing when considered fully. The contemporary references already given are rather uninformative, but are capable of the interpretation that the presence of the 'treasures' in the souterrains was in no small way connected to that of the raiders themselves. Further, references to digging strongly suggest that the entrances were being defended. The following references are more informative.

> In the life of St Maignenn we read how robbers *hid* portions of a butchered ram in a 'cave' under their house.
>
> An early story (of which more later) tells how the warriors defending a 'Cathair' (a stone Ringfort, see below) collected the wealth of the fort together when they came under attack and deposited it in a 'cave'.
>
> A story in the Norse Landnámabók relates how an Icelandic raider took riches from an Irish 'earth-house' (souterrain) after killing a man who was defending it.
>
> Another early source tells how, when famine hit Ireland (as it did frequently in the later Iron Age) the people made themselves 'strong cellars to save and hoard their victuals'.

It is therefore quite clear that the reason for storage of 'riches' (whether food or other) in a souterrain was specifically protective, and one of the sources is quite definite in telling us that only when danger threatened were the treasures thus hidden. This would explain why so few souterrains have contained contemporary valuables. A souterrain in a Co. Clare Ringfort contained a silver brooch of about A.D. 800; souterrains in Cos. Cork and Meath each produced a pair of silver Anglo-Saxon coins; a souterrain in Co. Sligo contained a valuable imported glass goblet and a souterrain in Co. Cork contained, carefully hidden under a flagstone in one of the chambers, a bronze-coated iron bell. We would expect that if a raid failed the defenders would retrieve their valuables, and if it was successful the attackers would take them. In normal circumstances a souterrain would have been, as we have seen, a most unsatisfactory place to store anything.

Refuge

Having discussed and dismissed the notion that Irish souterrains were constructed for *normal* storage, we may explore the alternative refuge explanation.

Familiarity with souterrains soon convinces one that they are extremely defensible structures. The creeps are often so well constructed that a small boy with a club could quite easily hold off an army of raiders, their only recourse being to dig for the chambers, as the contemporary sources tell us they did.

> The story already mentioned, in which the valuables of a fort were hidden in the 'cave' at the beginning of an attack, goes on to tell us that men and women belonging to the lower orders had also taken refuge in it, and were well prepared to defend it. Incidentally this souterrain had, according to the tale, a 'cave keeper'.
>
> In the Life of St Ruadhan, we read how the saint hid the king of a Connaught tribe (in the mid-sixth century, although the evidence of these stories relates more to the time of writing than to the alleged time of the event) in a 'cave in the ground', and that his pursuer attempted to dig him out. This supposedly happened in Co. Kilkenny.
>
> In a story belonging to the Finn cycle, two women hid from Finn in an 'underground cave' for a long time, until discovered and dug out by Finn's men.
>
> Yet more anecdotes and stories dating, in their written form, to the period between the ninth and thirteenth centuries, but referring, often, to an earlier time, tell of people hiding in 'caves'.

The main objection to the interpretation of souterrains as places of refuge has been that such structures, far from being safe refuges, are traps; that the occupants could be smoked or starved out. Such objection could equally well be made to any defensive structure, given that the raiding party was of sufficient strength to be able to wait around. The most common problem facing the ordinary farmer would have been the hit and run attack by a small party, intent on cattle on the hoof, slaves and small, easily portable valuables. For such a band to attempt to starve the occupants of a souterrain into submission would have been suicidal, for it would have given time for the surrounding district to rally (and the cattle would not, in any case, have been in the souterrain). It is clear from the annalistic entries that when successful souterrain plundering took place an extremely large group of raiders was involved (large enough not to fear the farmers of the immediate district), and that digging was the means of entry, not siege. In the discussion on chronology several well dated examples were given of the smothering of important persons in souterrains, but again it is clear that the enemy was present in force (the presence of the enemy king supports that) and had the leisure to undertake what would have been a clean (in the sense that the slayer's hands were not soiled), possibly almost ritual, killing of the victim (drowning was also a widely used method of royal execution).

Well preserved souterrains have frequently contained either air vents, leading (as has recently been shown in a well excavated example) to a hidden spot, or secondary exits, again to a secret place, such as a wooded hillside or the ditch of the fort. In no souterrain has the writer ever found anything but a fine air supply, even after many hours spent in the most inaccessible examples with several oxygen-consuming candles and a colleague. Smothering the occupants would, therefore, have been a time-consuming and difficult job. As for smoking the occupants out, it is quite obvious that the lighting of a fire at the entrance, even combustion of the house, would have had the effect of *increasing* the supply of good air to the *lower* souterrain. Far from being a trap, the souterrain would, in the usual circumstances of attack by a small band of cattle raiders, have been an extremely good defence for the non-combatants and their smaller possessions. It should be noted that besides the provision of escape passages in a number of souterrains, some have been found with blocked second entrances. That these were break-out points in case of blockage of the main entrance seems not impossible. The investigator of the souterrain at Donaghmore, Co. Louth, where a 'roomy', zig-zagging passage with two alternating 'drop hole' creeps (one up, one down), totalling 60 metres in length, finally led to a large chamber, noted that 'neither bright light nor loud noises' in the end chamber 'could be seen or heard' half way along the passage, and that the first upward 'drop hole' creep was invisible from within the passage leading to it, and indeed was missed by several visitors.

Perhaps the following is as clear a description of the protective value of a souterrain as could be found. It relates to the American mid-west in the late nineteenth century, to a typical small white settlement of about eight or nine families. On receipt of the first warning of a rising by Ute Indians, the men of the settlement being away on a distant cattle-drive, the women decided to retire every evening to a hastily provisioned small 'underground "fort" or cellar'. This was some $3\frac{1}{2}$ metres square, 2 metres high, with an earth covered rafter roof slightly raised above the surface but impossible to fire. The cellar, large enough for twelve or fifteen people, was connected to the largest log cabin in the settlement by a narrow passage, some 4 metres long and little more than 1 metre high, sloping slightly up towards the cabin.

Other Views

The view that souterrains were dwellings, not often expressed nowadays, can obviously be dismissed out of hand. But another suggestion, that they have, at least partially, a religious or ritual significance cannot so easily be ruled out. One of the most difficult features of souterrains to explain is their uneven distribution, areas in which they abound adjoining areas in which they are not found at all, even though all other material and structural evidence in the two areas is virtually identical and there is no reason to suppose that they were socio-economically different (to any great extent). Nor is it possible to call upon topographical or geological differences to explain uneven distribution (as can be done in the case of, say, the contemporary lake-dwellings).

The souterrain was an extremely sensible and useful method of defence, and given the cultural uniformity of the later Iron Age (as we will see), the most surprising thing must be its non-use in certain areas, rather than its use in others. Archaeologists are loath to use the 'ritual' or 'religious' explanation of things they do not understand, but it does not seem impossible that a heavy liking for, and equally a strong antipathy towards, souterrains might very well have had some underlying religious basis.

One of the 'three dark places of Ireland' was Uaim Cruachain (the cave of Cruachu) at Rathcroghan, Co. Roscommon, in a complex of secular and ritual earthworks of the earlier and later Iron Ages. The cave itself is, if identified correctly, a very long natural rock cleft, the first few yards of which has been made into a normal dry-stone souterrain passage. The souterrain part incorporates some Ogham stones, one of which bears a name extremely similar to that of a mythical person associated in the early literature (which has a pre-Christian basis) with this complex. It would be tempting to believe that the souterrain was part of the cave in its supernatural form, but it seems more likely that it relates to a secular use of the site long after its pagan heyday.

Human Remains

It might be felt that the refuge explanation would require human remains to be found, occasionally, in such structures. There have been some reports, though seldom well enough documented to be sure, that the bones, or bodies, were not thrown in at a later date (a souterrain in Co. Down seems to have been used at some time as a crypt judging by a report of oak coffins being found in it). In a souterrain in Co. Cork were found hundreds of skeletons (reportedly 500 in one chamber!), and the skeleton of a youth was found in apparently primary deposits in an excavated souterrain at Larne, Co. Antrim.

In one of the souterrains in the Ringfort at Cahercommaun, Co. Clare (which also produced the silver brooch) was found an adult skull, with an iron hook, carefully enclosed in a sort of stone box on the floor at the far end of the souterrain. The excavator suggested that it had been a prized head (pagan Iron Age practice that might well have survived into the Christian period) which had once been hung in a place of honour. We might suppose that its careful placing in the souterrain served first to hide it from critical Christian comment, and second to give protection to the fort and to the souterrain in times of danger. A number of skulls were found in a Scottish souterrain.

THE BACKGROUND

It has been shown that the date range within which the datable souterrains lie (and there is no reason to believe that the others are not of the same date) is between the sixth and twelfth centuries A.D. This period has been called, variously, the 'Dark Ages', the 'Early Historic Period', the 'Early Christian Period', the 'Late Celtic Period' and the 'Later Iron Age', and it is the last term which we shall use, while bearing in mind that the individual implications of the other terms are of no small importance. The beginning of the later Iron Age seems to have been revolutionary culturally, philosophically, socially and materially. The introduction of Christianity and the use of writing to record events, rather than simply memorials and spells were, although highly significant innovations, merely two amongst the huge number of changes, mostly drawing from the late, indeed collapsing, Roman world, from the late fourth century on. It can even be argued that it was this very collapse which gave the impetus to the movements of people and ideas of which Ireland was, perhaps, the most important recipient, and in whose earth the innovations took the most fruitful root. It is found, for instance, that the major part of the material culture of the fifth to the seventh centuries in Ireland has its origin in late Roman Britain and Gaul rather than in the Irish earlier Iron Age which preceded it. Interestingly though, there is evidence, both archaeological and 'historical', of a strong Irish element already present in some of these intrusions. Indeed it can be claimed that returning expatriate Irish formed the core of the intrusive peoples. We may take a single archaeological illustration.

In the second century there developed in the northern frontier zone of Roman Britain (between Hadrian's and the Antonine walls), by the fusion of a Romano-British brooch type and Irish earlier Iron Age technical and artistic bronze-casting ideas, a distinctive ornament called the 'Zoomorphic Penannular Brooch', a very suitable device for fastening the heavy cloaks necessary in the north. By the fourth century this brooch had taken root in Ireland, and over the next six centuries it developed numerous distinctive Irish forms. On the historical, or more correctly, pseudo-historical side (for we rely on legends and genealogies written down some centuries later) we find in the origin myths of those tribes who suddenly became dominant in the fifth or sixth centuries (and were often completely unknown before then) reference to a strong Hiberno–British element. There is much evidence that from before the fourth century until at least the sixth century, including the period of postulated intrusions, Ireland was in a state of extreme flux, undergoing a mini 'migration period' not unlike that on the Continent at the same time. Both the native and the intrusive people, jockeying for land and power, or pushed ahead of, and displaced by, stronger tribes, travelled large distances over Ireland (and even to western Britain).

From the seventh century a slowing down of this movement can be seen (although it never completely stopped), and the distribution and power-hierarchy of the people of Ireland began to take the general shape they would have until the Anglo–Norman invasion of the twelfth century. The material and social culture of the Irish (that is, of the upper classes) now showed a uniformity it was to keep until that same disruption. The reasons for this cultural homogeneity between tribes that were often at war, and which were proud of their ethnic and ancestral separateness, may lie in the rôle of the growing monastic communities as foci for craftsmen, scholars and traders and, at the same time, because of their common religion, as links between the often hostile tribes.

The origin and spread of the penannular brooch, an intrusive innovation of the fourth century which became one of the major Irish ornament types until at least the eleventh century, has already been mentioned. The products of a few closely linked workshops are found all over the country, paying no heed to the very strong political boundaries of the period. Similarly the major surviving monument of the later Iron Age, the Ringfort, is found in almost every corner of Ireland, yet it seems to have been unknown before the sixth century. The Ringfort is basically a defensive structure, an earth bank-and-ditch (or several concentric), or a considerable stone wall, surrounding a roughly circular area of between 25 and 60 metres internal diameter, containing the main house and sheds of a well-to-do farmer (in Irish bó-aire, literally 'cow lord'). Occasionally there are no major buildings, or signs of occupation, and the defensive structure may then be interpreted as a cattle stockade. Some 30000 Ringforts have been estimated to have survived to the early nineteenth century, although only a small proportion of these survive intact today. This response to the needs for individual defence by the farmer has several implications.

(1) That raiding (mainly for cattle but clearly any portable or on-the-hoof material could be taken, including slaves) was a common feature of the later Iron Age. This is borne out by annalistic entries and contemporary stories which make it evident that raiding was an accepted and inevitable part of life. This could take the form of major organised plundering raids in which the king of the tribe might take part, and which would often have severe political consequences, or hit and run raids by small bands of very mobile warriors, sometimes Scandinavians ('Vikings') but more often people from neighbouring territories.

(2) That the centralised tribal defence was unsatisfactory. This would be inevitable in the circumstances of hit-and-run raiding when the speed with which the surprise attack could

be carried out would make the chance of interception by a centralised force (even if such existed, which is doubtful) unlikely.

(3) That the 'free-farmer' had access to a large labour force, and skilled engineer-advisers. (This is even more relevant in the case of souterrains, below.)

(4) That by the time of the construction of the Ringforts the agricultural community had become settled.

This last point is important, for the migrationary conditions of the beginning of the period would hardly have been conducive to the construction of major defensive structures before the sixth century when the tribes began to settle. Therefore the innovatory nature of the Ringfort does not necessarily imply that the idea was intrusive (although this is not ruled out). Structures similar to Ringforts are found in Cornwall, south-west Wales and western Scotland during the British early Iron Age and Roman period, say up to the fourth century A.D. if not later. But the general cultures in which those 'parallels' are found are not found in Ireland.

The defensive bank, or wall, used by the farmers around a relatively small habitation area, was used by larger communities (such as, but not only, the monastic communities) to defend much larger areas, nearly a kilometre across in some of the large monastic towns after the ninth century.

The evidence from the structure of the souterrains must mean that they were, in most cases, constructed primarily for defensive purposes. The cultural context in which they stand, and the general purpose for which they were built is, therefore, the same as the Ringforts. We have seen that they are found in Ringforts, often demonstrably associated with a house, in the larger monastic enclosures, and in isolated contexts apparently unassociated with earthwork defences, though when excavated found to be associated with a dwelling. Souterrains, especially the complex stone-built ones, were major engineering feats which must have required the presence of a professional construction gang. The craftsman (or specialist, presumably the engineer in charge) who built a souterrain was, it seems, entitled to two cows as payment (the same as for a stone Ringfort). The implications of the construction, and the socio-economic considerations necessitating and allowing the construction, are exactly as has already been discussed for the Ringforts. Their association with Ringforts and defended monasteries is perfectly easily explained as a second level defence for the non-combatants and portable possessions. The non-Ringfort souterrains are rather more difficult to explain. The complexity of souterrains makes it hardly likely that a family, or small community, could afford a souterrain but not a Ringfort (the latter being more easily built by unskilled labour). Nor is it likely, if there was a straight choice, that a souterrain would be built rather than a Ringfort as the primary and only defence. We have no evidence that there was a specific law, in any Irish tribes, forbidding the construction of Ringforts by those below a certain social status, or by those belonging to an unfree or subordinate tribe, but it is not at all impossible that such laws existed, as they did with regard to castles in medieval Britain. In support of this explanation we would remember that there are whole areas, large enough, and clearly enough bounded by natural topographic features to be considered tribal, in which souterrains alone are found, others (even adjacent) in which souterrains, Ringforts and souterrains within Ringforts occur, and others in which Ringforts alone are found. Another possible explanation, that of a social or religious (tribal) favour for, or antipathy towards, souterrains was raised earlier.

SOUTERRAINS OUTSIDE IRELAND

If we regard a souterrain as an underground structure artificially created, in whatever fashion, with the aim of relatively extensive accessibility (for refuge, storage, habitation, ritual or a mixture of some or all of these), we find that the concept is widespread in time and space. Indeed the constructions, even down to fine detail, in different places at different times can be strikingly similar, and there is a temptation to draw conclusions of cultural connection which, on all the other evidence, are unfounded. It should be borne in mind that given the rather simple desire to make an underground construction, and the constraints provided by the required purpose and the available constructional abilities, similar results may be expected in completely unconnected cultures. The surprising feature about souterrains is the way they cluster, both in time and space, the examples being, often, evenly and densely packed within the area of immediate distribution, and rare or unknown outside an often clear geographical or temporal line of demarcation. It is not so much difficult to explain the presence of souterrains, as to explain their absence in areas of apparently similar socio-cultural or economic status, or similarly threatened by instability. We shall come to this again below. For the purpose of comparison reference will be made only to souterrains whose appearance, or cultural context, could be taken to imply a possible connection with those of Ireland. The widespread underground structures of medieval France and Germany are not discussed.

Brittany

The meandering rock- or clay-tunnelled 'souterrain refuges' of Brittany (or, as it is often called, in a late prehistoric context, Armorica), of which there are quite a large number, have been found to begin in about the eighth century B.C. and continue through the early Iron Age until (or perhaps just into) the Roman–Gaulish period (perhaps ending in the first century A.D.). These structures, often with hollowed out chambers separated by creeps, but rarely dry-stone built, can, in form and mode of construction, be paralleled in Ireland, particularly in Co. Cork. But the rich and distinctive material culture to which the Breton souterrains belong (the ceramic remains of which they contain in profusion) has no Irish counterpart, and we must be wary of drawing conclusions on the basis of such simple structures. Attempts have been made to point to other apparent parallels between Ireland and Brittany, such as pillar-stones decorated in 'Early-Celtic' art, or the distinctive coastal promontory forts common to both countries (and to Cornwall, which we shall come to below). Unfortunately these postulated connections do not bear close scrutiny. The artistic forms on the pillar-stones are only distantly related to the extent that they share a common ancestor, and the promontory forts in Ireland have, when excavated, been shown to be between 600 and 1600 years later than those of Armorica. The probable disparity between the dates of the Breton and Irish souterrains themselves is not stressed because, although it is argued that the Irish series cannot be shown to pre-date the sixth century A.D., it is the tunnelled Co. Cork examples which remain, for the most part, obstinately undated.

Cornwall

In the extreme west of Cornwall a number of dry-stone built souterrains are known bearing a striking resemblance to Irish examples. The similarities include construction techniques and details, such as the lintelled passages, small creeps (the Cornish ones are simple), corbelled 'beehive' chambers and the position of the souterrain within enclosed farmsteads, in one case (Trelowarren) lying partly under the defensive bank of the settlement and having a secondary exit into its outer face, as can be seen in a number of Irish examples. Their dates, however (perhaps between the second century B.C. and the first couple of centuries A.D.), and cultural background are quite dissimilar to the Irish souterrains, although the local economy, cattle raising, does bear comparison, as does the use of Ringforts in both areas.

Scotland

In Scotland a number of groups of souterrains occur, notable for the differences between the groups. In the south-east (what has been called 'Southern Pictland'), is a group distinguished by roomy curving passages, unrestricted accessibility, and paved and sometimes drained floors. They are, in common with most of the Scottish souterrains, build of dry-stone in a dug trench, and where excavation has been undertaken, have been found to be associated with a small, apparently undefended, settlement. The scanty dating evidence suggests that they were being constructed and used sometime between the first century B.C. and at least the second century A.D.

In the north-east, still on the mainland, is a group of much less roomy, rather simple, club-shaped passage-souterrains, and between these and the south-east group is a small mid-eastern group, sometimes passages of the northern type, but not infrequently expanded into a long chamber at the far end. These and the northern group lack the sophisticated features of the south-eastern series, and also lack acceptable dating evidence. They are found, when excavated, to be subsidiary to above-ground dwellings.

In the northern Isles of Orkney and Shetland a number of souterrains (or 'Earth Houses') have been found, typically consisting of a long, very restricted, low passage (with quite difficult surface access), leading to a polygonal, or roughly rectangular chamber. A feature of this chamber is that the roofing lintels are supported internally on a number of regularly placed stone pillars. Two typical 'Northern Isle' souterrains at the multi-period settlement of Jarlshof, Shetland, were associated with round-houses of the latest Bronze Age, or earliest Iron Age (a close date is not forthcoming, but one would suspect some time between the sixth and fourth centuries B.C.). Interestingly, and comparison may be made with Ireland, the souterrains were entered just inside the house-wall, and ran under and out. The same site produced a couple of simpler, irregular, 'passage' souterrains with rough side chambers, roomy enough to be described as 'passage-houses'. These were, apparently, roofed with organic matter rather than with stone, and were associated with distinctive surface 'Wheel Houses' belonging, as far as can be ascertained, to the first few centuries A.D.

The simple passage-souterrains, sometimes with subsidiary chambers, usually of restricted access with simple creeps, are typical of the Western Isles, or Hebridean, group, not infrequently associated with a settlement of 'Wheel Houses'. Again a date in the first few centuries A.D. is usually given, with little evidence, for these structures. It seems possible that many may be later.

Only Scotland approaches Ireland in the number of its souterrains, but the Scottish examples, whether for reasons of isolation, different dates or different cultural backgrounds (probably all three), show more striking regional differences than do those of Ireland. The Western group probably bear best comparison with the simplest Irish examples, although their cultural background has little similarity with that of Irish souterrains. It should be added that a number of stone-built defensive enclosures in western Scotland, the 'galleried duns', dated by different authorities to before, during, or after the Roman period, can be strikingly paralleled in the north and west of Ireland, particularly in areas where souterrains are not uncommon. A feature of these sites is that the stone walls contain passages, or galleries, often accessible through small creeps, which bear close comparison with souterrains.

Areas of Irish Colonisation
It is suggested that the areas in which souterrains might be expected, but in which none are found, need explanation. In the late fourth to the sixth centuries, during the period of major internal migration, Irish colonists settled much of western Britain. From the north-east of Ireland settlers from Dál Riada moved into south-western Scotland, as, it seems, a dominant aristocracy. Their Irish homeland is rich in souterrains, but they are rare in the areas of Scottish settlement. Southern Irish moved in considerable numbers to Wales and the south-west of England, but again (except for those of the extreme tip of Cornwall, which can be shown to belong to the native culture earlier than the Irish settlements) souterrains are completely unknown in these areas. By far the best explanation of this, that souterrains were not a *major* part of Irish culture before the sixth century is supported by discussion of the dates of Irish souterrains, but it may be, of course, that the emigrants were not themselves souterrain users.

A number of rock-cut souterrain-like structures in Iceland are interesting in the light of historical, and recently biological, evidence that Irish settlers (possibly slaves rather than freemen) played a major part in the occupation of Iceland in the ninth and early tenth centuries A.D.

CONCLUSIONS

It has been shown that the major period of the construction and use of souterrains in Ireland was between the sixth and twelfth centuries A.D., and that compared with other artifacts of that period their distribution, though widespread, is surprisingly uneven. In the discussion on the background to the period the innovative (and often intrusive) nature of much of the material and social culture of Ireland from the fifth century has been stressed, and it might therefore be supposed that the origin of the Irish souterrains lies in such an explanation. This would seem to have support in the dates of the souterrains outside Ireland, which can be shown to have extended until the first century A.D. at least, and their often close similarities to the Irish structures. Unfortunately the arguments against this conclusion are forceful (even if we ignore the apparently 500-year-long chronological gap). In the first place, the cultures within which the foreign souterrains lie are not represented in Ireland. Secondly, the major Irish groups of souterrains do not coincide with the known areas of primary, or ultimate, settlement by the tribes thought to represent the intrusive element (such as the Eoganacht of Munster, the Uí Néill and Airgialla of the north).

We might wonder, therefore, though lacking the dating evidence, if the souterrains were intrusive at an earlier period. Although no Irish souterrain can be shown to predate the sixth century, and although it has been suggested that the conditions did not exist before the sixth century for the widespread use of souterrains, we cannot argue on these grounds. In support of an early intrusion, one of the strongest souterrain clusters, that of the north-east, coincides with the early distribution of a number of tribal units going under the collective ethnic name of 'Cruithen'. These people were found in small groups elsewhere in Ireland, for instance in Co. Kerry (where souterrains are also found), and the name is, incidentally, that by which the Picts of Scotland were known to Irish writers of the later Iron Age. The other major cluster of souterrains, that of Co. Louth, seems to coincide with a group of people known as the 'Conaille' who, there are reasons to believe, were ethnically allied to the Cruithen. There is some evidence, mostly non-archaeological, that the Cruithen and the Conaille were intrusive, some centuries before the fifth century A.D., and that northern Britain might have played some part in this intrusion. But the absence of those cultural traits that should be present if the souterrain users had come from one of the known foreign souterrain areas is still a severe stumbling block. Should it be necessary to class the souterrains as an intrusive element it is suggested that the most that could be allowed, on present evidence, would be the arrival of a number of souterrain-craftsmen (there is evidence of migrating stone-fort engineers at this time).

There is usually a strong feeling against the concept of the independent invention of types with close similarities in cultures between which even the most tenuous links can be claimed (for instance the idea of 'Celticity', whatever that means in reality!). Sensibly however, the diffusionist obsessions of the past have quite given way to a realisation that, given societies with similar technological levels, and similar socio-economic backgrounds and problems, the chance of the development, independently, of comparable material artifacts, must be high. The significance that should be put on any degree of similarity is difficult to assess, but it is felt that the similarities between the souterrains within and without Ireland, given that the idea is a simple response to conditions, are not great enough to be given too much weight. What is perhaps more surprising is that other cultures, with apparently similar defensive needs, did not react in the same way. If we are right that there was an ethnic preference for, or antipathy towards, such structures, and that the Irish (and other) distributions can partly be explained in ethnic terms, we might be near a solution to that problem.

There is, in sum, no very good reason for rejecting the simplest explanation of the appearance of the souterrain: that the social conditions of the sixth century onwards created the need for defensive structures; that the increasingly settled nature of the population, and the amount of spare wealth, or labour, available to the upper ranks of society allowed these structures to be of strong, durable form; that the Ringfort and the souterrain were efficient responses to this need, within the technical capabilities of the time; that the spread of souterrains was rather more hampered by social or religious problems than that of Ringforts. Certainly such conclusions are all that the evidence will bear, and the rich inventiveness of Irish society shows that it was quite adequate to this task.

BIBLIOGRAPHY

No comprehensive work has yet been written on Irish souterrains, and an overview may only be had by a long search through scattered literature (particularly the *Ulster Journal of Archaeology*, the *County Louth Archaeological Journal* and the *Journal of the Cork Archaeological and Historical Society*), and an intimate knowledge of souterrains from field study. I have tried, when choosing an example, to refer to one that has been published. S. P. Ó Ríordáin has given a short summary in his *Antiquities of the Irish Countryside*, London, 3rd ed. from 1953, and A. Lucas has dealt very fully with the contemporary references in 'Souterrains: the Literary Evidence' in the journal *Béaloideas*, vol. 39/41, 1971/3, pp. 165–91. The most accessible, if now dated, account of the general cultural background to Irish souterrains is M. and L. de Paor's *Early Christian Ireland*, London 1960.

Scottish souterrains are usefully dealt with by F. T. Wainwright in 'Souterrains in Scotland' in *Antiquity*, vol. 27, 1953, pp. 219–32, and in his *Souterrains of Southern Pictland*, London 1963.

Cornish souterrains, and their cultural background are discussed by Hencken in his *Archaeology of Cornwall and Scilly*, London 1932, and a fuller, but less scholarly, descriptive account is E. Clark's *Cornish Fogous*, London 1961. The general discussion, and particularly the part on Irish souterrains, in this book should be ignored.

A short, general and rather personal view of the British and Irish souterrains is C. Thomas' 'Souterrains in the (Irish) Sea Province: a note' in *The Iron Age in the Irish Sea Province*, CBA, London 1972, pp. 75–8. A general and very useful account, with further references, of the Continental souterrains is to be found in eight papers in no. 2 of the 'Document' series of the French journal *Archéologia*, 1973. The issue is completely dedicated to this subject.

5
The Early Industrial Era

KENNETH HUDSON

The archaeology of mining is a complex affair. It includes the evidence both of underground workings and of all the associated activities which took place on the surface. 'Mining' is a loose and comprehensive term. It covers steam-engines, haulage railways and terraces of houses, just as much as shafts, galleries, pit-head installations and waste-tips but, over the period of approximately 2000 years during which anything that one can reasonably call mining has been carried on in Britain, most of the archaeological legacy which has been left for posterity has consisted of little more than holes in the ground and heaps of soil and rock on the ground round about. 'For the industrial archaeologist,' one of the profession has observed, 'coal-mining is normally an unrewarding study. Once a mine is closed, its shafts are covered or filled in, and usually its surface plant and buildings are removed. Mounds of debris and filled-in shafts are not, perhaps, the most exciting of archaeological remains, but they present a detective-type challenge and, properly interpreted, they have a contribution to make to the story of one of Britain's oldest and most important industries.' A very similar comment could be made about iron mining, lead mining, tin mining or stone quarrying. What generations of miners leave behind them for archaeologists to ponder over is essentially a disturbance of the earth's crust. So long as their tools and equipment remained primitive, they disturbed that crust very little; once they had steam, electricity and compressed air to help them, they began to disturb it a great deal and to create archaeology on an altogether larger scale.

In time, without doubt, we shall have scientific equipment which will allow us to remain safely and comfortably on the surface and to

A select bibliography is printed on page 172.

look down at old mine-workings concealed several hundred metres or so below. When that happens – it could quite well happen during the 1980s – the plans and drawings of eighteenth- and nineteenth-century mines will begin to come to life and we shall be astounded to see the conditions under which miners worked and the ingenuity with which they burrowed through the rock. Meanwhile, we have to content ourselves with what is actually in front of our eyes, and with contemporary descriptions.

MINING FOR COAL

In Britain, mining now means particularly the mining of coal. In 1844 M. Ross, describing the situation in the North-East, wrote: 'The face of the country is thickly studded with the engine-houses and coal-heaps attached to the respective pits, from which, at night, the sky is irradiated with a ruddy glow visible for miles around, and inducing the idea of some mighty conflagration, or, where the flaming heaps themselves are seen, appearing like the 'baleful watch-fires' of an immense army. The fields and roads are crossed and intersected in every direction by the "waggon-ways" connecting the pits with their respective places of shipment, and on which machinery of the most scientific and perfect description yet invented is employed to facilitate the transit of the coal to its destination.'

'The margins of our noble rivers,' Ross went on, 'are fringed with its staiths and machinery, often constructed on a most gigantic scale, necessary for effecting the shipment of the jetty treasure. The bosom of each stream is crowded with "keels" and other craft employed for the same purpose; as well as with steam-boats assisting in the removal of vessels to their berths, or conveying passengers between the various entrepôts of trade.' In Northumberland and Durham, as in a number of other parts of Britain, coal had created its own landscape, its own social pattern, its own range of ancillary industries. Now, 130 years later, the great majority of the mines have closed, as new and more profitable coalfields have been opened up elsewhere, and the culture based on getting and moving coal is becoming more a matter of folk-memory with each decade that passes. Very little of the surface equipment has been left, the great staithes, from which coal was dropped directly into the holds of ships below, have now all been demolished and the routes of the waggon-ways and railways which once served the pits have to be deduced from hedgerows, embankments and cuttings, much as one would plot the line of a Roman road.

The archaeology of coal, from the 300 years of its economic importance in Britain, falls into three parts: landscape disturbance; technological remains at the pit-head, and transport survivals; and buildings, such as houses, churches and chapels, public houses, schools and former miners' institutes and clubs which owe their existence entirely to the exploitation of coal within the area in which they are situated. All these types of evidence are abundant in the British Isles and in the space available here one can do no more than illustrate what is available and show its significance.

In medieval times, the quantity of coal used each year was very small. Reliable estimates are impossible but, as a rough guess, it may be that the figure was about 100 000 tonnes a year in 1400 and twice that amount in 1500. Largely because of the grates and chimneys available, it was not a popular fuel for domestic purposes. The fumes and smoke made life unpleasant in a room in which it was being burnt and wood and charcoal were, understandably, greatly preferred. The only people willing to use it were those who lived close to the coal workings and who were too poor to afford anything else. For similar reasons, it was not favoured for industrial purposes, especially for the smelting and fashioning of metals. Once the technique of producing coke had been discovered, so that the impurities in the coal could be removed, there was a great increase in the consumption of coal. The change of scale in coal production which took place between 1700 and 1900 can be shown by two figures, 3 million tonnes in 1700 and 200 million in 1900. Most of the archaeology of the industry was created between these two dates, the most important period of growth being 1850–1900, when production quadrupled.

Two types of working existed during the fifteenth and sixteenth centuries, in addition to the simple method of picking up pieces of coal from the ground when outcrops occurred. The first was to drive a gallery into the side of a hill or slope, so that the outcrop could be followed away from the surface of the ground. This kind of mine, the drift-mine, still exists, notably in the Forest of Dean in Gloucestershire (Fig. 5:1), and the techniques and equipment it requires are little different from those in use 500 years ago. A still-functioning drift-mine is an example of living archaeology. The second type of primitive mine, the bell-pit, has not been operated since the eighteenth century. It was possible only where the seam of coal was close to the surface. The miner dug a shaft up to 6 metres

Fig. 5:1 Drift-mining in the Forest of Dean, Gloucestershire. The tiny heaps of coal, the pit-props and the four trucks, pushed by hand out of the mine, illustrate the scale of working in these two- and three-man enterprises.   *Photo. Dean Forest Studios*

deep and, having hit the seam, cut out the coal by extending the bottom of the shaft downwards and sideways, so forming a bell-shaped hole in the ground. When the hole showed signs of collapsing, the miner abandoned his pit and started another one nearby. This form of coal mining produced pock-marked areas of ground, still to be seen in parts of Shropshire, Derbyshire and Lancashire, over which the little pits and the circle of earth and rock round them appear like huge ring-doughnuts, 6 or 9 metres across. Nothing illustrates the tiny scale of coal extraction at this time better than an aerial photograph of a bell-pit area, where one's thoughts are of children's sand-castles, rather than of coal mines.

From a labour point of view, bell-pits were an extremely wasteful method of working. The next development was therefore to carry the shaft down into the coal and then to cut short galleries outwards from it, leaving pillars of coal between each gallery to support the roof. As this technique progressed, the galleries became longer, timberprops being used to guard against the roof collapsing. Having followed the seam as far as possible – it might be dipping away too steeply or becoming too thin to extract easily – the group of miners worked backwards towards the shaft again, cutting away the pillars of coal as they went and allowing the roof to collapse. This method of mining, known as pillar-and-stall working, became normal in all the major coalfields in Britain during the nineteenth century and in some, particularly in the North-East, where tradition was very strong, it was still to be found in the 1950s. It inevitably produced subsidence, which in places has been very serious, causing deep pits to appear in roads and making houses so dangerous as to be uninhabitable. The underground archaeology of pillar-and-stall mining must certainly be abundant, but the archaeologist cannot, except in very rare instances, explore it for himself. He has to be content, so far as concrete evidence is concerned, with subsidence, cracks in buildings, and waste-tips.

Pillar-and-stall working was not safe in deep mines, that is, mines where the seams were at more than about 275 metres from the surface, partly because of ventilation problems, but also because the great weight of rock above the coal might cause the pillars to collapse. To meet this situation, a new way of extracting the coal, known as the longwall method, was developed. It came into widespread, if not general use, during the second half of the nineteenth century. Essentially, it consists of taking out a continuous wall of coal, up to 90 metres long, and packing back stone to form pillars immediately the coal is taken out. This is most easily done where layers of stone are found within the seam of coal, but in some cases stone is brought in from outside the pit to allow the pillars to be constructed. Machine-cutting, now universal in British pits, demands the use of the longwall method. In general, subsidence is much less likely to occur where longwall mining has been practised.

Occasionally, modern methods of extracting coal have produced evidence of early techniques. At Heage, in Derbyshire, for instance, a group of sixteenth-century bell-pits were discovered during the 1960s in the course of removing overburden for opencast mining. The pits went down to about 6 metres and were no more than $1\frac{1}{2}$–$3\frac{1}{2}$ metres apart. At about 45 metres below this, in another seam, galleries dating from the middle of the eighteenth century were revealed. This is archaeology of the crudest kind, however. The giant excavator and bulldozer are not well suited to scientific exploration.

So long as pits remained shallow, excavation of coal was on a small scale, the seam was soon exhausted and surface equipment was of the simplest type, being limited to little more than a windlass, turned by men or a horse, to raise the coal and lower men and supplies. Once the workings became deeper, the pits stayed in use longer and it was both worthwhile and necessary to erect permanent buildings at the pit-head. The first pits to go below 300 metres were in the North-East and in Cumberland, where, in the 1950s, it was not uncommon to find collieries with a continuous history of 100 years or more. Since then, however, closures have been very numerous, partly because all the available coal had been taken out of the seam, but even more frequently because the seams were too thin or too irregular or sloping to make mechanical cutting a reasonable proposition. During the 1950s and 1960s the obliteration of collieries, with all the surface installations demolished, was widespread and it is now very difficult to find examples of any winding gear earlier than the 1930s, although some of the smaller items can be seen in open-air museums. A winding-engine house and headstock of 1855 can, for instance, be inspected at the North of England Open-Air Museum at Beamish.

When a colliery is abandoned, it is usual, for safety reasons, to fill in the shaft or to seal it off in some way. Sufficient explorations of old pits have been carried out, however, to give a reliable picture of how the work of sinking and lining the shaft was carried out. Until the mid-eighteenth century, the shaft was driven down through the earth and rock by means of picks, shovels, hammers and wedges. After that time, explosives were frequently used. The early shafts were often lined with boards and made square-shaped or rectangular to allow this to be done more easily. In pits where there was a lot of water, the boards were placed upright around the sides of a circular shaft, like the staves of a barrel. This technique, known as tubbing, was being carried out with cast-iron sections, instead of wood, by the 1840s. Throughout the nineteenth century, however, brick-lining was the normal method, the bricks often being laid without mortar, so that they could easily be removed and used again when the shaft was abandoned.

Dry-lining could be dangerous. Until the late eighteenth century, the coal was hauled up the shaft in baskets, which swung freely on the rope and hit against the bricks, loosening them and sending them crashing below. Miners, travelling up and down the shaft sitting on chain-loops slipped over the basket hooks, were equally liable to knock against the bricks. In the 1780s, wooden shaft-guides came into use, with the baskets attached to cross-bars which slid up and down in the guides which were fixed to the sides of the shaft. Cages, instead of baskets, first appeared in the 1840s and they were in general use twenty years later. This development greatly increased both efficiency and safety, although accidents due to the winding chain or iron rope breaking were by no means uncommon.

By the end of the seventeenth century, the size and depth of mines, whether for coal, tin or lead, was limited by the ability of the owners and operators to keep the workings clear of water. In some cases, where the lie of the land was favourable, it was possible to achieve this by means of adits, underground drainage tunnels or ditches, but they were of little use in deep mines. Water continued to be the main problem facing mining engineers until the steam-engine provided the solution. The steam-engine was developed specifically to help to drain mines and it was being used for this purpose by the second decade of the eighteenth century. The Hawkesbury engine, designed by Newcomen, is the oldest steam-engine in existence. Originally installed during the 1720s at Griff Colliery, Warwickshire, it is now preserved at Dartmouth. The oldest drainage engine on its original site is at Elsecar, in Yorkshire. This beam pumping-engine worked from 1787 to 1923 and has been preserved by its owners, the National Coal Board.

Mine drainage systems could be elaborate. In some coalfields, the most effective way of going about the business was to drain not a single pit but a group of collieries. The Elsecar engine formed part of such a system. The most remarkable example of this kind, however, is to be found at Worsley, in Lancashire, where the drainage and transport systems were combined, by constructing an underground network of canals, linking up with the Bridgewater Canal. By 1840, there were forty-six miles of underground waterways in the areas of the collieries. They were on several levels, with shaft and inclined plane connections between the subsidiary and main canals. The deepest canal was dug more than 25 metres below the level of the entrance tunnel.

The development of efficient electrically-driven pumps during the present century virtually put the steam-engine out of business where drainage was concerned, but some veteran engines continued to work for a surprisingly long time and are still to be seen where they were first installed. The doyen of nineteenth-century engines is at Prestongrange, East Lothian, where the Cornish-built beam-engine kept the mine free of water from 1874 to 1954.

As mines became bigger and deeper, ventilation and the prevention of gas explosions proved more intractable problems than drainage. Until the eighteenth century, the only type of gas that miners had to concern themselves with was a suffocating mixture of nitrogen and carbon dioxide, which they called simply 'damp', and which we know today as blackdamp or chokedamp. When mines became deeper, a new kind of hazard had to be faced, the highly explosive mixture of air and methane known as firedamp. So long as miners had to rely for illumination on the naked flame of a lamp or candle, explosions were inevitable. Even the introduction in 1815 of Sir Humphrey Davy's safety lamp, which surrounded the flame with a very fine wire gauze, did not altogether remove the danger, although it greatly eased it. Firedamp was not always the culprit. After two particularly disastrous explosions in South Wales in the 1860s, it was discovered that the cause had been the ignition of fine coal-dust. The best way of combating this was found to be the spreading of stone dust over the floor of the mine and it is the usual practice nowadays. Anyone with a particular interest in this or any other human aspect of mining history does well to visit the churches and cemeteries in mining towns and villages, where the tombstones and memorial tablets record accidents and disasters in a way that makes it impossible to disregard the price that has to be paid for technical progress and industrial prosperity.

The increased size of coal mines made a forced-draught system of ventilation essential. To begin with, in the mid-seventeenth century, this was achieved by simply placing a brazier or 'fire-basket' underground at the bottom of the up-draught or 'up-cast' shaft. The hot gases rising up this shaft brought about a downward flow of fresh air through the down-draught or 'down-cast' shaft. The movement of air through the workings was controlled by boys who opened and shut trap-doors, so that pockets of gas were prevented from accumulating. The original system of underground furnace and flues still exists at Brinsley Colliery, Nottingham, although it has not been used for a century. In the larger collieries, steam-driven fans and air-pumps were being installed from the 1830s.

Steam-engines were invaluable for driving ventilation plant, for pumping and for hauling coal and men to the surface, but they were useless for actually cutting and loading the coal. Coal-cutting by machinery had to wait until the 1860s, when the first compressed-air cutter was introduced. Since then, electrically-driven cutting and loading machines have become commonplace. Changing mining technology, however, can only very rarely be documented by installations and equipment which have survived at the mine itself. The task has been undertaken by museums such as the National Museum of Wales, the Blist's Hill Open-Air Museum in Shropshire, and the North of England Open-Air Museum at Beamish.

In some ways, studying mining is very similar to studying prisons. Both fields of research rely a great deal on conversations with people who have actually undergone the experiences with which the investigator is concerned. It is not difficult for the specialist in industrial relations or the history of technology to visit a factory or a power-station for himself and to gain first-hand experience of how work in such places is organised and carried on. The world of the miner, however, is essentially different. Its special dangers, cameraderie and skills cannot be appreciated by anyone who has not shared them over a fairly long period. No-one in authority is going to arrange for the academic visitor to be buried by a roof-fall or blown up by a gas explosion, merely to add to his stock of useful experiences, but one cannot decently avoid the fact that mining, for those who earn a living by it, involves a life underground, and that to write about it solely in terms of tonnage, shafts, galleries and equipment is to exclude a large part of what is significant and to lessen the value of what one has actually included. The archaeology and history of mining are about scale, fears, skills and difficulties quite as much as about steam-pumps and haulage systems. Reminiscences are an essential part of the historian's raw material. Without their help, he can miss much of importance and make serious errors of judgment.

Unfortunately, we have practically no first-hand accounts of a miner's life before the middle of the nineteenth century. Most miners were probably illiterate and nobody bothered to collect and write down their descriptions of how they went about their work. In Victorian times, the combination of mining disasters and newspaper editors with an eye for sensational stories forced the general public to pay at least temporary attention to a kind of life which was normally beyond their imagination or caring. Within our own century, mining and the mining community have become a favourite subject for novelists, playwrights, sociologists and historians. The public nowadays knows about mining in a way that it did not a century ago. Or perhaps one should say, it thinks it knows, since by no means all the information about what actually goes on within the industry is either accurate or reliable. The media and sometimes the miners themselves are not always averse to a little sensationalism or exaggeration where mining is concerned.

But the careful historian, with a taste for the truth, can learn a great deal by talking to old miners, much as he can from talking to old farm labourers. The world has changed fast and radically in the past two generations and very often people with a lifetime's experience in a particular industry can provide information about superannuated techniques and customs which is obtainable in no other way. The story of the Bristol coalfield illustrates this very well. The last colliery in this area closed down in 1949 and most of the surface evidence of what was once one of Bristol's most important industries has been swept away during a general process of cleaning up, modernisation and rebuilding. No uninformed visitor to the district now could possibly guess that a hundred years ago there were pits and waste-tips dotted over a very wide area to the south and east of the centre of the city.

In 1970, a local historian, M. J. H. Southway, persuaded an old Bristol miner, A. H. Parsons, to put some of his memories down on paper. They have subsequently been published. Mr Parsons began work as a pit-boy in 1917, when he was fourteen, but much of what he has to say suggests the eighteenth century, rather than the twentieth. Having left home at four-thirty in the morning and cycled the five miles to the pit, 'we parked our cycles in a tin shed belonging to Mr Slocombe, for which we paid 3d. per week, then went to draw our candles from the candle house. Sometimes you drew tallow, sometimes wax candles. The tallow ones were meant for working where there was plenty of air, the wax ones for where there was little air, as they would last longer. Our cottage had boxes full of these candles, because sometimes we brought home spare candles. With tallow ones, we greased our boots and father his leggings.' Mr Parson's grandfather and even great-grandfather would have understood the situation without the slightest difficulty, although in their case the five miles to work would have had to be accomplished on foot, without the modern luxury of a bicycle.

MINING FOR METAL

In Britain, it is natural to think first of coal, in any discussion of mining. No other country in the world has had so much coal distributed over such a relatively small area. Britain, it has been said with only slight exaggeration, is a raft of coal floating in the sea, and its domination of world industrial development during the eighteenth and nineteenth centuries was due very largely to its abundant supplies of accessible coal. But without equally good supplies of iron the coal would have been largely useless. During the first phase of the Industrial Revolution, until about 1820, most of the commercially worked iron came from the Carboniferous ores found in association with the coal measures, in South Wales, the West Midlands, Derbyshire, South Yorkshire, and the Lowlands of Scotland. When these deposits had been worked out, the main centres of ore-extraction became located on the broad band of Jurassic ores which extends from North Yorkshire through the East Midlands to the Cotswolds. These ores are far from rich but they are easy to extract. The small area of good quality Jurassic ore in Kent and Sussex, on which the medieval iron industry in Britain largely depended, was worked out by the end of the sixteenth century. An excellent ore of the unstratified type occurs, as haematite, in the Forest of Dean, South Wales, Cumbria and the Furness district of Lancashire.

Until the nineteenth century, nearly all of the iron ore used in Britain was extracted from open pits, or from very short headings driven out from pits. In the northern part of the new areas which began to be exploited from the mid-nineteenth century onwards, however, mining was the general rule. At North Skelton, in Cleveland, the shaft went down to a depth of 220 metres. In the East Midlands, the deposits of Jurassic ore are found close to the surface and opencast excavation is normal. In the early workings, from about 1850 onwards, the ore was close to the surface and removing the overburden was a pick and shovel job, but by the end of the century, when the deeper strata had to be worked, the steam-shovel had providentially become available. Today, draglines strip off 30 metres and more of overburden as a matter of course. Modern opencast mining produces a different landscape from the one that was left behind a hundred years ago. Until about 1900 no attempt was made to restore the devastated countryside. The method was simply to dump the overburden in great ridges over the area from which the ore had already been removed. During most of the present century a more responsible and far-sighted policy has been followed, the excavated areas being carefully levelled, covered with soil and returned to farming use. What results, however, is an entirely new style of landscape, with fenced prairies instead of the more traditional English countryside of small fields, trees and hedges.

To connoisseurs, the regions where the more valuable metals, copper, tin, lead and silver have been mined are especially interesting, from both an economic and a technical point of view. The Lake

District is such a region. There was copper and iron mining here in Roman times, possibly earlier, and since then the local mines have produced lead, bismuth, wolfram, tungsten, zinc, iron and china clay, as well as large quantities of copper. The Lake District first became important from a mining point of view in 1565, when Queen Elizabeth invited the German engineer, Daniel Hochstetter, to come to England to develop the production of copper along the most modern lines. Hochstetter brought over experts from the Tyrol, established or re-opened mines at Caldbeck, Grasmere, Coniston and Keswick and built a smelter and rolling-mill at Keswick. The enterprise was on an unprecedented scale for England and employed a large number of men, especially in the provision of the enormous quantities of fuel required.

The works at Keswick were destroyed by Cromwell's soldiers in 1651, a completely pointless act, from which copper production took half a century to recover. Thereafter, the mining industry began a career of booms and slumps which has now almost come to an end, but which has made the Lake District one of the most rewarding of all areas for the industrial archaeologist with a special interest in mining. Some idea of the scale and speed of the decline can be seen from the number of workers at different dates. In 1870 there were more than 2000 men and boys directly employed in the mines. In 1890 there were 500, but by 1970 only six workers remained, all of them employed in the barytes mine at Force Crag. Of the many reasons why a revival has not been possible, the most important is certainly the successful campaign waged against further mining development by those concerned with the protection of Lakeland scenery, a factor which bothered the Elizabethans and Victorians not at all.

The Greenside mine illustrates very well the possible sources of conflict between the entrepreneur and the conservationists. Greenside mountain rises to a height of 790 metres. The county boundary runs, somewhat perversely, along its summit and the lead vein follows a north to south course through its eastern shoulder, ending at about 730 metres. The mine was operated continuously from the mid-seventeenth century until the vein was completely worked out in 1963. At one time, it was the most profitable mining venture in the North of England. A share that was worth £100 in 1827 had risen to £1000 ten years later, and at one time a 100 per cent dividend was paid for a period of only three months. A smelter was built at Alston Moor and there were so many carts bringing ore to it from the mountains that the authorities made a regulation that every fifth cart should have its wheels set wider apart on the axle than the rest, to help level out the ruts.

The most important point to make in connection with Greenside is that it was always an up-to-date mine, using the latest techniques and existing in order to make a profit. It was, for example, the first metal mine in Britain to have an electric winding engine and the first to use electric traction underground. Both pieces of pioneering took place in the 1890s. Much of the plant, including the crushing and dressing machinery, was high up on the mountain and very visible. When production finally came to an end in the 1960s, all the machinery, inside and outside the mine, was dismantled. The entrances were sealed and covered over, to prevent would-be explorers from getting into the honeycomb of shafts and galleries, many of which were old, decaying and dangerous, especially after the series of underground seismic tests undertaken by the Atomic Energy Commission in 1959–60. All the temporary buildings were removed, but the stone and slate offices and stores, and part of the old mill are now used as mountaineering huts. The former miners' lodging-house has been converted into a youth hostel, and the bare mountain remains as the permanent, impenetrable shroud for three centuries of intensive mining activity, during which it is estimated that three million tonnes of ore were removed and treated, and a quarter of a million tonnes of lead concentrate produced.

The Lake District does not, of course, have a monopoly of beautiful scenery and it is no doubt regrettable that such a high proportion of valuable metals and minerals should be found in mountainous country, where, at least nowadays, there is almost certain to be a conflict of interest between those whose primary concern is with earning a living and those who think first of appearance and amenity. Under modern conditions, the struggle between the two is refereed and ultimately decided by the planning authorities, but in previous centuries and indeed until the 1940s, the owners of the land and the mineral rights looked after such matters for themselves.

In the eighteenth century, copper-mining was carried out, for example, on the Quantocks, at Perry Hill, East Quantoxhead, now a highly protected area, officially and popularly considered to be of exceptional scenic beauty and where any form of industrial development would be extremely unlikely. Between 1786 and 1802, the Marquis of Buckingham, in association with the Fox family of Quakers, made a considerable investment in developing the mines on his estate here. New shafts were sunk and drainage adits driven, and the workings were further extended during the next fifty years. By 1846 there was a steam pumping-engine to look after the water in the mine, and additional workers were taken on. Soon afterwards, the company collapsed and mining operations in the Quantocks were never re-started. No permanent damage whatever was done to the local amenities and three buildings, on either side of the main Bridgwater–Minehead road, near Nether Stowey, are the only surviving evidence that mining was ever carried on in the district at all. Two of these buildings are ruined engine-houses and make picturesque and entirely acceptable additions to the landscape. The third was once the mine office, the counting-house, and has been a private residence for many years.

The Welsh metal mines, scattered over an area which stretches southwards from Anglesey to Brecon and Cardigan, have been less considerate to the landscape. Their legacy of huge waste-tips and ruinous buildings is, in many places, all too apparent. In Flintshire, lead and silver were worked in Roman times and throughout the Middle Ages. Considerable fortunes were made from lead mining in the seventeenth and eighteenth centuries, the county being stripped of trees by the insatiable demands of the smelters for fuel until, early in the eighteenth century, coal, of which Flintshire had an ample supply, began to be used for smelting, at the great new works at Gadlys, near Bagillt. Between 1704 and 1744 Bagillt produced 430 604 ounces of silver, and Queen Anne permitted silver coins made from Flintshire silver to carry the Welsh plume of feathers on the reverse side. In many ores, lead and silver are found together and, with reasonable luck, the cost of producing both metals was covered by the sale of the silver, leaving the lead as clear profit.

The famous iron-master, John Wilkinson, prudently bought a lead mine in Flintshire at the beginning of the Napoleonic Wars. In 1800 it was described by a visitor, Richard Warner, as 'the most considerable lead-mining speculation in England'. Mr Warner was greatly impressed, both by the site and by what Mr Wilkinson had created. Of the first, he wrote: 'The scenery of this place is wonderfully wild and romantic; a deep valley, rude and rocky, shut in by abrupt banks, clothed with the darkest shade of wood'; and of one of the four steam-engines installed to drain the mine: 'It has a particularly striking effect, from the singularity of its situation, standing detached from every other trace of human art, in the bottom of the valley, immediately at the foot of a huge perpendicular lime-stone rock which rears its broad white face above the apparatus to a considerable height.'

This aspect of mining, its romantic appeal during the earlier days of the Industrial Revolution, should not be forgotten. The owners and operators of mines and factories were not, at that time, seen as vandals and destroyers of beauty. They were, on the contrary, entitled to be honoured and respected as the creators of new sights, which were both fine and even noble in themselves and which should be a source of national pride. As the landscape acquired more and larger industrial accretions, and the air grew thicker with smoke, the euphoria faded and horror began to take its place. But it is fair to say that in parts of Britain like mid-Wales and the West Country, where industry never achieved the terrifying, dominating scale that it did in South Lancashire, the Black Country and the North-East, mining and manufacturing remained relatively unobtrusive and good-mannered and, to that extent, unobjectionable.

At the site of all long-closed mining enterprises, what one sees depends to a great extent on what one knows. One of the most important and productive of Welsh mines, Cwmstwyth, near the Ystwyth river, south of Devil's Bridge, is an excellent case in point. The steep mountains here have been worked for copper and lead for more than two thousand years. Stone implements found here provide a clue to the age of the workings and the enormous waste-heaps to be seen over a wide area are an indication of the quantity of ore that has been removed. The metal-bearing lodes cut across the mountains at a number of levels and until the nineteenth century the ore was extracted from them entirely by means of horizontal and opencast workings. The opencast pit at Graig Fawr is spectacular. Subsequently, shafts were driven to tap the ore lying deeper in the mountain at lower levels. If it were possible to X-ray the mountain or to cut a section through it, the resemblance to a giant wasp-nest would be very marked.

A crude but effective method of prospecting, known as hushing, was practised here during the seventeenth century and the evidence of it is still to be seen. The technique was to release a great volume of water from a reservoir, so that it would wash away all the soil and loose overburden and scour the surface down to the bedrock, leaving any outcrop of ore immediately visible. A reservoir built for this purpose can still be seen at Graig Fawr at a height of about 450 metres, with ravine-like channels radiating down the hillside from it.

In the early nineteenth century there were four entirely separate sets of workings here. By the 1840s all of them were semi-derelict. At that point, however, a new company took over the whole site

EAST POOL WHIM AND HEADGEAR ABOUT 1895

Fig. 5:2 Surface installations at the East Pool copper mine, near Camborne, in about 1895. The engine and engine-house have been restored by the Cornish Engines Preservation Society and are now in the care of the National Trust.   *Photo. The Trevithick Society*

and, by sinking deep shafts, found previously unknown reserves of rich ore. Between 1886 and its final closure in 1921, the Cwmystwyth mining complex had six different owners, each trying to discover the secret of making a profit in a period of falling world prices for lead and each contributing something – a new leat (a trench for carrying water to a mill-wheel), a large crushing mill, a system of tramways and inclined planes – aimed at increasing efficiency and reducing costs. What one is faced with here, as at many other sites in the old metal-working areas of Britain, is a kind of economic and technical sedimentation, illustrating the movement of the mining industry through a succession of stages of development, from the times when the market was assured and costs were relatively unimportant, to the later period from about 1870 onwards, when supplies were available from the whole world at a price the British producers were unable to meet.

The double economic cycle, from boom to depression and, in

160

Fig. 5:3 Workings at the 70 fathom level (128 metres) at East Pool mine. The photograph, taken in the early years of the present century, shows the slope and thickness of the lode and the type of timbering used to support the roof. *Photo. The Trevithick Society*

recent years, back to boom again, which the Cornish tin industry has had to face, provides a classic illustration of this. Cornwall is a heavily mineralised region, very roughly divided into a tin area in the west and a copper area in the east and around Camborne (Figs. 5:2 and 5:3) and Redruth. Cornish tin was a sought-after product in Phoenician and Roman times, but it was not mined on any scale until the seventeenth century. In this period, and throughout the eighteenth century, the main centre of activity was on the Atlantic coast at St Just. There were two reasons for this. It was easy to drive galleries from the high cliffs straight into the tin lodes and the heavy winter rainfall provided abundant reserves of water-power to drive the water wheels used for draining the mines and processing the ore. Many of these wheel-pits and adit openings are still to be seen, as are the remains of stamp-mills, smelters, buddle-houses for washing ore, dams, leats, tramways and, above all, engine-houses and chimneys, all the ghostly evidence of a once prosperous industry that died from an overdose of foreign competition. The best-preserved memento of all is the town of St Just itself, which owes its existence, its solid and elegant appearance, entirely to tin. Its two most significant monuments are possibly the former Capital and Counties Bank, now a butcher's shop, and, also in the main square, the site of the former Post Office. The first is a symbol of the industry's need in its heyday for locally provided credit and at the second, when the depression was giving Cornish miners the choice of emigration or starvation, it was possibly to buy a one-way through ticket to Johannesburg or Michigan.

The most complex set of mining remains is to be found at Botallack, where three separate workings can be distinguished on a very confined cliff-side site. Small-scale copper mining was carried on here during the late eighteenth century, through a deep cut made in the cliff on its seaward side, the ore being pulled up in buckets by means of a windlass. An engine-house was built at this point in 1816 and another was added higher up the cliff in 1858, when the copper was becoming exhausted and it was decided to go deeper for tin. This section of the Botallack Mine was closed in 1895 and very little now remains of its once elaborate surface buildings, apart from the engine-house.

In 1906 a new company was formed to reopen the old workings. It constructed buildings on a ridiculously lavish scale, at a time when intense competition from both South America and Malaysia made it essential to cut costs in every possible way. The engine-house stack was never used, since the pumps were always driven by gas-engines, not steam-engines. Botallack 3 was an expensively built industrial folly. Despite years of excavation, no tin was ever brought to the surface, and in 1914 the machinery was all sold off.

Tin was the glamour-metal in Cornwall, the metal with a long history, but it was copper that laid the foundations of the region's industrial importance. Its power lasted only from about 1700 to 1870. It made vast profits for landowners and entrepreneurs, it was responsible for the construction of Cornwall's railways, engineering works and foundries and many of its harbours and, like tin, it fell a victim to cheaper and much larger deposits overseas. For 150 years, the copper-miners could not go wrong. There was a steadily increasing market for the metal, for all types of copper, brass and bronze products, ranging from buttons to sheathing for ships' hulls and from slave bangles to rum stills. Cornwall was churned over and burrowed through to meet the demand, and its battered landscape, littered with the ruins of old engine-houses, proves it.

From so many mines, it is difficult to select any one for particular attention, but Dolcoath, in the parish of Camborne, would have as strong a claim as any. It was worked continuously for a longer period than any other mine in Cornwall; it was the deepest mine in the county, it produced both copper and tin and it was always in the forefront where the installation of new types of machinery was concerned. Newcomen atmospheric engines were used for de-watering the mine before 1758 and a much bigger engine, with a 1600 mm cylinder, was supplied by the Coalbrookdale Company in 1768. A Boulton and Watt engine was working here by 1781. The eighteenth-century records relating to the mine have survived. They show that in 1778–9 coal for the steam-engine cost 13 per cent of the total amount spent on working the mine. There was consequently every reason to invest in the more up-to-date and economical engines being designed by James Watt. The new engine was able, in fact, to halve the mine's coal consumption. During the 1780s, however, the price of copper fell to a point at which it was no longer economic to work the comparatively low-grade ore at Dolcoath. The mine was closed, the 595 employees – about half of them were women and children – were paid off, and the Boulton and Watt engine sold to a neighbouring mine, Wheal Gons, which had a much richer lode of ore.

In 1790 the market for copper greatly improved and Dolcoath was reopened. By the 1820s the workings had reached nearly 450 metres and 800 men were employed underground, with about the same number engaged in a variety of tasks on the surface. At that time the mine was producing about a tenth of all the copper raised in the county. In 1850, when the copper ore was almost exhausted, new and deeper workings were begun, and Dolcoath became a tin mine once again. When the members of the Royal Institution of Cornwall visited the surface workings in 1869, they were told that Dolcoath was 'the richest mine in the world, the deepest and most productive of all tin-mines.'

WORKING CONDITIONS

This is perhaps a suitable moment to draw attention to the fact that for the whole of the nineteenth century, and for the first two decades of the twentieth, mining of all kinds in Britain provided an income for the whole family. Men went underground and women and children did a large part of the breaking, crushing, sorting and processing on the surface. At Dolcoath, girls armed with small sledge-hammers broke up the lumps into pieces small enough for the stamps to handle. These girls, and their mothers, were paid at a very low rate, ninepence a day. Visitors to Dolcoath remarked on their 'presentable and pleasant appearance' and found them, for the most part, 'healthy good-looking girls', but wondered why they chose such heavy work, which after a year or two spent shovelling fifteen tonnes of ore a day, often resulted in severe deformation of the shoulders. The answer was simple. Here, as in the coal-mining areas, it was shovel or starve, a point not always well understood by later generations.

It was noticeable that the introduction of modern methods into the mind at Dolcoath, especially mechanical drilling, brought an increase in disease. Here, too, what was happening at Dolcoath was typical of mining as a whole. The early miners, working in shallow pits, had little more to fear than the roof falling in on them. Their successors, compelled to go deeper and deeper each decade, were gassed, blown up, drowned and choked in what to us seems frightening numbers, but which those carrying out the work at the time accepted more or less fatalistically as an inevitable part of the job. In Cornwall at the beginning of the present century, Miners' phthisis and ankylostomiosis were widespread, largely as a result of the dust created by dry-drilling, and, although it was proved that the risk could be greatly reduced by spraying the workings with water, the management for some time found it far from easy to persuade the men to co-operate. The changing attitude of the miner to his work is one of the most important aspects of the history of mining in modern times. So long as men willing to go underground were in ample supply, because no alternative employment was available, an appallingly high rate of casualties was accepted by all parties. Once this situation changed – the dividing line between the old and the new industrial worlds was the outbreak of World War II in 1939 – the miner was able to argue from a position of strength, and to insist on wages and working conditions which would have been unbelievable even twenty-five years earlier. Dolcoath itself did not remain productive quite long enough to experience the miner's new status in the community. It depended throughout its career on the highly skilled, low-paid miner who was bred and trained to put up with his lot.

The Cornish miner was the most resourceful and the most highly skilled in the world. He learned his craft under unusually difficult conditions and, when employment failed him in Cornwall, he emigrated, to dig for metals in America, Australia, South Africa or

Fig. 5:4 The social effects of mining. This Durham coal miner, photographed *c.* 1900, earned 34*s* for a six-shift week.

wherever else there was mining to be done. If there was no mining, he drove railway tunnels. He was a natural burrower. Very often, he came home to Cornwall to die, after foreign mines had eaten his lungs away. The late Treve Holman, of the great Camborne firm of mining engineers, once told the present author that a memory that never left him was of hearing returned miners, 'coughing up their lungs at street corners in Camborne on a Saturday evening'. The history of mining is about this, quite as much as of tonnage raised, profits made or not made, and steam engines installed.

The British, as has been said earlier, tend to think instinctively of coal whenever the word 'mining' is mentioned. A hundred years ago they would have reacted differently, because metal mining, although in some difficulty, was still widespread and still very much part of the national consciousness. Today, however, the extraction of metals, with the single exception of the opencast working of iron ore, is largely a matter of ruined buildings and weathered, half-obliterated heaps on the surface. Sometimes, as at Laxey, in the Isle of Man, and in Cornwall, the remains are as spectacular as anything Rome or Athens has to offer, but more often they reveal themselves only after a careful search, supported by a good deal of imagination and previous knowledge. The mining archaeology of Cornwall is essentially collective – engine-houses scattered thickly over a landscape – and the remains of the nineteenth-century lead industry in Shropshire, running south from Minsterley, produce a similar effect, although in a gentler area.

At Laxey, few people would pay the slightest attention to this once-great mine if it were not for the giant water wheel which dominates the valley above Laxey village and, like the Colosseum in Rome, makes a popular tourist attraction by reason of its sheer size, if for no other reason. But, just as the Colosseum loses much of its interest if one considers it as an isolated phenomenon, without any knowledge of the culture from which it sprang, so the Great Laxey Wheel is largely meaningless on its own. Out of context, it is no more than a mammoth piece of sculpture or an entry in the *Guinness Book of Records*, nearly 20 metres in diameter and the largest water wheel in the United Kingdom. In context, it became the wheel constructed in 1854 for the Great Laxey Mining Company, which owned and operated the lead mines; and which wanted to reduce the cost of importing coal to drive the steam-engine. The Isle of

Man has no coal resources, but ample supplies of water, so that even in 1854 to construct a water wheel on this scale was an entirely sensible procedure.

The wheel itself is in public ownership and has been carefully restored, but the rods connecting it to the pumping machines at the mineshaft were removed for scrap during World War II. The viaduct carrying the rods over the stream between the wheel and the mine remains, however; so, too, does the leat bringing water to drive the wheel and the ruins of a building known locally as the Machine House, which originally contained a beam-engine for the winding gear and was then converted to house a man-riding engine powered by a water-turbine. The mine closed in the late 1920s and most of the surface buildings have since been cleared away, but one has only to look at the immense wheel and walk along the track which leads from it to the mine to marvel at the ingenuity of such an installation and to begin to understand the small margin which divides profit from loss in a mining enterprise, so that it was worth, for the sake of avoiding expenditure on coal, investing in a water wheel and a lengthy system of pumping rods, all of which would cost a small fortune today, but which were cheap enough in Victorian Britain.

When mining ends the visible evidence disappears fast. To illustrate this, one can usefully consider what happened in and around Morwellham, in the Tamar Valley. In 1800 it was an insignificant hamlet. Fifty years later, it had become a prosperous river port, serving a group of copper mines. Fifty years after that, it had ceased to be a port, and the Tamar Valley had sunk back into obscurity again.

Very rich copper deposits were discovered in 1844, about 8 kilometres north of Morwellham. The lode was more than 9 metres thick and the ore yielded 17 per cent of copper. Within a few years a string of mines, nearly 5 kilometres long, had been established to exploit it – Wheal Fanny, Wheal Anna Maria, Wheal Josiah and Wheal Emma. In 1846 they were amalgamated to form the Devonshire Great Consolidated Mining Company, popularly known as Devon Great Consols. For ten years, it was the richest copper mine in Europe. Between 1844, when the original discovery was made, until 1865, shareholders received £1 million in dividends – £923 for each £1 share – and the Duke of Bedford, who owned the land and the mineral rights, had benefited by £210 000 in dues, some of which was devoted to rebuilding the centre of Tavistock. Without copper mining, the Bedford Arms Hotel would not have existed. Devon Great Consols was by far the biggest employer in the Tavistock area. At its peak, it provided work for more than 1500 people. Its success led to appallingly overcrowded living conditions in the district, where a serious cholera epidemic broke out in 1849.

The copper ores were closely associated with arsenic, which occurred in the form of arsenical pyrites. In the 1840s and 1850s, this was a waste product, which was either dumped or used for wall-building or road repairs. During the remainder of the century, however, arsenic became sought after and profitable, for insecticides, dyes, paints and other purposes. By 1871, Devon Great Consols was obtaining a fifth of its income from arsenic and by 1800 it was producing half the world's requirements of arsenic. Sufficient arsenic was stored at Devon Great Consols at any given time to poison every man, woman and child in the world, but the intended victims were, in fact, insects, not people. A major market for Tamar Valley arsenic was the cotton plantation area of the United States, where it was used to spray the crop against the destructive boll-weevil. In 1901 the mine ceased working for good. Between 1861 and 1901 the population of Tavistock declined by over 3000 and, in the area from which the mines drew their labour, Calstock lost 1000 people and Callington 500. A large proportion of the people who left went to the United States and Canada.

To offset rising costs after mining activity had developed on a major scale, it was decided to avoid the use of steam-engines wherever possible and to take water from the Tamar to provide the power for pumping and haulage. Two leats were built, a total of $10\frac{1}{2}$ kilometres between them, and the 12-metre wheels they drove powered pump-rods nearly a kilometre long. Other wheels worked foundry machinery, saw-mills and workshop equipment. Altogether, the Tamar supplied the power for thirty-three water wheels at the mine.

In 1902 the mine went into liquidation. The surface buildings were levelled, the machinery disposed of, the shafts filled in and the Duke of Bedford planted trees over the site. Today it is difficult to distinguish the 55 hectares of the mine from the woodland surrounding it. Few of the great mining enterprises have disappeared more completely.

QUARRYING FOR STONE

The use of the word 'quarry' in connection with stone is apt to suggest that stone is always and necessarily extracted from an open pit, since that is what most people understand by a quarry. Stone has been extensively mined, however, in the strict sense of the term. Shafts have been sunk, galleries driven, and all the normal mining procedures followed. Two examples can be taken to illustrate this, the slate mines of North Wales and the limestone mines which lie between Box and Corsham, on the north-western edge of Wiltshire.

In Wales, the roofing-slate industry is now virtually extinct, but some block slate is still produced for walling and there is a not unimportant market for slate powder which is used as a filler for a number of manufacturing purposes. The once-prosperous mines and quarries were developed during the nineteenth century to provide builders with a cheap, reliable roofing material. Slate roofs, however, require a good deal of maintenance if they are to remain weather-tight. They were eventually priced out of the market for this reason and also because the hand-labour needed to split and trim them had become impossibly expensive and difficult to find.

In its heyday, however, the industry produced some impressive underground workings. Maenofferen quarry, north of Blaenau Ffestiniog, was being operated mainly by means of tunnels in the 1860s. A visitor here in 1873 reported afterwards that it was dangerous for a stranger to venture into the galleries alone, 'for by missing a turning one might be precipitated down one of the shafts sunk for ventilation purposes'. The nearby Oakesley quarries were visited by the proprietors of the various slate companies on the occasion of their annual congress. Equipped with lanterns, they descended by the water balance shaft and reached a gallery 450 metres down inside the mountain. From here, said the congress reporter, 'the party was taken in single file something like one and a half miles along this subterranean passage, here and there passing through chambers which were being worked. Above and below could be seen quarrymen, with a candle as their only light, carrying on their daily avocations.' It is interesting to observe in this connection that in 1937, although the underground inclines, landings and most of the tunnels were lit by electricity, the miners in the workings had to rely on nothing more up-to-date than primitive tallow-dips.

In slate mining, as in tin and copper mining, mechanisation produced more dust, more respiratory diseases, more tuberculosis. Governments move slowly and cautiously in these matters, however, and the provisions of the silicosis compensation scheme were not extended to slate workers until 1939, although the causes of the disease had been perfectly well known for two generations before that.

The reason for mining, rather than quarrying the slate in the Ffestiniog area is interesting. In this part of Wales there is usually a layer of granite above the bed of slate. It was therefore a fairly simple matter to drive tunnels under the granite roof and then to cut chambers about 9 metres wide out of the slate on either side. New chambers were cut below the old ones, as the miners worked downwards from the top to the bottom of the mountain. The method was very wasteful, since very thick pillars of slate were left to support the roof. A new technique was introduced in about 1900 at the Rhiwback quarry, near Blaenau Ffestiniog. It consisted of taking a great slice off the face of the rock by means of a thin steel rope pulled backwards and forwards by compressed air. The quarrymen moved up the mountain in steps, splitting the mechanically cut slice into blocks with wedges.

The accident rate among quarrymen and stone miners has always been high, a fact normally overlooked by those whose interests are confined to the coal industry and who may, for sectarian reasons, wish to present coal mining as the most dangerous of all occupations. All mining is inherently dangerous, but coal mining is regarded as particularly unpleasant by the community as a whole, mainly, one suspects, because it is dirty as well as dangerous. A coal-miner coming up from the pit looks less like a human being than a copper-miner or a gold-miner does.

It therefore seems a kindly and reassuring gesture to end this brief survey of mining in Britain by describing a type of mine in which conditions are agreeable and in which accidents have been remarkably few. Between 1838 and 1841, during the construction of Box Tunnel, on the main railway line from London to Bath and Bristol, it was discovered that the whole district was a solid bed of excellent building limestone. With the new railway available to take the stone away, mining operations began almost immediately. By 1900 more than 85 000 cubic metres of stone a year were being removed from the mines and in 1904 it was said that there were 100 kilometres of passage-ways. Until 1939, when parts of this great underground system were used for defence purposes, one could walk a distance of about 5 kilometres from Clift Quarry, Box, to Tunnel Quarry, Corsham, in a straight line.

Three forms of entry into the mines were used, shafts, adits and slopes. The workings are not deep and the temperature remains at a pleasant 15·5°C (60°F), summer and winter. Until more recent years, when mechanical cutting was introduced, the method of extracting the stone was to pick out a narrow layer just below the roof, saw down from the slot produced in this way until the bottom of the bed was reached and then split off the blocks with wedges. As the work proceeded, pillars $1\frac{1}{2}$-$2\frac{1}{2}$ metres wide were left to support the roof. Props were rarely used, but between 1883 and 1968 there were only fourteen fatal accidents, a record almost certainly unequalled in any other group of mines. There have been no ventilation problems in any of the Box–Corsham mines and the air in them is so fresh that celebration dinners and parties have been held in them without the slightest discomfort to even the most fragile of guests. Only one mine, Monks Park, is still working and this is now the sole remaining source of new Bath stone, a development which would have seemed hardly possible to those who were involved in the industry at the beginning of this century.

Two general points can usefully be made. The first is that innovations usually take place in the more profitable types of mining, where the investment is likely to be higher and the rewards of success greater. It is no accident that, in the sixteenth century, the most notable technical inventiveness and pioneering were to be found in the silver mines of Saxony and Bohemia, or that the seventeenth-century Cornish tin adventurers showed particular enterprise in installing steam-engines. The second observation is that, seen from an historical perspective, mining appears much more as a single entity than it probably did at the time. Capital, enterprise, ideas and engineers have moved from one branch of mining to another, so that a technical development which has proved its value in the working of, say, tin or copper, is very likely to find its way, suitably adapted, into coal or diamonds. At different periods, the carriers of ideas have been, for example, emigrants, designers and builders of steam-engines, manufacturers of wire ropes, doctors, politicians and trade papers. A classic instance of the transfer of technology from one field to another can be seen at Monks Park stone mine. During the early years of World War II, when the British government was trying to increase coal production by every possible means, coal mines were equipped with a number of different cutting machines. When the war was over, the stone industry found itself faced with serious cost and labour problems. In an attempt to deal with the situation, the Bath and Portland Stone firms bought a couple of second-hand and, by then, decidedly obsolescent 'Sampson' coal-cutters and set them to work in their mines at Corsham. They have given excellent service ever since. At that stage in the fortunes of the stone industry, however, it is doubtful if any machinery manufacturers would have considered it worthwhile to design a machine specifically for cutting stone. The low-investment industry had to content itself with the crumbs from the high-investment industry's table, which is a normal feature of technical progress.

BIBLIOGRAPHY

ALLEN, J.S. *et al* Article on early steam engines in *Transactions of the Newcomen Society* vol. XLI, 1968–9.

BICK, DAVID *Old Metal Mines of Mid-Wales* Part 1, 1974.

BIRD, R.H. *Yesterday's Golcondas*: notable British metal mines, 1976.

BOOKER, FRANK *Morwellham*, 1970.
  Industrial Archaeology of the Tamar Valley, 1967

GRIFFIN, A.R. 'Bell pits and soughs: some East Midland examples' *Industrial Archaeology* Nov. 1969, p. 382.

HAIR, T.H. *A Series of Views of the Collieries in the counties of Northumberland and Durham.* With descriptive sketches and a preliminary essay on coal and the coal trade by M. Ross, London 1844.

HARRIS, T.R. *Dolcoath; Queen of the Cornish Mines* Trevithick Society 1974.

HENSON, F.A. and SMITH, R. S. 'Detecting colliery workings from the air' *Colliery Engineering* June 1955.

LINDSAY, JEAN *A History of the North Wales Slate Industry* 1974.

NEEDHAM, JOSEPH, *et al.* Article on early steam engines in *Transactions of the Newcomen Society*, Vol. XXXV, 1962–3.

PARSONS, A.H. As recorded by M.J.H. Southway in *The Journal of the Bristol Industrial Archaeological Society* 1970.

SHAW, W.T. *Mining in the Lake Counties* 1972.

TODD, A.C. and LAWS, PETER *The Industrial Archaeology of Cornwall* 1972.

TUCKER, ROGER J. 'Box Quarries, Wiltshire' *Industrial Archaeology* vol. 5, no. 2, May 1968.

WARNER, Rev. RICHARD, *A Second Walk through Wales* 1800.

6

Some Medieval and Eighteenth Century Curiosities and Utilities

BARBARA JONES

Excavation is hard work, and to make a place for oneself under the ground is no trivial enterprise. Most children are bewitched by the mystery of caves and want a small one of their own to be a private place away from the house, which is not truly their own territory. A natural cave to hand is unlikely, so many start to dig. Few persevere. Some of those who do may go on digging, perhaps scraping a further room, perhaps delving a deeper one, which imposes a floor and steps; considerable enterprises. Occasionally there is applied or incised decoration, but imagination is more practical, effortlessly transforming a pirates' jolly lair into a horrid dungeon. 'I want, therefore I have', is the whole of the law.

But making the cave itself is always hard work, and only a few serious excavators go on moling away into adult life. In Britain, tunnelling for mood began in the seventeenth century when melancholy was modish. Then, in the eighteenth century, tunnelling became fashionable for those who not only desired but could afford it as a last sublime touch to the landscape park, and in the nineteenth century it returned to mood.

Royston Cave, Hertfordshire

Before these tunnels, though, came a number of medieval excavations, small caves or tunnels cut in soft rock or chalk as hiding places, or cold stores, or hermitages or chapels to commemorate hermits; their uses are now obscured by legends or by later embellishments, and I know of only one which is really worth visiting – Royston Cave in Hertfordshire. This is a bell-shaped cave

A select bibliography is printed on page 196.

173

hollowed out of the chalk almost directly under the centre of the town where the Icknield Way crosses Ermine Street. It was rediscovered by accident in 1742, under a buried millstone. When the earth that half filled it had been cleared, the searchers found a skull, a few other bones, fragments of a small decorated earthenware cup and a piece of brass. Later, animal bones and more pieces of pottery were found, but nothing to suggest the origins or purposes of the cave, which remain mysterious, and still invite interpretation. It is over $7\frac{1}{2}$ metres high and over 5 metres across, cool, a little damp, and well preserved; the graffiti of more than two centuries have textured the carvings over, but they keep most of the detail drawn by the early antiquaries. The bas-relief and incised carvings run round the cave to a height of about $2\frac{1}{2}$ metres. Above them are traces of a floor, and below them is a low octagonal podium. There are dozens of human figures that range in style and scale from a large St Christopher with infant Christ, carved by someone familiar with, say, thirteenth-century representations of the saint, to tiny figures that are scarcely more than ideograms of humanity, and remind one of the figures on the doors of lavatories in public places. There are saints and their symbols, crosses, crucifixions, swords, shields, a bird, a horse, hands, groups, hearts, moons, globes, scratches, and very faint traces of red and yellow colouring (Fig. 6:1).

There are many theories about the origins of the carvings; one of two Norman noblewomen, both called Lady Roisia, was an early contender, either as artist or as patron of a hermit artist; later, a hermitage was referred to in Henry VIII's grant of the Priory estate to the Chester family which may refer to the cave. Joseph Beldam in 1852 opted for a Roman columbarium, among other suggestions, and other interpreters have suggested a grain-store, a flint mine or a refuge. One could also argue it was a hidden place for worship by a heretical sect, and some of the symbols could be interpreted as Manichaean. Each visitor is free to choose. The most scholarly work on the cave has been done recently by Sylvia P. Beamon, who suggests that it might have been a chapel and warehouse for the Knights Templar, who held lands at Baldock, Shingay and other places in the neighbourhood, and would have needed a cool store for the produce they sold at the weekly market at this important crossroads. The store would have had to be secure as well as cool, for in the middle of the thirteenth century the Knights were in constant dispute with the Abbot of Westminster, claiming exemption from all the market dues demanded by the Abbey. Knights

Fig. 6:1 General view of Royston Cave
carvings. St Catherine and her wheel are
easily discernible. The smaller picture
shows St Christopher carrying the infant
Christ. *Photos. Cambridge Evening News
and Royston and District Local History
Society*

protecting the store would then have needed a place nearby for their regular devotions, and Mrs Beamon draws attention to strong similarities in design between Royston Cave and the Holy Sepulchre in Jerusalem. Other copies of the Sepulchre exist in Europe, and at the Templar's Tour du Coudray at Chinon there is a mixture of sophisticated and simple work and similar cult images. Personally, I find it difficult to believe that such travelled and worldly men as the Templars would have either executed or commissioned quite such artless work as Royston. They may have made a cool store though, and based its shape on foreign models. A succession of warehouse keepers might then have decorated it, either in the boredom of the six days between markets, or from the almost universal human desire to decorate one's environment.

When the country began to settle down after the long wars of the Middle Ages, peace was reflected in the architecture of the great houses; fortification was abandoned, arrow slits became large windows and, of more importance to us here, the gardens spread beyond the walls, further and further out, in straight noble avenues and canals. Not everyone wished to impress, though, and idiosyncratic gardeners did not copy the gazebos and summer-houses from which their neighbours complacently surveyed their formal, geometrical gardens. Instead they built what their temperaments suggested, things that the neighbours came to call 'follies', and folly tunelling began early in the seventeenth century. William Harvey, who died in 1657, had caves in his garden at Combe in Surrey where he meditated in summer, and two brothers of the Howard family dug tunnels on their estates, which were also in Surrey. (Culture-carrying began early on the folly scene, and so did family addiction; the Howards and their relations built follies far and wide.) Henry Howard, later sixth Duke of Norfolk, owned Albury Park, where John and George Evelyn from nearby Wotton laid out the grounds for him in the late 1650s, with a 'crypta', or subterranean passage, 150 metres long, tunnelled through the bottom of a hill north of the house. A cavern to imitate a Roman bath was dated 1676. Most of the Albury work remains, but for Charles Howard's tunnelling at Deepdene near Dorking we must rely on Aubrey's *Brief Lives*:

> In the hill on the left hand, being sandy ground is a cave digged thirty six paces long, four broad, and five yards high; and

at about two thirds of the hill (where the crook, or bowing, is) he hath dug another subterranean walk or passage, to be pierced through the hill; through which as through a tube you have the vista over all the south part of Surrey and Sussex to the sea. The south side of this hill is converted into a vineyard of many acres of ground which faceth the south and south west. The vaulting or upper part of those caves are not made semicircular, but parabolical, which is the strongest figure for bearing and which sandy ground naturally falls into then stands. And thus we may see that the conies (by instinct of nature) make their holes so. Here are caves for beer etc.

Early in the eighteenth century, fashion turned from the formal gardens, and the age of the great landscaped parks began, parks that extended ever further away from the house and were designed for 'picturesque' views and constant variety. Follies were very fashionable for these parks, and a set might include an eye-catcher, a pagoda, a prospect tower, a sham ruin, a hermitage and a grotto. It was soon obvious that the really lucky landowner already had a ruined castle or abbey standing unregarded on his estate; nothing, it was realised, looked better at the end of a valley or a vista. Those who did not own a real ruin could easily build a false one, while for those who could afford it a tunnel, labyrinth or grotto (above or below ground) might be the crowning glory of the park. Curiously, although a live hermit was occasionally employed to sit in the hermitage, and legends were invented about mythical tunnels made by the monks of old from the ruin to the house, the real tunnels do not seem to have been decorated to match; even if the tunnel vaults were Gothick in shape, they were decorated with shells, felspar and minerals.

The first shell-decorated tunnel was probably the one that connected Alexander Pope's villa at Twickenham with his garden on the other side of the road, a tunnel at once useful and ornamental. Pope, a witty enemy of formal gardens, began his own picturesque works in 1718, but the tunnel is not picturesque at all. It is on the simple plan of a trident-head with a very long centre tine. The side aisles do not connect with the main one in any cunning way; there is not even the surprise of a window opening between them. There are no traces of those stalactites from Wookey Hole (one is shown the stumps) which Mr Pope's friends shot down like sitting pheasants and presented to him for his grot. There are no shells, only petrifications and rock, a few pieces of medieval carving and a little quartz. All is dark and dim, even the two mirrors in which Pope is said to have watched the world go by on the river, sitting with his back to the door. It has suffered more than one would expect the work of so great a poet to be allowed to suffer; it simply cannot be recognised from the contemporary descriptions; it has been kept, and that is all. There were doors at each end and when these were closed, wrote the Swedish minister Gyllenborg in 1725, the grotto became 'on the instant a *camera obscura*, on the walls of which all the objects of the river, hills, woods, and boats are forming a moving picture in their visible radiations.' Some part must have been smooth and white to achieve this; Pope does not say. He describes the sparkle of luminous minerals, ores, 'Cornish diamonds', 'Brazilian pebbles', crystal, amethyst, quartz, and the angular pieces of looking-glass, now so dead. In the roof was a mirror star with a single lamp hanging, 'an orbicular figure of thin alabaster'. And there was a little spring for the sound of water.

Goldney, Bristol

In the 1730s Thomas Goldney began elaborate and splendid works at Clifton in Bristol. His memorandum book does not say when excavations began, but in 1737 he 'finished the Subterraneous Passage to the Grotto and began upon the Grotto the same year'. In 1753 he began a Great Terras, and in 1757 finished the Rotunda – for things above ground with plants go faster than below with shells

Fig. 6:2 Goldney Grotto. The Lions' Den.   *Drawing by Barbara Jones*

– and at last at the end of 1764, after many years of effort, he finished the grotto, which carries the date 1739 in shells. During that summer he had made a tower, a pretty castellated one with a fine view, for the fire-engine that supplied water to the grotto and a lily pond. The grotto waters still run (but now by electricity), and the noise of the cascade does not murmur but fills the whole place, echoing over the pool and singing in the great shells. The entrance is through a yew hedge from the lawn into a tunnel, silent and dark till we turn a corner to hear the roar of water for the first time. Four pillars encrusted with minerals support the roof whose vaults are hacked in rough grotesques from limestone. On one side The Lions' Den is formed of curious rocks, to shelter a marble lion and lioness who glare whitely at the visitor with blind eighteenth-century eyes. Past them, the grotto ends abruptly at a pool and, halted, we look on up a narrow cleft. Apparently far away, greenly-lit past the jagged teeth of wonderfully eroded rock which mask the opening, a marble Neptune reclines in an elaborate cave. His right arm rests on an urn from which the water spouts, to leap and tumble over the rocks, ending with a cascade from the flutes of two giant clams into the pool at our feet. The whole of the grotto is delightful, but the cascade is particularly theatrical and fine, a masterpiece of shifting light and water, sound and shadow.

It is possible to climb up a dark passage parallel to the cascade and see Neptune in profile, even more dramatically lit, through an opening among the rocks. The bright stillness of the figure is a long way from Bristol, and this is surely what a grotto is for, the evocation of a new world. The pleasant cool house and its sunny garden are superbly set above the city, but as we walk down the lawn our pleasure in it is of our daily world; then before the expected green terrace can display the tremendous view, the path descends into darkness and opens, not on to the hot landscape but on to tortuous rocks in a cold gloom, and the enclosed echoes of the cascade. Ultimately, Goldney is terrifying; however fine the shell-work, however cunning the scale of the cascade, the water dominates everything; at last the damp air chills the spine and the crash of the waters turns every meek little shell into a tiger's mouth.

Ascot Place, Berkshire

Those whose estates offered the softer rocks, especially chalk, were of course able to make tunnels merely by laborious and expensive excavation, but determined troglodytes managed very well with earth and imported hard rocks; this technique had the advantage

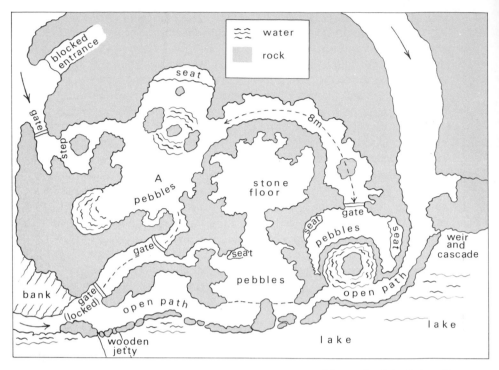

Fig. 6:3 A plan of the grotto at Ascot Place.   *Prepared from a sketch by Barbara Jones*

that the overground could be made exactly where art decreed it, without reference to the natural scene. One of the finest examples of an overground underground is at Ascot Place in Berkshire. Nothing seems known of its history except a nineteenth-century statement that it was made for a Daniel Agace. At first glance its spar and sparkle suggest the work of Joseph and Josiah Lane of Tisbury in Wiltshire, a father and son who made, wholly or in part, most of the great overground grottoes of the southern counties. But the marvellously preserved work at Ascot lacks something of their airy delicacy; instead it is fierce and feels very subterranean indeed.

Fortunately for its safety, the grotto is near the house, from which it can be seen across the lake as a fine pile of great rocks and a large cave-mouth. The mound is high, and skilfully built with a crown of standing rocks at the top which conceal until the last moment a lantern of eight delicately leaded windows to light the grotto. At ground level, an entrance winds on each side of a rock and tufa pier into the largest chamber (A in Fig. 6:3) which is about 10 metres long, contrived with bewildering asymmetry of all floors, walls and ceilings except for a fine arch of huge flints with a 3-metre span across a pool with a seat behind, but even this is on no axis, even of the scattered octagons and circles set in the pebble floor. There is another pool and several simple seats. Certainly the grotto was lit, for all round, both at floor level and high on the walls and niches, are holes in the grot-work, and today there are electric lamps, white below and red above, an effect that the eighteenth century would have loved and that may indeed have been suggested by remaining fragments of red glass. The ceiling is all stalactites of felspar, decorated with zig-zags of a sparkling brown mineral and the spar glitters and shines overhead, under the big arch and off into a corridor beside it. Up among the stalactities are a few eyes for daylight, and the blue sky reflects with the red lamps to turn the glitter of the spar to mauve. Glitter draws one on, down an obvious or down a concealed passage, into the two more elaborate, differing, chambers. These open onto views of the lake, but great fangs of zig-zagged felspar seem to hold the visitor firmly inside and under.

West Wycombe, Buckinghamshire

Many follies or folly groups are famous, like the sham castle on the hills above Bath, but the most famous of them all, at West Wycombe in Buckinghamshire, is a most entertaining group of assorted follies, with over everything the glamorous spell of the legends of the Hell-Fire Club and its assorted sins. Sir Francis Dashwood's considerable works at West Wycombe began in about 1739 and continued until his death as Lord Le Despencer in 1781. Some of the architectural conceits in the park were altered, and some were later swept away by Repton as 'useless and unmeaning', but the Hell-Fire Cave seems to have survived intact: tunnels are not so easily altered as buildings.

Between 1750 and 1752, Sir Francis made a fine new road from the town of High Wycombe three kilometres away. To build it he used chalk taken by local labour from the steep spur of the Chilterns that ends north of the house and as the road grew the excavation became more than 400 metres of tunnel winding down under the hill. The cave, closed when I first saw it, has a black entrance in an elaborate flint screen. The side walls have pointed arches and short obelisks, and between them is a tripartite façade with curved triangular wings to a three-storeyed central wall with a pointed arch at each level, but the top ruinous. Inside, the white tunnel leads clammily on via a chilly first room to a simple labyrinth and the bed of a dry stream. Beyond is a very large vaulted circular hall with six recessed chambers and the tunnel leading on to end in a little circular room. The various openings are now alive with *son et lumière* and peopled with Hell-Fire waxworks, which have the power of all waxworks to dominate their environment. There are names too: the Robing Chamber, where club members changed into the habits of Franciscan monks; the Catacombs; the River Styx (it was not always dry); the Banqueting Hall, with four Monk's Cells; a Buttery and a Cursing Well. The little room at the end is the Inner Temple, for the most sophisticated initiates only. Some of these names may linger from a long tradition, but it must have taken a lot of fires and furs and soft divans to make the cave a cosy place for orgies. Outside again, the flint façade is now almost invisible behind an ice-cream parlour and a Chinoiserie café.

Ware, Hertfordshire

The Hell-Fire Cave is chiefly interesting as a tunnel to complete a good and varied group of follies; even the legends cannot make it as exciting as the remarkable grotto that John Scott built for himself at Ware in the 1770s, a frightening grotto like a decorated, gleaming coal mine. Beside the house a hill rises sharply to a wooded summit crowned with a small octagonal summer-house reached by winding paths through a typical nineteenth-century shrubbery, while at the foot sunken paths between flint walls covered with ivy and hart's tongue ferns lead to the grass enclosure in front of the elaborate, concealing main entrance to the grotto. An antechamber leads to a square room with arched windows and alcoves. Patterns of pale shells cover even the doors and the floor is patterned in shells and wood. Steps under a narrow light-shaft lead to the black copper slag of the passage down and a Soane-like complexity begins, for from the first room lined with knapped flints a narrow shaft runs down for glimpses of two others far below the chalk. Rooms suggested but beyond access would have been a good horror; it is a pity that Scott only made the illusion of them.

After this the complexity of the tunnelling makes description difficult; it descends via a circular room and then a square room with simple flint- and shell-decorated walls to the two rooms below the shaft. The Committee Room is domed and a terrifying echo forces speech back into the brain and the illusion of entombment is complete. The walls here are only spotted with shells pressed into the cement, but at least the passage rises, and leads to the big Council Chamber. This has a patterned pebble floor and, for the councillors, six niches of the usual grotto discomfort cut into the walls. The entire chamber is covered with shells, coal and other minerals, set in circles, stars and octagons. The roof is again a dome, covered with the same decoration, though it is above ground and has lights let into it. From outside it is a flattish cone of purple slates. Steps rise from another door to an entrance on the other side of the porch; if you *enter* the grotto this way a Soane-like trap leads to a blind, patterned niche while the real entrance is unnoticed. Scott was a most industrious mole who left us a mystery; all the rooms in his grotto have names, like the rooms at West Wycombe, and indeed both caves have a Robing Room, but what went on at Ware? There is not even the ghost of a legend.

Hawkstone, Shropshire

One of the last great landscaped parks of the eighteenth century also has its most ambitious excavation, the Labyrinth at Hawkstone in Salop. Here the work on the park must have been done with remarkable speed, with workmen and architects and churned-up earth all over the place, for Sir Richard Hill only inherited the estate from his father in 1783, and the family has a beautiful black book, a *Survey and Particulars of the Manor*, illustrated with most exquisite watercolour drawings which show that most of the existing conceits, as well as the destroyed heather-hermitage and moss temple, were all there in 1787, though of course it is always possible that the painter ran a little ahead of performance.

The map shows that the natural site was perfect, with water, a complex arrangement of hills, a lot of red sandstone and a real castle. This and the surrounding landscaping are probably as fine now as they have ever been, a piece of picturesque design in the naturalistic style that has turned even its conversion into a golf course to advantage, for the great green sweeps are thus well cared for, and from the heights of Grotto Hill the little figures of the golfers with their tiny cries and red flags animate the scene.

From the lower slopes of Grotto Hill, the obvious path takes us over a rock bridge across the Gulph, 'calculated to inspire solemnity', but another very narrow and unobtrusive path winds steeply up the back of the hill, pausing among the heavy rhododendrons at a semicircular stone seat, and then on through a cleft in the rock, thick with moss and ferns, floored with skeleton leaves, getting steadily darker and narrower. A great carved gothic stone lies across the path, which is then closed by the rock. The path cuts through it, opens again for a moment to the sky, and then runs straight into the rock face, into absolute darkness. The narrow tunnel is about 2 metres high, but the silence and blackness are so complete that it is difficult to walk upright under the intangible pressure of the rock. The tunnel winds on for nearly 60 metres, but at last patches of mere darkness show in the black, and the tunnel turns into a round chamber lit faintly from a distant eye in the roof. The gloom and earthly terror are complete until at last the eye begins to pick out an enormous, clumsily-hewn arch, beyond which the way divides and then returns on each side. Dimly seen, the rustications of both the arch and the recess have been picked out with black paint. Further on is another room, larger, with two exits and three false ones, again lit from the distant sky by dim eyes and hewn into vaults that arch straight down into four great piers of rock. The most hidden dark hole, squeezed behind the heaviest pier, opens at last to the green subterranean light of a gallery 25 metres long, still all in the rock, and supported by pillars cunningly cut to emphasise the natural strata, so that they spiral and twist uneasily away from us. Once the whole gallery was painted bright emerald green; much of the paint has gone – it is stronger at the far end, increasing the perspective – but even today it is the Palace of King Neptune from the pantomime. Everywhere, circular openings and lepers' slits give vistas into darker or brighter parts of the cave, through into the ruined grotto or up through sun-bleached grass to the sky. One crevice in the roof leads to darkness filled with the rustling and squeaking of innumerable bats. At the far end of the gallery is an exit on to a series of rock galleries in the sun, but opposite the entrance from the labyrinth is another exit through the grotto, still cut in the rock but now well lit; a ruin, destroyed, said the proprietor of the hotel, by some cyclists who were refused tea. It is about 6 metres square with little caves at the sides. Once the rock pillars were covered with shells and stalactites and crystals, there was a dome of coloured glass, glass in the Gothick fenestration of the door, and the 'wax effigy of the ancestor of a neighbour'. Now only a handful of shells remains, and the fossils of shells in the plaster. The empty door opens on to a terrace looking out over the sunny park, up the Elysian Hill. The drop is absolutely sheer. The *Survey* says:

> Through a part of this rock the present owner has with great exertions and much taste made an extensive cavern and grotto,

supported within by several rude pillars which were left of the stone in forming it and curiously ornamented with spar petrifications, stained and painted glass and other suitable appendages, and at the west end is a door opening to a gallery in the rock so immediate on the precipice as to strike the visitor with terror in looking down, and yet so far is it beneath the summit, that Ravens build their nests in the spontaneous growing wood on the Knob above, thence denominated the Ravens' Shelf.

Today, the *Survey* seems to have understated the cavern and overstated the gallery; perhaps the author suffered from vertigo, just as I fear the dark.

Margate Grotto, Kent

So far, we have seen the grottoes and tunnels of the wealthy upper classes, and the inventors of legends have worked only at West Wycombe. But they have been very busy weaving their spells around a more plebian grotto, where written history only records that it was made, lost and found again. This near-vacuum is now not only filled, but overflowing with stories and strife almost on the scale of Borley Rectory, and also demonstrating the lure of the Orient for the British.

Commonsense and the look of the thing itself both suggest that Margate grotto is English work of the late eighteenth or very early nineteenth century. But this is not so. The place attracts like a magnet every possible archaeological theory, especially diffusionist – very surprisingly it has not been suggested that it was built by Joseph of Arimathea. No one seems able to bear the simple thought that Margate might possess a very good English shell grotto – this far-eastern corner of England is determinedly, and widely, exotic. Romans, Danes, Persians, Phoenicians, Essenes, Moors, Mithras, Tibetans and Cretans all jostle for supremacy as the builders, though the Druids and some vague monks uphold the insular claim, and it has been connected with Avebury and Coldrum. The Cretans seem to be the favourite candidates; no attempt is made to prove that they built the grotto – instead, the grotto is taken as proof that priest–kings were sent from Crete to Kent for instruction and initiation.

What *is* known is that the grotto was found in 1834 or 1835 by Joshua Newlove when he was helping to dig a duck-pond for his father, a schoolmaster who rented and afterwards bought the land. All attempts so far to find earlier printed references have failed and so have researches into the ownership of the land. But one piece of plain testimony to the origin of the grotto exists which is always brushed aside by the exoticists on the lines of how-could-a-poacher-have-written-Shakespeare. It is known that, early in the 1800s, a child named Thomas Bowles used his little cart to transport loads of shells from nearby Shell Ness to the site. According to the account given by his great-grand-daughter (who was still alive in 1956) he and his family lived in a cottage near the grotto, and when the Newloves found it in 1835 Bowles told them that the work had been done on an existing excavation by two brothers, his uncles. (This existing excavation was probably, on stylistic grounds, simply an earlier grotto that the tunneller had no time or money to decorate.) But no one would listen to Thomas Bowles. Mr Newlove wanted it to be *old*; 2800 B.C. seems to be the longest guess so far. I prefer the Bowles brothers. It is certainly odd that the grotto was lost, but not nearly so odd as the Cretans.

The shell work takes the form of pointed arches separated by wide pilasters all the way to the last rectangular chamber. This once had an arched roof but unfortunately Mr Newlove, extending his school, replaced this by a flat plaster roof because the high one would have interfered with his new foundations. Three of the walls of this room, however, are intact; the fourth was damaged by a bomb and is plaster, like the ceiling. On my first visit this was covered with a most distressing mural of purple priestesses performing some ancient rite, but this has now gone (Fig. 6:4). The remaining walls, except for an arched niche and the entrance, are divided by wide bands of shells into big squares, two deep all round. The designs here are mostly geometrical; stars, diamonds, circles and their various segments, and a few floral arrangements. In the passages there are vases with flowering plants climbing out of them, various curves and spirals, two crude representations of human forms, and a great number of curving and interlacing plants, flowers and stars. They are indeed just the simple shapes, themes and variations that one would expect an untrained artist to use, the shapes that have been used in decorations since decorations began; they are the universal themes, they are the doodling on the blotting-paper.

But here, some curious alchemy in the soil of Margate goes to everyone's head and remarkable transformations occur; photographs have been ruthlessly retouched, so that a vase of flowers becomes the Cretan Mother-Pot; part of an ordinary diamond pattern is isolated as The Double-Headed Axe; a plant is a Sacred

Fig. 6:4 Margate Grotto.
The Dome. *The proprietors*

Palm of the Bo Tree of Buddha, while every star is Indian, every
flower Biblical and every vase Bacchic. 'Isis is here. Pythagoras,
Aldebaran with the Ankh . . .'

There is really only one difference between Margate and all the
other shell grottoes and that is its colour. For many years it was lit
by gas, and the whole mosaic was smoked brown, shiny here and
there from the passing of visitors, but brown all over; a rich,
ancient, mummy-coloured, bone-dry brown.

ICE-HOUSES

All through the last three-quarters of the eighteenth century, when follies (or at least garden architecture of some sort) were almost mandatory, economical follies were popular – sham castles or ecclesiastical façades to farms, stables, cow-sheds and cottages killed two building birds with one set of stones, and, at a distance, looked very much like the real shams. One common subterranean building that was often turned into ornamental use was the ice-house.

Britain came late to the idea of storing ice. Charles II is said to have introduced it from the Continent, and after a century or so ice-houses had passed from the grounds of royal to great to ordinary country houses. There were a number of recommended constructions to achieve good insulation. An ice-house might face north to avoid the sun, or south, so that the sun might keep it dry. The plan was usually circular, but the walls might be straight or tapered; an egg- or cone-shape, narrow end down, was popular. The roof might be underground, or overground below a mound of earth, or heavily thatched. A passage or tunnel with double doors was the usual entrance, and brick was the usual material. Cavity walls were favoured but not universal; only two things were essential – earth rising to at least half-way up the house, and good drainage at the bottom. Drainage was the first consideration of the site, and sometimes the ice-house was a long way from both the river or lake and the house; no matter, there were plenty of gardeners. If ice was not available, snow could be packed firmly down and layered with reeds or straw. A last thick layer of reeds or straw, moved and replaced daily as the ice was fetched, covered everything, perhaps up to forty tonnes of ice.

If the ice-house stood under a natural or artificial mound it became the obvious setting for some small piece of ornamental architecture, a temple or a summer-house. A particularly splendid and interesting crown to an ice-house is the Temple of the Winds at West Wycombe which, in 1759, was the first building in Britain based on the Horologium of Andronikos Cyrrhestes. Later, careful copies of the Horologium were made at Shugborough in Staffordshire and at Mount Stewart House in Co. Down, but here is the first, much freer version, elegantly trimmed with flint, a very un-Athenian material (Fig. 6:5).

Another handsome ice-house stands at Buckland House in Oxfordshire, built of brick with a thatched roof and a stone

Fig. 6:5 The Ice-house. Temple of the Winds, West Wycombe.

soakaway at the bottom. It has for ornament in front a fine pedimented porch with a slate roof and plain stone dressings on very knobbly tufa walls. Few ice-houses were given such noble entrances and very few are now more than a hole in the ground, but this one is safely near the house. Moreover, there is a written account telling how it was for the men who filled it one particularly late spring:

THE ICE HOUSE

Mr Painter remembers filling the ice house on his birthday, 6th April 1913. I remember clearly because it was my sixteenth birthday. Two men went out in a punt and broke the ring of ice and then got two long poles with iron spikes on the end and pulled the ice into the bank.

Two other men standing on the bank with wooden mallets broke up the ice into small bits and the two who were in the punt had two mesh sieves, wired into a forked stick and they dipped the ice out in the sieves and put it into a wheelbarrow. Six men and wheelbarrows, on a chain, wheelbarrowed the ice up the hill and tipped it. Two more in the ice house shoved the ice in, and two more in the ice house levelling it out.

The head gardener, Mr Gough, heated beer for us and also provided bread and cheese.

The ice was wheeled from the ice house to Buckland House every morning and washed before use and the ice lasted practically until the next winter's ice was brought in.

Bobby Kinch, who lived in Mildenhalls, offered me a clay pipe and some twist tobacco. I have smoked a pipe ever since. The other people working with me were

Mr Dick Clark	Tommy Wells
Joe Fear	Billy Wells
Joe Whiting	Dick Fear
Alfred Jordan	Ted Eley, senior

(signed) F. G. Painter

The ice-houses survived until the end of the nineteenth century, being gradually replaced as clearer ice was imported from North America or Norway and by manufactured ice, though a few were in use until World War I.

MOLING

Margate grotto in its original bright state was one of the last excavations to combine charm with alarm. Later moles were blind to the gleam of shells and made plain excavations, labyrinths and catacombs that plunged down into the earth as far as they could go, ignoring in their progress most decoration and all entertainment.

The changed mood is darkly seen at Banwell on Mendip, where a natural cave 45 metres long was discovered by miners in 1780 on land belonging to George Henry Law, who later became Bishop of Bath and Wells. The miners closed the shaft to the cave, but later a skeleton was discovered, the shaft was re-opened, and another cave found nearby with a large collection of animal bones; it was one of the largest prehistoric finds ever made in this country. The most interesting bones are in Taunton Museum, but the happy Bishop nevertheless gave the cave an entrance chamber with coffin-shaped niches and a central table, and decorated it at a lower level with some sad bone architecture.

But the first true mole after the early tunnellers in Surrey was Joseph Williamson who tunnelled in plain brick far and elaborately

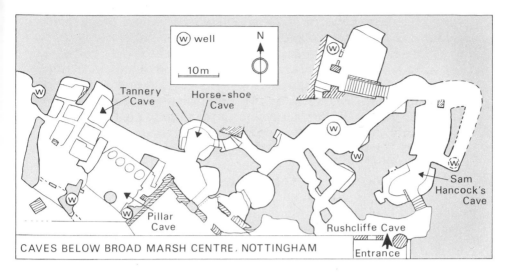

Fig. 6:6 *Redrawn from printed references*

under Liverpool, until his team, it is said, heard noises ahead in the rock and fled, crying that they had dug down to the Devil. Actually it was a gang of Stephenson's men making a tunnel for the railway and, as usual, utility won the day, so Mr Williamson's tunnels had to stop.

There are other city tunnels in Nottingham, and caves as well, mostly put to industrial or domestic uses (Fig. 6:6). Alderman Herbert had a house on one side of the Ropewalk (then Victoria Street) and a garden running down to a park on the other. So in 1856 he had a tunnel driven from his cellars through the rock under the road. There were several pockets of loose earth on the way, and when these were removed, a series of caves was left, several of which overlook the garden. Unfortunately we do not know the name of Mr Herbert's sculptor, who was probably local and possibly a stonemason. He carved both along the tunnel walls and inside the caves, one of which was a conservatory with animals among the plants and ferns. Another was an Egyptian Temple, with sphinxes, and there were Druids, but the climax was Daniel in the Lions' Den, a spirited group of lions and lionesses, three pairs, roaring and sleepy and Daniel flung back tense at the top of the pile, an acceptable change from the usual placid uncle-with-pussies of the period. All are cleverly lit from concealed windows of coloured glass; a nice echo of Goldney.*

At Welbeck are the famous underground works of the fifth Duke of Portland. We read of a huge underground ballroom, a suite of libraries, glass-houses and more than 6 kilometres of tunnels. The ballroom, three libraries, all *c.* 1875, and a long corridor lined with huge portraits of heavily-maned horses are bitterly disappointing at first, as they are sunk only so far that their ceilings are on ground level, and we had expected so much – quite literally, the earth – and there are the rooms lit by normal daylight pouring through the sky-lights. But the walk underground through curving passages, their railtracks giving an illicit feeling of trespassing on the Tube, and then the great empty rooms and the enormous horses, all remain desolately in the memory. The railway lines are set into the floor of the passages, so that food could be driven to the underground rooms. At junctions, there are points levers in the walls and past the last room the rails still go curving on into the darkness. Old postcards show the ballroom, which was said to be the largest room in Europe, with its cut-glass gasoliers, conifers in tubs down the centre, and dozens of sofas and chairs (we can see changing fashion in the shapes and chintzes), not set in conversational groups or towards the dancers, but all facing outwards in a great rectangle to the walls (Fig. 6:7).

About 2 kilometres of tunnel actually run under the lake. Through this the Duke would drive to Worksop Station, where his closed carriage was taken straight on to a truck and thence to London.

In London, privacy continued. The sewers and mains services under the city were already so complex that undoubtedly even a duke was not allowed to tunnel, but I have been told that until about 1905 there was at the south end of Wimpole Street a sham façade continuing the line of houses, its windows thick with dust, that hid part of a garden for the Duke.

No disappointment of any sort attends the Catacombs at High Beech in Epping Forest, an indescribable tumble of masonry into a hole in the earth. It is said to have been made in the 1860s from the stones of Chelmsford gaol, and indeed entablatures and dentils here and there in the chaos were clearly part of some older buildings, but

---

*EDITORIAL NOTE The Alderman Herbert's caves are now sealed off. The plan (Fig. 6:6) shows some of the Broad Marsh Centre caves south-west of the ones described by Barbara Jones.

Fig. 6:7 The underground supper room at Welbeck Abbey.

now their original purposes are lost. The Catacombs are under a mound in the garden of the house and were once a popular show place. They start quite gradually with a circular court, open to the sky, formed of six pillars carrying an arcading of stone in which holes have been cut as if by a huge leather-punch. In the niches between the pillars there is some spar and there used to be statues, and once there was purple stained glass in the windows above. Through one niche, the symmetry breaks and the stones begin to spiral downwards. Neither walls nor ceiling nor floor present normal surfaces; the blocks of stone roughly piled, the piles twisted, and the twists pushed over. The instability is emphasised by the use of *almost* normal features – the roof is supported here and there on columns built of blocks of stone piled one on the other – but these are thin at the base, massive at the top and nowhere regular. Blocks of stone make haphazard steps down into the gloom, which is lightened here and there, at longer and longer intervals, by light shafts from the ground above. At the bottom, darkness is complete.

The last mole was Whitaker Wright, a financier who promoted mining companies on a large scale in the 1890s. In 1904, he was sentenced to seven years for fraud and killed himself. During his prosperous times in the early 1890s he bought Lea House near Godalming in Surrey and set out to transform it. His new house was gutted by fire in 1952 and has since been demolished, but much of his work in the park remains, and, in a number of *The Royal Magazine* for 1903, appears 'The only Authentic Account that has ever been Published of the Wonderful Way in which Mr. Whitaker Wright "Improved Nature" at his Home, Lea Park, in Surrey. Full and True Details are given for the First Time of the Marvellous Palace . . . . of the Construction of the Grottoes and the Great Artificial Lakes, with their Fairy-like Houses under the Water; and of the other Wonderful Surprises that were Prepared for Visitors, which are said to have Cost, in all, £1,250,000.'

In the course of six or seven years workmen utterly changed the face of Lea Park, making three artificial lakes, a square lake, a bathing lake, and the big lake, with many statues and fountains. . . .

But one must go beneath the surface of the big lake to see the wonder of wonders at Lea Park – the houses under the water, the retreats, built of iron and glass, where the Master loved to think of seclusion from the cares of the world, to smoke his cigars in peace.

On the lawn, by the lake side, is to be seen a little erection sheltering the head of a spiral staircase. Descending the stairs one comes to a subway, 400 feet long, lighted by rows of electric lamps. The passage, which is wide enough for four people to walk abreast, leads into a great chamber of glass 80 feet in height – a beautiful conservatory with a wondrous mosaic floor, settees and chairs, palms, and little tables. [Fig. 6:8]

It is a wonderful place – a fairy palace. In summer it is delightfully cool – in winter, delightfully warm, for the temperature is always fairly even. Outside the clear crystal glass is a curtain of green water – deep, beautiful green at the bottom, fading away to the palest, faintest green at the top, where little white wavelets ripple. Goldfish come and press their faces against the glass, peering at you with strangely magnified eyes. On summer nights one looks through the green water at the stars and the moon, which appear extraordinarily bright and large, for they are magnified quite ten times by the curved glass and the water.

This submerged fairy-room with appendages cost fully £20,000. It was built, of course, with the utmost care – for if one of the square panes of three-inch glass should break, the place would be filled with water within five minutes.

Sailing round the lake, one would come unexpectedly upon an opening in the bank almost hidden by shrubs and trees. This gave entrance to a subterranean passage, lined with white tiles, covered in places with creepers, deep water rippling at the bottom. Proceeding cautiously up this strange channel running underground, one was reassured by the sight of daylight at the end; and pushing on, came at length to a wondrous grotto, a fairy-like cavern, with trees, high above, forming a roof with their branches. Leaving the boat, one stepped on to a path carved out of the solid rock, which led, by steps, into an extraordinary labyrinth of galleries and hidden chambers, some of which were beautifully fitted with Oriental decorations.

The sad half-tone illustrations of 1903 show the house, the site of the big lake before and after (with a temple on the bank), and also the lake drained of water showing the outside of the submarine passage and the domed smoking room on top of which stands the giant Neptune which normally appeared surrounded by water. The last picture shows the interior with a palm tree in the middle, a button-upholstered bench, electric lights and a lady and gentleman. The dome is stark lattice; it must have looked better with the goldfish.

Fig. 6:8 Lea Park. Section through the lake, showing the position of the conservatory. *Rough sketch by the author, uncompleted at the time of her death.*

Today, the park is still a routine late Surrey one, landscaped with considerable Japonaiserie round a series of big lakes. In the pine trees beyond the farthest lake is the entrance to the grotto.

A large descending spiral of concrete enclosing a circle of glass lies almost sunk in the ground, like a submerged snail. In the mouth of the shell stands an arched wooden door in a wide concrete frame. Inside, the starkest possible concrete passage sinks slowly round and down, with openings on the right looking into a circular room under the glass into which the passage eventually opens, a bare drum of cold light. The ramp goes on, becomes steps, and opens into another room below the first, semicircular this time, lit from the room above. Behind the diameter is an echoing vaulted chamber, 7 or 8 metres long, bare dark concrete, but three of the walls are broken with niches, that, utterly plain though they are, seem all Versailles after the bare ramp. The fourth wall opens into a water-floored tunnel to the lake.

No record or tradition remains of any intention to decorate any part of the 'grotto', as the smoking room was called, or of any use for it; the entrance suggests purpose, extreme utility, a fuel store or an arsenal perhaps, and then at the bottom of the ramp are the odd blank rooms and the water. Perhaps there was no time. There is nothing to say except that Whitaker Wright was the last mole.

BIBLIOGRAPHY

BEAMON, SYLVIA P. 'L'énigmatique cave aux sculptures de Royston' *Archaeologia* June 1973.
    'Ice houses' *The Rickmansworth Historian* No. 32 Autumn 1976.
JONES, BARBARA *Follies and Grottoes* Constable, London 1974 (Messrs Constable and Co. have kindly allowed me to include some quotations and illustrations from this book, which has a bibliography on the architectural ornaments of the landscaped parks.)
LOCKE, GEOFFREY 'Ice houses' *National Trust* No. 24 Autumn 1975.

GENERAL BIBLIOGRAPHY

ASHBEE, PAUL *The Bronze Age Round Barrow in Britain* London 1960.
The Earthen Long Barrow in Britain London 1970.
DANIEL, GLYN *Lascaux and Carnac* London 1955.
GRINSELL, L.V. *Barrow, Pyramid and Tomb; ancient burial customs in Egypt, the Mediterranean and the British Isles* London 1975.
RUDOFSKY, BERNARD *Architecture without Architects* New York 1964.
SOLECKI, R.S. *SHANIDAR The Humanity of Neanderthal Man* London 1972.
UCKO, P. and ROSENFELD, A. *Palaeolithic Cave Art* London 1967.

Index